Ch. 8

Human Factors in Project Management

JB JOSSEY-BASS

Human Factors
in Project Management
CONCEPTS, TOOLS, AND
TECHNIQUES FOR INSPIRING
TEAMWORK AND MOTIVATION

Zachary Wong

BICENTENNIAL
1807
WILEY
2007
BICENTENNIAL

Published by Jossey-Bass
A Wiley Imprint
989 Market Street, San Francisco, CA 94103-1741   www.josseybass.com

Jossey-Bass books and products are available through most bookstores. To contact Jossey-Bass directly call our Customer Care Department within the U.S. at 800-956-7739, outside the U.S. at 317-572-3986, or fax 317-572-4002.

Jossey-Bass also publishes its books in a variety of electronic formats. Some content that appears in print may not be available in electronic books.

Library of Congress Cataloging-in-Publication Data

Wong, Zachary.
   Human factors in project management : concepts, tools, and techniques for inspiring teamwork and motivation / Zachary Wong. — 1st ed.
       p. cm.
   Includes bibliographical references and index.
   ISBN 978-0-7879-9629-1 (cloth)
  1. Project management. 2. Teams in the workplace. 3. Employee motivation.
4. Personnel management. I. Title.
   HD69.P75.W656 2007
   658.4'04—dc22   2007010273

Printed in the United States of America
FIRST EDITION
HB Printing   10 9 8 7 6 5 4 3 2 1

CONTENTS

ACKNOWLEDGMENTS

This book would not have been possible without the love and support from my family. I owe my deepest happiness and success to my wife, Elaine, a dedicated teacher, the heart of our family, and a loving mother to our two daughters, Amy and Sarah. To Amy, my idealist and athlete of the family, thanks for showing me what teamwork really means and what it means to have a great heart for others. Sarah, my favorite artisan and running buddy, you have always been the spirit and fun behind my book. I have learned much from our life experiences together as a family, and I look forward to many more adventures. I thank my dear mom and dad; my grandmother; my siblings, Reynold, Pamela, and Gary, who all remain important in my life; and my extended family, Bob, Marilyn, Tom, and Marguerite, for their affectionate support, and my nephews and nieces.

Special thanks to my friend and best colleague for over thirty-five years, Rich Clark, who has never forgiven me for spewing water all over him in organic chemistry and continues to be there for me. To my good friends at Chevron who helped shape my career and thinking, with sincere gratitude to Judith MacGregor; Manfred Michlmayr; Kathy Dougherty; Mark Keller; Jeet Bindra; Pete Stonebraker; my colleagues in health, environment, and safety; and my team in Toxicology and Health Risk Assessment, pound for pound the best team in Chevron. It is a pleasure to share this book with longtime friends, Steve and Mary Jane Lundin and Chuck and Cathy McGinnis. Thanks for your friendship.

This book was in my head for many years but did not come to light until I was given an opportunity to present it at the University of California at Berkeley. My gratitude to the many dedicated people there, especially Clara Piloto, for giving me the opportunity to teach. My sincere appreciation to Cindy Andallo and Michelle Ragozzino and my fellow instructors: Jim O'Donnell, Terry Hird, Cheryl Allen, Pamela Dryer, Martha Haywood, Barbara Blalock, and Lifong Liu.

My personal thanks to my colleagues for reading the manuscript and giving valuable feedback: Rich Clark, Jerry Miller, Wendy and Vernon Harmon, Jim O'Donnell, Hank McDermott, and Elizabeth King. I want to recognize my editor, Neal Maillet, for believing in this book and making it happen, and the team at Jossey-Bass: Jessie Mandle, Beverly Miller, Cathy Mallon, Bernadette Walter, Diane Turso, Amie Wong, and Brian Grimm. Special thanks to Jonathan Rose, who took my idea forward at Wiley.

Finally, this book was truly inspired by my students in Human Factors and Team Dynamics for Project Management at UC Berkeley. You gave me the energy and insights to create it. You helped me rise to a higher level.

To my wife, Elaine, and our daughters, Amy and Sarah

Zachary Wong is a manager at the Chevron Energy Technology Company in Richmond, California. He is a highly acclaimed instructor of human factors and team dynamics at the University of California at Berkeley Extension. Wong has over thirty years of managerial and project management experience. He has held senior positions in research and technology, strategic planning, business analysis, and risk assessment. He has extensive experience as a team facilitator and project leader.

In 2002, Wong was selected as an Honored Instructor by the University of California at Berkeley Extension and has received numerous teaching awards. For over fifteen years, he has taught a wide range of courses in health sciences, economics, business management, leadership, and human factors. In 1978, he received his Ph.D. in toxicology and pharmacology from the University of California at Davis. He has served extensively on project teams, executive leadership teams, and decision review boards of public committees, industry associations, and academia.

Human Factors in Project Management

This book is a synthesis of key concepts, tools, and techniques for motivating high performance in self-managed project teams. Over the past three decades, project management has benefited from numerous people-based strategies, such as quality management, facilitative leadership, reinforcement-based leadership, and performance management. These strategies have resulted in greater employee empowerment and dependency on self-motivated project teams, cross-functional teams, and global networks. Despite this tremendous growth in using teams, there has been a lag in new thinking about team motivation. This book presents new ideas and models in team motivation and applies them to the most challenging issues facing project managers today: motivating a diverse workforce, facilitating team decisions, resolving interpersonal conflicts, managing difficult people, and strengthening team accountability, processes, and leadership. It integrates the most significant concepts in team motivation and behaviors into a single set of principles called human factors. A simple definition of *human factors* is the study of the interactions among people and systems. Human factors are the underlying elements of human behavior that affect organizational performance. This book is designed for people who want to improve their interpersonal skills and techniques when working in a team environment. It provides strategies and techniques for strengthening personal competencies and confidence when working with others. Regardless of your occupation, background, and work experience, this book will increase your ability and power to influence others in more positive ways.

This is a handbook for managers, supervisors, team leaders, project managers, and people who want to improve their teamwork and motivational skills. It explores individual management styles, leadership skills, team facilitation techniques, conflict resolution, decision making, and project team management.

Historically, human factors have been applied to engineering, design, construction, mechanical systems, and industrial processes. Its application to these processes was driven by the need to ensure that equipment and operations were efficient, safe, and compatible with employees' work habits and physical ergonomics. It is now recognized that human factors are important not only in design and operations but also in how people work together within a given system. *System* refers to a group of interrelated things that operate together, such as an organization. The interactions among people are simply the collective behaviors of those people. Behaviors are the things that we see, hear, and feel from others. Organizations are composed of structure, processes, and technology. The key structure in essentially all organizations is the team. So in the context of this book, the objective of human factors is to maximize teamwork and relationships in an organization toward achieving common goals.

The subject of human factors is not formally taught, and most people are not aware of them. Yet human factors are the most important keys in building relationships, teamwork, and motivation. We spend a great deal of time in relationships at work, yet we know little about what motivates our colleagues or what may motivate our own behaviors. We judge others only through our own eyes and quickly draw conclusions about them. We are inclined to compare and contrast behaviors against our own values.

In business today, the emphasis is not on behaviors but on strategies, projects, and time lines. Behavioral elements are often ignored. Yet behaviors—not strategies, processes, and structures—make or break organizational performance.

Most companies recognize diversity as a key corporate value. They sponsor employee clubs, networks, cultural events, and even ethnic lunches to celebrate diversity. These activities help to raise awareness and intracultural sensitivity, but how well do companies promote and integrate diversity in business and project management? Do we truly value diversity in our organizations and teams? Diversity goes well beyond differences in ethnic, cultural, and professional backgrounds, extending deep into human factors. Human factors are the values, work styles, emotions, and experiences that power behaviors and relationships with other people. Human factors are about individual differences and similarities and the need to consider these factors when working in an organization or team. Nothing is more important to our success than being able to recognize and understand human similarities and differences. We recognize human differences all the time, but do we understand them? Why do we like or dislike certain behaviors? Why do we enjoy or disdain certain types of work? Why do we respond to stress differently? Why are we afraid of conflict? Why are some people aggressive, or timid, at work? Learning the strategies and techniques of human factors will help broaden your awareness and understanding of the differences and similarities that exist among people. These differences and similarities are the basis for understanding interpersonal behaviors and motivation.

Behaviors are elements that have an emotional and lasting impact on teams and people. It is true that what you see is what you get, but it is those things that we do not see which matter most. These are the underlying elements that trigger behaviors. We are born with a set of behavioral tendencies that are shaped by life's experiences and human interactions. Human factors are inside all of us but hidden from view. If we could see them, we would be more understanding and forgiving of others. We would have much better relationships, teamwork, and managerial abilities. It would be very powerful to possess such insights into others. Managing human factors is an art rather than a science, because it requires insights into and understanding of human expression. What would you give to have the power to see the motivations behind people's behaviors? This is the power of human factors and the key to project success.

Human factors bring out the best and worst in people. Some people are naturally competitive, which gives them great drive to succeed and win. Yet too much competitiveness can drive others away and reduce teamwork and success. Increasing our knowledge of human factors increases our ability to cope, influence, and motivate. It is the foundation of teamwork, collaboration, leadership, and personal power. Collectively, human factors are the set of relationships, behaviors, and interactions of an organization or project team. It is about our interface with our work environment on a day-to-day basis. They are the relationships and interactions that we look forward to or dread each day. Ultimately it is about how we feel about ourselves when we finally leave the organization.

Many books and articles have been written about teamwork, diversity, quality management, personality types, organizational behaviors, project management, facilitation, and organizational capabilities. But none puts all of these topics together. This book takes concepts from all of these areas and organizes them into simple strategies that can be used daily. The intent of this book is to help people develop their managerial skills and interpersonal relationships. These concepts are aimed at helping people improve their view and understanding of themselves and others and how they can use that knowledge to maximize their influence and happiness.

ORGANIZATION OF THIS BOOK

The key concepts of human factors are presented in a sequence of seventeen chapters. Each chapter builds on the previous one and expands on concepts presented earlier. Therefore, it is best to read the chapters in the order presented.

Chapter One reviews the emergence of human factors and discusses the important changes in management styles and team dynamics. We have gone from a top-down, rules-based, autocratic management style in the pre-1970s to one that is team based, values driven, and participative. Companies are no longer driven by fiats and autocrats but by systems and teams. In the past, the approach was to impose rules, policies, and standard operating procedures to standardize behaviors—to shape people to fit processes rather than shape processes to fit people. We have learned that when power is restricted to the top few, creativity and discretionary performance suffer. Because of the rising cost of doing business, the pace of globalization, and increased workforce diversity, companies have been forced to shift from a hierarchical system to a more leveraged, cross-functional, team-based system of operation. This new interdependent structure demands greater skills in teamwork, motivation, and organizational behaviors. When people understand each other and processes are in place to support them, enormous energy and productivity are created. When people are in conflict or are forced to fit into processes, tremendous opportunity is lost.

Chapter Two clarifies the role of human factors and team dynamics in project management, both critical elements in project management. Every team has the same basic goal: to meet the objectives and expectations of the project. Yet each project team is unique and works on a project differently. Also, each person is unique and pursues the goals of the project differently. Project teams are influenced by three conceptual spaces: organizational space, team space, and personal space. These are the interactive spaces of project management. To bring out the best in people, we must have a good management system and a work environment that supports the diversity of human factors. Our challenge is to learn how to operationalize diversity in our work environment and integrate diversity in our management of projects.

Organizational space encompasses the project's objectives, strategies, goals, work plan, technology, budget, time schedules, policies, performance standards, and procedures, all defined by the organization. These are the hard skills and processes of project management. These areas of project management are enormous and well covered in many books, articles, and periodicals, and are outside the scope of this book. This book focuses on the two primary spaces of human behavior in project management: team space and personal space.

Chapters Three, Four, and Five reveal the three key elements essential in running a successful team: content, process, and behavior. These three elements apply to all industries, companies, organizations, and projects. They are interdependent variables and must be managed well for the team to be successful. When things break down on a project, this failure can be attributed to one or more of these three elements. To achieve high performance, a team must learn how to recognize and distinguish these three factors when problem solving and making decisions. The strength of the team lies in the management of these three elements.

Chapter Six presents the secrets of managing the three key elements of team performance. These are the motivators and demotivators of people and drive the level of collaboration and success of a team. Knowing how to separate and manage these three elements is key. This chapter provides tools, techniques, and strategies on how to use these elements to diagnose and solve relationship and team problems.

Chapter Seven examines the five key stages of team development. It is natural for teams and organizations to go through periods of good and bad teamwork. This chapter breaks down this natural cycle into five distinct stages of team development and productivity: forming, storming, norming, reforming, and performing. Each stage is unique and requires skills in team building, leadership, communications, conflict and stress management, management of change, and achieving team expectations. Understanding this team development cycle helps us better manage team conflicts and work pressures.

Chapter Eight covers the secrets to moving a team forward and describes many of the best tools and techniques in facilitation. It brings together the best team processes for opening and closing team discussions. Team leaders tend to spend too much time on forming content and too little time on forming team processes. People seem to know how to set up a team meeting and know what they want it to accomplish, but it is facilitating the people to get there that is hard: this is process. Having the right processes enables a team to convert strategies and information into decisions and actions.

Chapter Nine demonstrates how personal space and values drive behaviors. How people act and work with others may appear to be natural and spontaneous, but they actually come from a set of acquired and learned responses driven by basic individual values. Values are fundamentally created and shaped by genetic makeup, life experiences, and culture, and these values are inherent in behaviors. Values are what people believe in and demonstrate in their everyday interactions. These values are the underlying human factors of behaviors—the hidden truths. A key determinant of values and behaviors is temperament type. There are four distinct temperament types as identified by David Keirsey: Rational, Idealist, Guardian, and Artisan. Each type has distinct preferences for learning, processing information, communicating, and interacting with others. Each temperament brings different but very valuable skills to a work team. If the goal is to bring out the best in people, maximize performance, and build high-performing teams, then we must respect and understand individual differences in personal values. This chapter reveals the power of life experiences, culture, and temperament types in shaping personal space and values.

Chapter Ten offers effective strategies in understanding and managing team conflicts. The majority of conflicts fall into three main areas: change, values, and behavior. A change conflict usually originates from organizational space and challenges people's abilities to adapt to a new environment. Values conflicts occur between people or between people and an organization. An organization imposes values through its system of policies, decisions, and actions. The most common conflict is behavioral: people do not get along. Behavioral conflicts come from personal space. In conflict situations, each temperament type demonstrates different coping and interactive behaviors. In a team setting, certain conflicts are healthy, but taken to an extreme, each can lead to antagonism and team breakdown. The desired state is team synergy, where breakthrough performance is achieved.

Chapter Eleven explains how fear of conflict affects personal space. Behaviors are often driven by fear: fear of conflict, rejection, failure, embarrassment, and accountability. Nothing grips a team more than conflict. People avoid confrontation and conflict because they often lack the emotional strength, skills, and confidence to resolve it. Fear is a human factor that creates bad team behaviors. It can even drive people to behave contrary to their own beliefs. When they let outside factors drive their behaviors, they lose personal space and self-confidence. Each personality type displays a different set of fearful behaviors. By understanding them, teams are able to address team conflicts more effectively.

Chapter Twelve discusses how to expand personal space to strengthen your abilities to influence others and manage conflict. Expanding space means to reach beyond yourself with positive influence into team space and organizational space, where behaviors have a positive impact on others. Expanding personal space builds informal power, reduces incoming conflicts, motivates others to want to work with you, and gives you inner strength. This chapter provides seven key strategies for expanding your space.

Chapter Thirteen examines the good and bad levels of personal space. Each temperament type has strengths and weaknesses. Everyone possesses positive upper-level behaviors and negative lower-level behaviors. This chapter defines the upper and lower states of human factors and how these states drive behaviors and interactions with others on project teams.

Chapter Fourteen provides strategies and techniques on raising your performance level in teams (in other words, raising your game). Each personality type has a different set of upper- and lower-level behaviors. Whether a person is upper-level dominated or lower-level dominated at any given time is a matter of personal choice. People in their lower state are poor listeners, impatient, self-centered, defensive, frustrated, and fearful. People in their upper-level state are open-minded, tolerant, giving, and collaborative. They naturally move to their lower state when they are stressed and insecure. People reside in their lower levels because they choose to be there. Ironically, people are less stressed and more secure when they are in their upper state. To avoid the lower level, people have the skills and internal strength to take the upper path or receive help from others to do so. This chapter shares numerous techniques to raise your behaviors.

Chapter Fifteen presents the stories of five people of different temperament types and the power of human factors in improving their personal behaviors. These are people who struggled with longtime personal issues, adopted the concepts of human factors, and experienced breakthroughs in their lives.

Chapter Sixteen explores the hearts and minds of human factors. The continuing need for intellectual and emotional fulfillment is the basis for motivation. High-performing teams always show two strong intellectual traits—clear vision and an ability to solve problems and two emotional traits—a positive mind-set and inclusive behaviors. Intellectually, people want to be challenged and connected to the team's content and processes. Emotionally, they want to feel appreciated and valued by others. Each temperament type has certain intellectual and emotional needs. In seeking to fulfill those needs, they send messages through their behaviors, which can have positive and negative impacts on others.

Chapter Seventeen shares the human factors behind personal leadership. Personal leadership has influence in all three spaces and makes things happen. It has power, authority, and great influence on behaviors. Leaders guide behaviors by setting the vision, direction, expectations, and processes. Each personality type brings different leadership styles to an organization, and each can make good team leaders. Yet all good leaders seem to share some common human factors and leadership behaviors. No matter how strong a team is, good leadership is essential in achieving team success, and poor leadership can single-handedly bring a project down. Leaders can bring out the best and the worst in people.

ADDITIONAL ASPECTS OF THE BOOK

In the future, a key organizational challenge will be managing human factors. Teamwork and collaboration will remain core values in successful organizations. Teams are a group of people who have been assembled to work toward a common purpose or project. An entire company can be viewed as a team with a common purpose or a small group of people working on a project. In this book, team refers to a group of people with a shared objective.

One aspect of this book that I am sensitive about is the use of generalizations and stereotypes. I believe generalizations, when used constructively to raise awareness and sensitivity, are educational and justified. Diversity is about differences, but it is also about similarities. Observing and understanding different types of personalities, generations of people, and behaviors increases our social and behavioral intelligence. We are all diverse in the same way. We seek the same things in life and work: to be appreciated, loved, valued, and accepted. However, each of us pursues it differently. That pursuit consumes and generates a lot of human energy. That is what gives power to human factors.

Too often, books tell you what you need to do but never any specifics on how to do it. This book covers both the whats and the hows in managing behaviors and team dynamics. It is intended to increase awareness of individual diversity and behaviors. It contains strategies, concepts, and techniques for improving interpersonal skills and team management. In this book, the concepts are presented in the context of an interactive project team, where a high level of human interaction occurs. Projects fail because of poor execution, and poor execution occurs because of poor people management and performance. To put it simply, projects fail because we fail to manage human factors.

Emergence of Human Factors

For over two decades, the successful teachings and practices of Edward Deming, Joseph Juran, Quality Management, Total Quality Management, and Six Sigma have been key drivers in shaping business culture. They have helped improve business productivity and enabled change through greater strategic alignment, customer focus, and continuous process improvement. These concepts have greatly contributed to the global competitiveness and success of international companies. They have provided philosophies for effective strategic leadership, systematic methods for improving business processes, and tools for driving performance improvements. Most important, they have advanced the concepts of teamwork in organizational performance.

In the past three decades, business management has dramatically changed. Prior to 1970, management was predominantly top down, rules based, and autocratic. A militaristic philosophy was common. This changed as companies realized that when power was restricted to the top few, creativity and discretionary performance suffered. In the 1980s, team-based, values-driven organizations appeared. More employee participative philosophies were introduced. Companies were no longer driven by rules and autocrats but by systems and teams. They were still managed by rules, policies, and standard operating procedures. The effect was to standardize behaviors and shape people to fit processes. The visionary 1990s inspired a shared mission, vision, values, and objectives approach and opened the process for greater employee participation. With a shared vision and plan, people were considered in sync with the direction and priorities of management—a new shared ownership of objectives. But this shared ownership turned out to be insufficient, and new tools and processes to execute these objectives were needed. Enlightened companies soon recognized that old command-and-control processes did not work well with their shared strategies. Also, companies faced pressures of rising costs, product cycles, globalization, and a rapidly changing workforce and were forced to adopt a more distributed, leveraged system of operation. In other words, they had to make every employee count. A key enabler of this change was technology, which provided the connectivity and critical tools to make dramatic improvements in information sharing, work productivity, communications, and rate of change. Another key was building organizational capabilities around core businesses and technologies.

These business developments resulted in a profound change in organizational structures and how work was being managed. The traditional hierarchical structure was replaced with natural teams, self-managed teams, cross-functional teams, employee networks, and project teams. A team operated as a group of people with shared objectives and processes and possessed complementary skills, knowledge, and experiences. Some of these team structures, such as project teams and cross-functional teams, were not necessarily new, but how the teams operated and the impact of these teams on organizations were far different and much more empowered than in the past to make changes.

The team-based structure quickly became a norm in organizations. Businesses and projects benefited when people worked together well as a team. Successful team-based companies saw higher employee morale, innovation, and financial success. But creating a productive, sustainable team environment took more work. In addition to strategies and processes, a third need was identified: an improved system for managing people's behaviors. Modifying and adopting new behaviors to facilitate strategies and processes were not keeping pace with the structural changes that were occurring. Behavioral management was an intangible, the soft side of business. Yet it is critical to success. Companies knew this but did not know how to do it.

In the past decade, the focus on strategies and processes has significantly shifted to team behaviors and project execution. It has been recognized that successful execution requires a stronger emphasis on people skills such as leadership and collaboration, and team behaviors around decision making, problem solving, and conflict resolution. To help, companies began personalizing their value statements by defining specific behaviors that supported those values. These values define how people will work together on a day-to-day basis. Companies have sought to build a community of workers dedicated to common behavioral norms (the GE Values, The Nokia Way and Values, the Chevron Way), cast as the things they believe in. They seek not just to get results but to get results the right way, meaning that people walk away feeling good about the project and themselves, including their relationships with others and their contributions to the team. Feelings and relationships are the motivating human factors that carry over into future projects. These motivating factors generate human energy and discretionary performance and produce sustained success. The new definition of success in project management is "getting results and feeling good about it."

As Figure 1.1 shows, project success has two dimensions of performance. First is meeting project expectations. This means that the results meet project objectives, which includes being on time, on spec, and within budget. Second is meeting people's expectations: this means that values are respected, people feel fulfilled, and they succeed together as a team. High performance in one or the other is only partial success; true project success requires meeting both people and project expectations. Project managers lead both projects and people.

We are in the midst of learning how best to manage employees in a changing global business environment. A team-based work environment still fits well in a rapidly changing global marketplace. However, there is a strong drive to maximize knowledge, skills, and behaviors across the enterprise. The focus on shaping workforce behaviors has resulted in greater profit sharing, individual and team incentives, greater team recognitions and awards, and employee development programs.

With a new emphasis on team behaviors, human factors have emerged as a critical element. The study of human factors has extended beyond ergonomics and engineering and into team behaviors as it relates to organizational performance. Human factors are clearly a business issue today. The issue has grown in large part due to globalization and workforce reductions: employee downsizings, right sizing, rationalizing, optimizing, restructuring, delayering, and offshoring. These "ings" have reshaped how we work and reshaped our view of the work environment forever. These developments have changed not only the competitive landscape but also the human landscape: the relationship between employees and employer and how people behave on the job. Companies that recognize this change and respond to it successfully will be the winners.

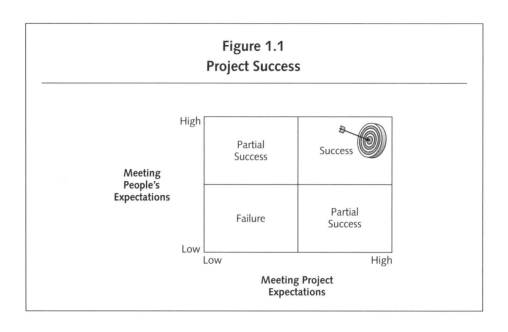

Figure 1.1
Project Success

Organizational success will continue to depend on how people work and interact with each other. Human factors help by bringing effective behavioral elements into structure and process. The power of human factors is understanding motivation. How we motivate and develop people is determined by their talents and dynamics, as well as the competitive challenges of company objectives and strategies. When people understand each other and processes are in place to support them, enormous human energy and productivity are created. When they are in conflict or are forced to fit into processes, tremendous opportunity is lost. For example, a major movement in business today is to standardize and institutionalize processes to get the best and most efficient results. So companies continue to streamline, reengineer, right-size, and rationalize their enterprises to achieve superior business results for the shareholders. What this approach fails to recognize is that people are not standardized, and trying to force-fit people into standardized processes can limit success by limiting human creativity, motivation, and freedom to operate. Work becomes a compliant, punishable activity.

When setting organizational standards, it is important to ask which human elements are being affected and which behaviors are critical for the execution of these standards. Respecting diversity and individuality are essential. For example, does a strict nine-to-five work schedule respect individual needs? Does placing employees in standardized work cubicles maximize employee performance and creativity? How will an open work environment affect people's values, personal stress, and emotions? Standardization is good as long as human factors are considered and integrated into these processes. Processes become best practices when they are aligned with business objectives, human elements, and the culture of the organization. That is why best practices in one organization are so difficult to adopt in other companies. In order for an organization to be successful, the human element must be factored into operational and management systems. When human factors are well integrated into the objectives, strategies, and processes of the organization, then people are engaged and performing at their best.

The motivational power of human factors comes from meeting the intellectual and emotional needs of people, valuing people for who they are, and respecting the diversity of their backgrounds, cultures, and experiences. Project objectives need to align to processes, but they also need to align to people if projects are to be planned and executed successfully. People, not objectives and processes, create success. Objectives and content provide direction and processes enable action, but ultimately human factors make or break a project. Only people can generate the needed motivation and human energy to get the job done. In today's complex work environment, people must be good collaborators and facilitators, because no one has direct control over everyone they work with. As time goes on, we must depend more and more on the cooperation of others to get our own job done. At the same time, organizations are functionally more integrated, and departments and divisions are more leveraged in their operations and work processes. Basically, companies are becoming more dependent on internal and external partnerships to meet their business goals.

The dynamics of individual values versus organizational values creates an opportunity for both great successes and deep disappointments. When people are asked to work in close quarters with others, there is a potential risk because of the many uncertainties and personalities involved. They are brought together to work on a common goal, yet their interests, background, commitment, competencies, and personalities may be quite different and unknown to others. In the absence of this knowledge, people will make assumptions and judgments based on their personal experiences, culture, and psychological types. Each of us copes with change and new challenges in a different way. Typically we all carry our emotional highs and lows from past team experiences, hoping for the best but also braced for the worst.

Teams within the same company are usually fairly successful, probably due to shared organizational structure, policies, and behavioral norms. Also, people generally like to work on teams. Maybe they like the safety in numbers, a break from normal routines, or the promise of great achievement, but the idea of joining a team has always had a certain special allure. Being selected to serve on a team is a special commitment. In most cases, people are asked to do something beyond their current job. As they move out of the comfort and familiarity of their own work group, they are challenged with intercompany and intercultural differences among people. Misunderstandings and even conflicts may result. Misunderstandings may be intellectual, but conflicts are emotionally consuming and take people to places that can be very deep and regretful. Working on a new team can truly test a person's intellectual and emotional strengths.

SUMMARY

Over the past three decades, organizational structures have made the transition from a top-down, autocratic structure to a team-based, values-based structure. This shift has caused a change in how people view and execute projects. How team members treat each other is more important than procedures and work plans. The ideal goal in project management is to "achieve results and feel good about it." Human factors are the driving force behind project success. Projects fail when there is a failure to motivate and respect human factors. When human intellectual and emotional needs are met and systems are in place to support those needs, enormous human energy and productivity are created. When people are in conflict or are forced to fit into processes, tremendous opportunity is lost. The motivation and human energy needed to execute projects successfully are generated by people.

Human Factors and Team Dynamics in Project Management

A project is a planned undertaking that requires a set of human tasks and activities toward achieving a specific objective within a defined time period. Projects are temporary, though they may last from a few hours to many years. A team project involves a group of people with complementary skills and experiences, working together to accomplish the goals and objectives of the project. The purpose of the team is to develop and execute a work plan that will meet the expectations of the project. Everyone on the team is committed and dedicated to the same thing: meeting the goals of the project. Although the goals may be same, how the team elects to execute the work plan is variable.

Different teams run the same project differently. This variation is attributable to differences in people, processes, and interactions. The interactions of a team are dependent on the collective knowledge, skills, experiences, personalities, and behaviors of the group. Each person has personal preferences regarding how to run the project and how to work within the project. People have different work and communication styles, and these personal preferences and differences represent the diversity of the team. All team members want the same thing (to achieve the project goals), but each goes after it differently due to their diversity. This can generate both positive and negative interactions. How well we manage human interactions is the key to the success of any project.

The dynamics of a project is determined by the project's strategies, work plan, team processes, team behaviors, and individual human factors. These components are integrated, but they operate at three different planes or spaces. *Space* refers to a conceptual boundary of human interaction. First, the interaction of people and systems occurs in a broad organizational space. Second, people's interactions with each other occur within a smaller space, referred to as team space. Finally, there is a third space: each team member's inner self or personal space where internal interactive thinking occurs and human factors are formed. Thus, a project has three types of interactive spaces: organizational space, team space, and personal space. I call these the three spaces of project management (Figure 2.1).

Once project objectives and goals are defined, the role of a project team is to plan, execute, and control the project. Organizational space encompasses the project's goals, strategies, business plan, budget, schedule requirements, policies, performance standards, procedures, and deliverables, all defined by the organization. The organization has ultimate control of this space. The business plan and resources represent the overall management system of the organization and project.

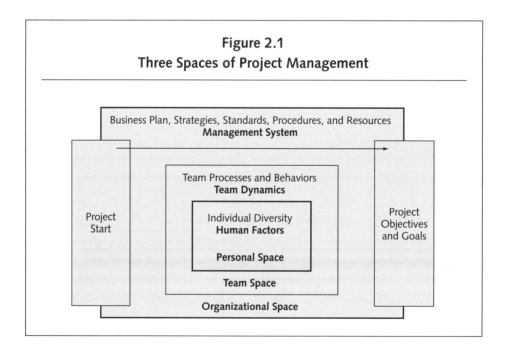

Figure 2.1
Three Spaces of Project Management

Business Plan, Strategies, Standards, Procedures, and Resources
Management System

Team Processes and Behaviors
Team Dynamics

Individual Diversity
Human Factors

Personal Space

Team Space

Project
Start

Project
Objectives
and Goals

Organizational Space

Critical tools and skills needed to operate this system include project planning, strategic thinking, budgeting, scheduling, information management, and logistics. These are the so-called hard skills of project management. Also, going from start to finish in accordance with the team's work plan and schedule is a results-oriented, linear process. In other words, it is a set of time-dependent activities, and the project is driven by a deadline. The team's goal is to complete the project on time, on spec, and within budget. Organizational space is therefore unemotional, logical, and objective based.

Supporting this organizational space are team processes and team behaviors, which the team owns and controls. For example, team meetings and communication processes are defined and operated by the team. How the work is performed depends on the teamwork and collaboration among team members. This space represents team dynamics. It is an interactive space with shared responsibilities based on team agreements and decisions. What occurs in this space has direct influence on project management. Positive team dynamics certainly increases project performance and success. Each individual has influence and partial control of this space. Sharing space requires individual compromise and accommodation. It is not a linear, time-dependent process but a behavior-based process. Team space is where individual behaviors are exhibited. The management system motivates team behaviors. Team processes drive individual behaviors. In business today, the emphasis is not on behaviors but on strategies, projects, and time lines. Behavioral elements are often ignored. Yet people's behaviors, not strategies, processes, and structures, are what make or break organizational performance. Project management requires good management of team behaviors. Personal preferences may have to be relinquished for the greater good. Roles and responsibilities, team facilitation, decision-making processes, ground rules, feedback, work coordination, and accountability are all critical elements in a shared system. Good team dynamics are essential to successful project management.

Team behaviors are the collective behaviors of individual team members. Individual behaviors are formed by internal factors—the human factors that make us unique: our genetics, values, personalities, experiences, culture, and beliefs. No two people have the same makeup. The way we respond to people and things externally is a reflection of our internal human factors. We have full authority and control over how we respond and interact with others. This is personal space. It is not shared or owned by an organization or team. We choose how we want to respond to the world each day. Our perception and response are filtered and shaped by our human factors. Human factors have tremendous power and influence over team dynamics. They are at the core of successful project management.

People operate in these three spaces every day regardless of whether they are involved in a project. Their organizational space is defined by their employers as well as by government institutions, legal systems, and various authorities. Each organization or institution must comply with governmental and legal requirements. Also, each organization has objectives, goals, strategies, policies, work ethics, and procedures that define its work culture and behavioral norms. To do well in these organizations, workers must conform and behave according to these rules, policies, and expectations.

The workplace environment is unique. People are expected to be cooperative, friendly, and respectful, and workplace regulations prevent people from discriminating, harassing, or hurting each other. Procedures, policies, and reporting relationships control behavior. Any nonconforming behaviors are deselected in some direct or indirect way by the organization, which strives to create a work space where people are treated lawfully and fairly.

Personal space is a private place where we have full control over what we think, do, or say. We have no rules, policies, requirements, or procedures in how we must think, store, or process information. If we want to be optimistic, we can be optimistic. If we want to be excited, we can be excited. Motivation comes from this personal space. We define our own space, and that space is always occupied by our human factors. This space contains our memories, learnings, senses, and feelings drawn from our culture, experiences, and personality type. For example, our feelings of compassion may be drawn from our experiences with people who are poor and disadvantaged. It is a space that helps us see, interpret, and respond to the world. External information is internalized in personal space and intellectually and emotionally processed through internal dialogue. We define our personal space as a place where internal interactive thinking occurs and human factors are formed. Internal dialogue occurs as we mentally process new information, interpret its meaning against our human factors, and express those perceptions in our behaviors. The content of our space helps us generate compassion, empathy, and competitiveness, as well as disappointments, sadness, and insecurities. This space is where our self-confidence, self-motivation, and self-esteem are generated and maintained. Personal space can generate enormous desire and human energy.

Research has shown that desired employee behaviors are motivated from all three spaces in our project management model. Theories on employee motivation have existed since the nineteenth century, beginning with Elton Mayo's famous studies at the Hawthorne factory of the Western Electric Company in Chicago from 1924 to 1932. Mayo's research revealed that workers were not solely driven by monetary benefits (organizational space) but were motivated by social elements as well (team space). In fact, social elements like communications, teamwork, and employee involvement can lead to better work performance, even when work conditions are worsening. The Hawthorne studies gave birth to the study of employee management and highlighted the importance of addressing the human needs of workers.

Following Mayo's classic work, numerous long-standing theories have been developed about motivation. Abraham Maslow's hierarchy of human needs (1954; Figure 2.2) focuses on the inner space and posits that people are motivated by five

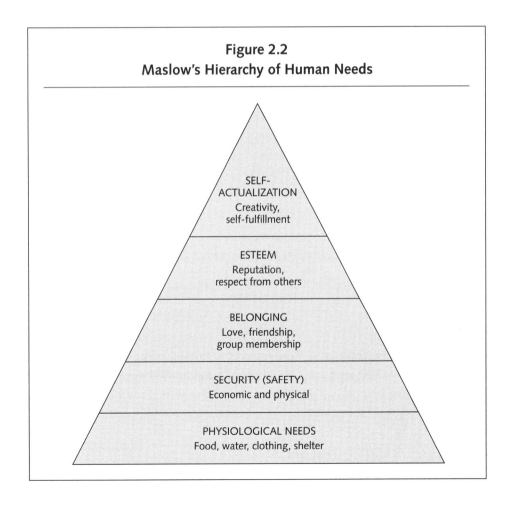

Figure 2.2
Maslow's Hierarchy of Human Needs

SELF-ACTUALIZATION
Creativity, self-fulfillment

ESTEEM
Reputation, respect from others

BELONGING
Love, friendship, group membership

SECURITY (SAFETY)
Economic and physical

PHYSIOLOGICAL NEEDS
Food, water, clothing, shelter

psychological levels of needs: physiological, security, social, esteem, and self-actualization. These five levels are treated as a hierarchy where basic physiological needs are sought first, then security, social, esteem, and, finally, self-actualization. People must satisfy the lower level before moving to the next higher level. Not everyone aspires to the same level of human need or achieves self-fulfillment. These five areas may be common to everyone; however, people operate at different levels, and organizations need to support their workers in satisfying their desired level of need. Organizational space needs to provide a work environment that helps employees transcend their hierarchy. It recognizes that each person (personal space) is motivated in different ways in satisfying his or her needs.

Frederick Herzberg's dual factor theory (Herzberg, Mausner, and Snyderman, 1959) distinguished between factors causing satisfaction (motivators) and those causing dissatisfaction (hygiene factors) (Table 2.1). Hygiene factors are employment factors that prevent dissatisfaction and are expected to be adequately provided. Motivators are more personalized factors (personal space) that give people feelings of achievement, recognition, enrichment, and growth. This may include job responsibilities, position, title, authority, and learning opportunities. In the three-space model, hygiene factors represent things found in organizational space, such as salary, benefits, job security, work conditions, policies, and safety, and also team space such as interpersonal relationships and supervision.

Table 2.1
Herzberg's Dual Factors

Hygiene Factors	Motivators
• Salary	• Recognition
• Policies	• Responsibilities
• Work conditions	• Advancement
• Administration	• Personal achievement
• Security	• Interest in the work
• Safety	
• Supervision	
• Interpersonal relationships	

Victor Vroom's expectancy theory (1995) deals with the concept of effort, performance, and reward—how the level of individual effort on a given task will translate into success and personal reward. Before committing to a task, people tend to weigh the level of effort required versus probable benefits. They need to know that the job task will likely lead to better results and that the results will lead to a benefit that is meaningful to the employee.

Motivation is an inner judgment process of effort (personal space) and expected outcomes. It is similar to a personal cost-benefit analysis:

Effort on Task → Probable Outcome → Personal Reward

David McClelland's achievement theory (McClelland, Atkinson, Clark, and Lowell, 1953) believes that people are motivated by three basic needs: (1) achievement—attain realistic but challenging goals and gain advancement in the job; (2) power—lead and have their ideas prevail; and (3) affiliation—cooperative relationships with others. These three needs are not mutually exclusive; people may be motivated by one, two, or all three elements. Some people may be motivated by achievement and affiliation, while others are partially motivated by all three. An organization should try to formulate jobs and responsibilities that best fit the individual's needs (that is, the person's personal space).

John Stacy Adam's equity theory (1963) states the importance of fairness when managing groups of employees. Workers seek a fair balance between what they put into their jobs (inputs) and what they get out of it (outcomes). Employees want to be treated fairly and are likely to compare their treatment to that of their peers. This theory recognizes the motivational force of organizational space when rewarding for performance and how favoritism and inequities in the system can lead to job dissatisfaction and demotivation.

Douglas McGregor's theory X and Y (1960) presents two opposing sets of assumptions regarding the attitudes of managers and employees (Figure 2.3). Basically, theory X assumes that workers are lazy and will avoid work if given the choice, while theory Y assumes that workers are creative and want to do a good job. If we believe theory X is correct, then management needs to be authoritative and motivate employees through strict control of the work environment with clear negative consequences for nonperformance. It requires a task-oriented, fear-based system of management (top-down, organizational space control). In contrast, theory Y workers want to create, contribute, and participate in work planning and

Figure 2.3
McGregor's Theory X and Y

Theory X

Assumes people are not self-motivated in their jobs, and that most people:

- Dislike their work and will avoid it
- Lack ambition and have little capacity for problem solving and creativity
- Prefer direction and avoid taking responsibility and initiative
- Are motivated only by Maslow's lower level of needs (physiological and safety)
- Are self-centered or indifferent to organizational needs and resistant to change

Theory Y

Assumes people want to do well and that most workers:

- Meet high-performance expectations when appropriately motivated in a supportive climate
- Are creative, imaginative, ambitious, and committed to meeting organizational goals
- Are self-disciplined and self-directed, desire responsibility, and accept them willingly
- Are motivated by Maslow's higher-level needs (self-esteem and self-actualization)

decision making. They are self-starters who desire more responsibilities and direct involvement. Far more workers behave like theory Y than theory X.

No one of these theories can be expected to capture the essence of motivation perfectly. However, there are some common themes among them:

- Historic motivational theories are more centered on organizational space and responsibility of management in motivating its workers. However, early research found that social roles and employee involvement were important factors.

- Earlier theories focused on organizational management, with little treatment on team-based motivations and behaviors. Before 1980, team-based organizational concepts were scarce.

- Motivation is highly individualistic and situational.

A good project manager has a positive influence in all three spaces. Management systems are easier to influence because they are visible and standardized, while human factors are much more difficult to manage because they are invisible and unique to each individual. Good managers have the hard and soft skills to meet people's core needs. Project success is not only about meeting deadlines and goals but also about meeting the expectations of people. An organization can sacrifice the latter now and then, but to be successful in the long term, it needs to keep, develop, and motivate people. A sustaining organization relies on human energy and motivation. Human factors provide the energy and motivation to achieve success. By having a better understanding of this energy, we can tap it and draw out the best in people. More important, we can draw out the best in ourselves.

Human factors represent the diversity in people. It is well accepted that workforce diversity creates better results and higher organizational performance. Creating an inclusive work environment generates better ideas, production, and quality products. Many companies consider diversity a corporate value and say they value and respect it. Yet how well are they operationalizing diversity in the workplace by integrating and factoring it in conducting business, developing people, and executing projects? How do they put diversity into action? Sponsoring cultural events, hiring more ethnic minorities, supporting diversity networks, holding special cultural celebrations, and providing diversity awareness training are all well-intended activities, but how is diversity truly valued and respected in the organization? Having people on the team who think differently is a good practice, but what more can organizations do? How do we expand our understanding of diversity to inspire greater performance? In the following chapters, we explore the spaces of the organization, team dynamics, and diversity in maximizing the power of human factors. Each chapter presents key concepts, tools, and techniques for improving management knowledge and people skills.

SUMMARY

Team dynamics and human factors are critical elements in project management. Every team has the same basic goal: to meet the objectives and expectations of the project. Yet each project team is unique and operates a project differently. Also, each person is unique and pursues the goals of the project differently.

Project teams are influenced by three conceptual spaces: organizational, team, and personal. These are the interactive spaces of project management. Organizational space represents the management system; it directs and controls the project externally. Team space is where team dynamics and interpersonal behaviors reside. Personal space contains the human factors that define and drive each person's behaviors. All three spaces are critical to project management.

To bring out the best in people, an organization must have a good management system and a work environment that support its diversity of human factors. The challenge is to learn how to operationalize diversity in the work environment and integrate diversity in planning, execution, and control of projects. The following chapters discuss strategies, techniques, and tools for understanding and valuing diversity in project teams.

Key Elements
of Team Performance
Content

Three key elements are required to run a successful team: content, process, and behavior. These three elements apply to all types of organizations, projects, and work teams. Human factors are embodied in all three elements.

The content is the "what" or intent of the team—the vision, objectives, direction, opportunities, strategies, and assumptions. Vision represents the highest motivating force for the team. Teams are inspired by vision and the hope for success, and the objectives and strategies provide direction to that vision. Process is the "how"—the tools and procedures that help a team reach its objectives. Behavior is the collective human interactions of the team.

Content defines the team's purpose and work plan, and process converts the team's purpose and work plans into actions. Process also influences behaviors, which drive team performance. Most important, these three elements are motivators and

demotivators of people and determine the level of success of the team. Team performance is high when all three elements are operating well.

The key to any high-performing team is the team's ability to develop and agree on the key purpose, goals, and plans of the project (content); use the right tools, techniques, and procedures to implement the team's work plan (process); and communicate, collaborate, and work in synergy (behavior). These three factors are interdependent variables and must be in place and working in synergy for a project team to be successful. It is a system. Content does not stand alone.

To accomplish the purpose of the project, effective processes and the right behaviors are needed. When things break down on a team project, the breakdown can be attributed to one or more of these three elements. If one element changes or breaks down, the other two elements are affected. For example, when the goals of the project suddenly change, it is certain that the work processes and behaviors will change in response to this disruption. That is why the three elements are shown as three overlapping circles. In order to be a high-performing project team, the team must learn how to recognize the element that is changing and distinguish among the three factors when problem solving and making decisions.

I have found that people are predominantly content focused. They prefer to address the subject matter and goals more than anything else. People are programmed to be content driven by our educational systems and the general business culture. Content is regarded as the hard stuff, while processes and behaviors are perceived as soft. Also, people are more conscious of content. They decide to do things for a reason, and they will not fully engage without first knowing the purpose and "what's in it for me." No doubt, understanding expectations and objectives, defining the problem, and developing work strategies are indeed important. Yet in reality, processes and behaviors are harder to address, and content is actually the easiest. More important, process operationalizes a team's content and drives behaviors. It is easier to align people to the objectives of an organization than it is to align people to processes and desired behaviors. What needs to be done is usually explicit; how people do it and how people treat each other in the process are not always very explicit because people have different individual values, perceptions, work styles, and personalities.

DEFINING CONTENT

Content is the rallying point for the team. It is the reason the team was formed. The content refers to the purpose, intent, or subject matter of the project. The pur-

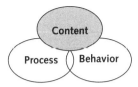

pose of the project may be around improving a process, restructuring an organization, introducing a new product, or building a new company. The content also
covers the work outputs, decisions, and expectations of the team. Most large team
projects are formally commissioned by management, who define the purpose and
objectives. Content is an output of organizational space. A company may have a
need to expand or improve an asset, policy, or process, and it fulfills that need
through a continuous series of projects. Projects are executed by a team of people
who each have their own unique set of team dynamics and human factors.

Content is probably the most tangible and the most visible of the three elements
because it is the reason the team was formed. Typically team members are stakeholders and subject matter experts of the content. Content is the most familiar element to a team. Since many teams are given the purpose of the team, the content
is the joining force and the one element that requires full agreement and clarity
from the start. All high-performing teams have a strong common purpose and
shared goals (Katzenbach and Smith, 1993). There must be explicit team agreement, and each person must have a stake in the success of the outcome. The toughest situation is when people do not want to be on the team but feel they "have to"
participate. A "have-to" attitude weakens a team's commitment. It is not fatal, but
it is a factor that needs to be addressed rather than ignored.

The core content of any project team is the compelling business case. A business case contains all the reasons for doing this project: What is compelling us to do
this project at this time? The key questions of a business case are

- What are the benefits to me and the organization?
- Is there a window of opportunity in effect?
- In what way does this project have to do with the company's strategic objectives?
- In what way will this project affect the organization?

If the reasons for the team are highly relevant and timely to the individual, commitment to the project will follow. However, commitment to the team is another matter. Commitment is the ability to engage with trust. A team must have a compelling vision to inspire personal commitment. Inspiration is taking purpose to the highest level and sustains a team through good and bad times. A critical aspect of building a high-performing team is developing the team's commitment, which can be accomplished in a number of ways—for example

- Articulating how each person is vital to the success of the project
- Highlighting the complementary knowledge and skills of the team members
- Taking the time and effort to get to know each other
- Clarifying roles and responsibilities
- Making sure everyone has a stake in the work plan and outcome

Debate helps clarify the team's purpose. Teams need to debate their team's purpose and direction. Creative tension is healthy, especially in problem solving. Getting diverse opinions and perspectives from stakeholders, management, and team members is critical for ensuring that the project will address key concerns and issues. Teams often make the mistake of assuming that everyone knows the purpose of the project and no one wants to second-guess management. People are typically eager to get to the solution. Debate, challenge, and skepticism are required to yield a robust and sustainable point of direction and purpose. A team should always welcome constructive disagreement and challenges. There are four key reasons for debating content:

- Ensure any individual biases are fleshed out.
- Achieve a shared understanding of the purpose and content. Poor clarity leads to confusion and conflict later, and fuzzy content produces fuzzy performance.
- Define good behaviors and team dynamics for resolving differences.
- Uncover any hidden agendas (differing objectives).

CREATING CONTENT

Effective tools and practices help project teams support content.

Project Team Charter

No one tool is more effective in defining the content of the project than the team's written charter or terms of reference document, which embodies the team's understanding of what they are being asked to do. The document is written by the project team and endorsed by the organization's management. Depending on the project, the charter may be derived from a formal contract, work order, or service agreement. It should be a stand-alone document that captures the full understanding of the project team and is owned by the team. The charter is the document that drives the team's process and, in some ways, the team's behaviors. Nothing focuses the minds of a team more than written team agreements.

A team charter has these key components:

- Objective: A statement on the purpose of the project.
- Problem statement or opportunity statement: A sentence that explains why it is important to solve this issue and what the benefits will be for the company.
- Current state: A description of the current status of the problem or opportunity and why it is beneficial to take action.
- Key drivers: The key factors that cause this problem to exist and are motivating the team to address it now.
- Project value: The tangible benefits of solving this issue and what the potential size of the prize will be in terms of quantitative value (for example, cash or rate of return).
- Project sponsor: The person or organization that is leading the formation and support of this project.
- Team members and roles: A list of formal team members and support personnel and what role each person is playing on the team (team leader, facilitator, expert adviser, voting and nonvoting members, and part-time members, for example).
- Customers and stakeholders: The people who will be affected by the outcome of this project.
- Project boundaries: The scope of the project in terms of subject matter, the depth of study, the areas of study, and other factors such as which organizations are involved, geographical boundaries, and time frame.
- Key team decisions: The specific decisions that the project team is being asked to make.

ject assumptions: The strategic and tactical factors that the team believes are ~ or will be true concerning the content of the project and the responsibilities of the team. For example, if the goal of the project is to improve an accounting process, the team may assume that the accounting process will stay in-house and not be contracted out; if the project is to build a new office complex, the project team will assume the office complex will be built to accommodate "the current population of employees plus 20 percent," the employee growth forecast in the company's most recent business plan.

- Deliverables: The specific work outputs of the team to the project sponsors. A deliverable can range from a verbal recommendation to a lengthy written report. Each deliverable carries a firm deadline.

- Success metrics: The measures that the team will use to gauge the progress and success of the project.

- Resources: A list of additional people, equipment, budget, and assets that will be available to the team.

Air Cover for the Team

Air cover refers to the power and protection that management can give to a project team. Management can provide company resources, funding, time to work on the project, decisions on matters outside the reach of the team, and authorization to access and process information. When the team runs into barriers, management can work to remove them and influence others to support the project. No project can operate successfully without the support of management. The key is to get specific individuals from management to back up the team. This may take the form of a decision review board, steering committee, governance board, or executive sponsor. The project team itself needs to define the role and expectations of the management team in the project. The team members must not assume that management knows what the team needs. It is important to clarify expectations. A management confidant or management committee can be valuable in serving as a sounding board to test the team's ideas and directions.

Some team members may resist air cover and say, "I was assigned to this project, and they are looking to us to get the job done." They see management involvement as unnecessary and a hindrance that might stifle their creativity, dilute their authority and power to act, make the team appear weak, or increase pressure on the team to follow their guidance. These are common reactions for people who feel insecure. Air cover works very well: it reduces the team's risk of failure and positions the team for better communications and management buy-in.

Another reason for air cover is to gain a better view of the political minefield. Typically every major project has some sort of political element to it—that is, sensitive organizational factors that fall outside the scope and control of the team but have a major influence on the context, if not the content, of the team project. They may include turf issues, management processes, legal concerns, management biases, strategic changes, and other confidential issues. A team cannot work in a vacuum; these minefields have a way of attaching themselves to the project. A management contact can serve as a good political adviser to the project team. If nothing else, management support can serve as a shield to protect the team from getting misdirected.

Identifying Biases Early

Project teams are more effective when they share a common objective. Yet the factors driving each team member to commit to the project may be different. When I was assigned to a project team to reorganize an internal service group, I understood the intent as to realign the service group functions to their internal customers and improve cycle time. Two other team members had the same understanding, but with the underlying intent to reduce staffing and costs, and another thought that the intent was to relocate the function to another department. These hidden differences in our intents did not surface until our third meeting and were a major cause of conflict, disagreement, and uncooperative behaviors.

These are the hidden agendas that often surface in teams because team members have information that they are unwilling to entrust to the team. People in unfamiliar surroundings naturally hold back information until they feel safe to do so. In the meantime, there could be a lot of testing and probing that goes on initially. Team leadership, openness, and preparedness can help reduce the problems of hidden agendas.

It is important to encourage openness and establish a shared vision of the team's mission and objectives. The key is to recognize that not everyone is starting from the same point. To help avoid this problem, in the first meeting, each team member should share what he or she knows about the project and what assumptions and biases may exist. All assumptions and biases should be captured and summarized. Conflicting team assumptions and potential biases should be discussed with management sponsors. Depending on the sensitivity of an issue, sometimes one-on-one discussions with management can be effective, followed by a team meeting with

agement. The important point is to capture all assumptions at the start and
___m with management before proceeding. Clarity of purpose and intents goes
a long way to avoiding team misunderstandings, conflict, and distrust. Explicit team
assumptions help avoid conflicts in team objectives.

Communicating the Charter

Once a team has its purpose and content of the project, both should be communicated right away—to the sponsor, managers, and peers. Communication should be both verbal and in writing and occur in a timely fashion.

Requiring a team to put its purpose in writing forces the team not only to clarify and explicitly agree on what they are doing but also focuses and pinpoints the key reasons for doing the project. Naturally, everyone wants to know why the project is being done, who is involved, how it may affect them, and what the time line is for results.

It helps to communicate the formation and purpose of the project team throughout the organization. This not only gives legitimacy and power to the team but also sets realistic expectations. Since all projects involve some degree of change, the announcement starts a change process: a series of actions that an organization takes to address the impact of change to people.

Change processes need to be managed well. Some people enjoy the opportunities of change, and others fear it. The threat of change can be more worrisome than change itself. Heavy resistance may result, for example, and reactions can range from fear, denial, and anger to full acceptance and support. Because of these negative reactions, some organizations may elect not to communicate anything. Some managers may say, "Let's wait until something is decided" or "Let's not get the workforce all riled up; it will be a distraction we can't afford." Rationalizing inaction is easy. Open communications and sharing information build trust and respect in an organization. Also, communicating in a timely manner strengthens the credibility of the message. If the subject matter is highly sensitive, the communication needs to be more limited.

SUMMARY

Three key elements are required to run a successful team project: content, process, and behavior. These three factors are interdependent variables and must be in place and working in synergy for a project team to be successful. When a project breaks down, the failure can usually be attributed to one or more of these elements.

Content is the purpose and intent of the project—the vision, objectives, direction, opportunities, strategies, and assumptions. These directives are most commonly captured in a team charter or terms of reference. The initial goal of a team is to establish a shared view of the team's expectations and understand the different motivations and perspectives that each member brings to the project. The project should be communicated to stakeholders outside the team in order to strengthen the visibility and buy-in for the project. Teams are inspired by vision and the hope for success, and the objectives and strategies provide direction to that vision. A team must have a compelling vision to inspire personal commitment. Inspiration is taking purpose to the highest level and sustains a team through good times and bad.

Key Elements
of Team Performance

Process

The second key element in team performance is process. Most text-books define processes as the tools, techniques, and procedures that people use to reach their goals. In organizational space, processes are high-level procedures in planning, finance, human resources, safety, and legal. These organizational processes help to ensure compliance to company policies and legal requirements. Many are long-standing and are adjusted as the organization evolves. Project teams are expected to comply with these organizational processes and requirements. This may affect how a team communicates with management, how project expenses are managed, how the team behaves in working with outside contractors, and how rewards and recognitions are given. Processes

that reside in organizational space can have a significant effect on team behaviors.

In team space, processes are temporary and are defined by the team to fit the needs of the project. Team processes are the most underestimated power in influencing people's behavior. Process plays a much greater and influential role in team dynamics and human factors than content.

Process plays three critical roles:

- Converts the team's charter and work plan into actions
- Influences individual and team behaviors
- Helps to reveal the intent behind behaviors

Processes are the expressways for the team. They can take the team quickly to a desired destination or bog it down in confusing traffic. A good process feels like a smooth ride down the interstate, and team members feel energetic and in control. A bad process saps energy from people; they feel that the process rather than the team is in control. Processes can be used to uncover disagreement, hidden agendas, contrary thinking, conspiracy, and destructive behaviors. They can expand thinking and help develop team consensus. All in all, processes shape team behaviors.

Once the charter of the team is decided, execution is accomplished by implementing the team's work plan and motivating desired behaviors. Without good team processes, people are on their own. Obviously this is not teamwork, and nothing much will get accomplished as a team. Process takes the plan from words to actions and influences how people will behave in executing the plan. Processes are determined by the purpose and content of the work plan. For example, constructing a new facility requires a planning process, permitting process, environmental reviews, governmental approvals, financial systems, contracts administration, procurement, and good project management. These processes must all be in place, working well, and consistent with one another.

GOOD AND BAD PROCESSES

There are two famous twin castles nestled above the Rhine River in Germany called Sterrenberg and Liebenstein, but they are more notoriously known as "the hostile brothers." These two nine-hundred-year-old castles are separated by a wall and moat, and legend has it that they were once owned by two rather antagonistic brothers who battled each other over a fair maiden. The rivalry and distrust were so intense that they erected a defensive barrier to keep themselves separated from one another. They fought each other for years. Finally, in an attempt to reconcile their differences and heal their relationship, they agreed to meet for a hunting trip the next morning. The one who woke first was to awaken the other by shooting an arrow at the other's window shutters. One brother awoke first and shot an arrow at his brother's shutter. At the very moment when the arrow was in the air, the shutter opened, and the bowman was horrified to see the arrow pierce his brother's heart. This legend illustrates an important lesson about team processes: despite best intentions (to awaken his brother to go hunting together), bad processes (awaken each other by striking an arrow against the shutter) create bad behaviors (shooting an arrow that killed his brother).

Having the right tools makes things fair. It makes speaking out and contributing safe and rewarding. Good processes bring a team together, while bad processes take a team down. For example, if a team does not have a good process for decision making, team decisions may be dominated by one or two outspoken individuals. A poor process can discourage participation and creativity. People may withdraw from a team if things are not running smoothly. Bad processes increase the chances for team problems. For example, if a team does not have a good feedback and assessment process, the team will not learn together as quickly, and there will be less transparency and trust among team members. Thus, bad processes can lead to distrust and negative behaviors.

In contrast to content, process is more variable and less tangible because processes are defined by the requirements and composition of the team. The number and complexity of processes required to run a team project largely depend on the collective skills, experience level, and size of the team. For example, a small team or a team where people already know how to work together well may not need a lot of formal processes. However, for large, diverse projects, processes are important in terms of efficiency, consistency, and organization. Managing the logistics of meetings, communications, data and information, decision making, and team conflicts become major processes.

A good team process has five key attributes:

1. It depersonalizes the topic or issue.
2. It increases transparency among team members.

3. It makes the discussion more objective and less emotional.

4. It creates an inclusive, participative environment.

5. It gives each team member equal power.

For example, companies often form a job selection team to recruit and find a good candidate for a key position. There will be a written job description, a slate of job applicants, and a process for interviewing and selecting the successful candidate. This requires a good decision-making process. A good team process for identifying the best candidate for the job is to use a selection criteria process. The team agrees to a list of qualifications, skills, and experiences that are needed for the job. This list contains the selection criteria for the team. Each criterion may be equally valued in the decision making, or each may be given different weights of importance. Selection criteria are objective and depersonalized. Each team member then scores each candidate against each criterion on the list. This is done in an open session so that each team member can hear the opinions and score from each member. No matter how strongly a team member may feel about a given candidate, everyone participates and has an equal vote. The open discussion format allows all team members to express their preferences in a transparent manner and helps to neutralize any individual biases, unequal influences, and hidden agendas. The process drives good behaviors, and the team makes a good decision.

ESTABLISHING GOOD PROCESSES

Good processes build team alignment and organization. The key to success is to agree on team processes early in the project and to use specific tools and techniques to help facilitate those processes. The team should reach agreement on how they want to manage themselves and install the infrastructure that they will need to run an effective team.

Nevertheless, too many teams improvise and use a just-in-time strategy for installing team processes. The result is that the team will struggle. (This is rather like giving swimming lessons after the person has already jumped into the water.) The just-in-time processing can work on occasion, but over time, the chance of success is slim. Teams that take the time to agree on team processes from the start are more successful and encounter much less conflict and delays in getting their work done on time.

CORE PROCESSES OF A HIGH-PERFORMING TEAM

To succeed, a team requires effective processes in six main areas:

- Team meetings
- Roles and responsibilities
- Communications
- Decision making
- Measuring performance
- Team feedback

Team Meetings

This is the primary venue where the team interacts, discusses issues, defines the work, resolves conflicts, and makes decisions. The team meeting is where the behaviors and personality of the team are developed and reinforced. Team meeting processes are usually established early and are essential for well-focused, productive meetings. Good team meetings follow these best practices.

Have a Formal Meeting Agenda The most vital tool for team meetings is the meeting agenda, which defines the purpose, content, and priorities for the meeting. The format should identify the topic, the discussion leader for that topic, the time allotted, and the desired outcome. Some agendas specify the type of process that will be used for each topic. The agenda should clearly state what decisions are expected from the participants.

Include everyone on the agenda whenever possible and ensure every topic has an owner. This ensures that everyone plays a leadership role to some extent and will be engaged. A meeting should have full participation. If the team is large, each topic may have co-owners or a team of people who will speak to the issue. The key is to create an inclusive, participative agenda. Leaving people off the agenda sends a subtle message of exclusion and irrelevance, and no one wants to feel irrelevant on a team. Every team meeting should include at least one inclusive process (for example, brainstorming, roundtable discussions, team feedback, or individual voting) to help draw the team together and create opportunities for everyone to contribute.

Establish Key Issues and Decisions Effective meetings have clear objectives and well-prepared participants. To achieve this, an agenda should be drafted early and circulated to team members for their thoughts in advance of the meeting. This gives everyone a chance to contribute to the content of the agenda and creates shared ownership of the meeting. Along with the agenda, premeeting reading materials are distributed to support the agenda topics and any specific decisions. This is a great help for those who may not be up to speed on the issues and allows people some time to test and solidify their thoughts prior to the meeting. Advance work results in a more focused and productive meeting, greater team participation, and a readiness to make decisions.

Reground the Team by Summarizing Team Agreements and Pinpointing Decisions   At the start of the meeting, the team reviews key decisions and agreements made at the previous meeting. Then the facilitator reviews the topics, outputs, and decisions that will be addressed in the current meeting. This grounds everyone, avoids revisiting old issues, and sets the focus and expectations for the current meeting. This takes five to ten minutes and is well worth the time.

Review Feedback from the Previous Meeting   If the team conducted a meeting assessment at the previous meeting, it should review the feedback and reinforce what has worked well and determine what needs improvement. A feedback review accomplishes two important things: captures continuous learnings and reinforces desired team behaviors. The type of meeting assessments should be decided and scheduled early in the project. Without this agreement, the team may bypass it or lack the team discipline to do it. Scheduling the activity ensures a commitment.

Use Meeting Ground Rules   Ground rules are the team's code of conduct: an agreement among team members on how the team will operate and what behaviors are valued. Common meeting rules include no side conversations, no one dominates, be willing to compromise, listen while others speak, be action-minded, start and end on time, and speak frankly. The best ground rules are short and pinpoint specific behaviors.

Ground rules are a key tool for defining desired team behaviors. After developing a list of ground rules, the team should periodically review the list to refresh the rules. Rules that are not revisited will become extinct.

Assign a Facilitator   For large and complex projects, a third-party facilitator is highly recommended. Someone who is experienced and skilled in meeting processes and managing behaviors is invaluable.

If the team elects to self-facilitate (someone on the team plays that role), the following conditions need to be met:

- A clear understanding on who plays that role during each meeting or topic—for example, "The topic owner will play the role of facilitator"
- Clear agreement by the team that they will respect and honor that role at all times
- Individuals on the team have facilitation skills and know how to step in and step out of that role

Close the Meeting with Great Clarity   Most teams are so tired and bored by the end of the meeting that the close of the meeting is nothing more than, "Okay, we're finished." If this occurs, the team will risk team agreements that either will not be remembered or remembered in different versions, no opportunity to give team recognition to people who volunteered for actions or performed well in the meeting, and team learnings that are not captured. Reaching closure means having complete clarity around the actions and expectations of the team going forward. It is important to confirm action items and deliverables for the next meeting.

Close each meeting in this way:

1. Review team agreements.
2. Confirm action items and owners.
3. Do a meeting assessment to capture what went well and what needs improvement next time.
4. Agree on the date, time, place, and owner for the next meeting.

Closing should take no more than five to ten minutes. It takes team discipline to close out a meeting well. A strong close is a sign of a well-run team.

Close the Meeting on a Positive Note   High-performing teams make a habit of acknowledging and thanking people who made significant contributions to the meeting. They recognize those who helped organize the meeting, prepared the agenda and advance reading, facilitated the discussions, and arranged for the room, equipment, and any refreshments. Recognizing people is an important team activity and deserves a place on every agenda.

Roles and Responsibilities

The key roles on a project team are team leader, facilitator, timekeeper, knowledge manager, and team representative or specialist. Depending on the team, one person may play more than one role, and more than one person may play a given role. For example, a team may want the role of facilitator and knowledge manager to be handled by one person, or a team may elect to rotate the facilitation function among its team members. The importance is having an organizational structure in place to help operate the team.

There are no hard-and-fast rules about the division of labor, but the following roles are useful in supporting most project teams.

Team Project Leader The project leader organizes the team meetings, leads the meetings, provides direction and communications, ensures work is consistent with the team's charter and management expectations, manages team resources, supports desired team behaviors, and stewards the team's deliverables. This leader may have the authority from the team to make the final call when the team is split on decisions. The project leader is also responsible for assigning roles and responsibilities.

Facilitator The team facilitator is a process expert who guides the team toward its project objectives and team expectations. This person keeps the team focused on objectives, captures action items, acts as a neutral process monitor, helps to ensure fair and balanced participation, and assists the team leader in developing meeting agendas and processes to help achieve team objectives and teamwork. On occasion, the facilitator may need to play referee and help avoid team conflicts, personal attacks, and process battles. The facilitator is the key support person for the team project leader.

An important role for the facilitator is to ensure that the team processes used will support the team objectives and goals. The facilitator clarifies the team's decision-making process, which may be different for different issues. Also, the person needs to assess the fluency and experience level of the project team members to determine if any training is needed. The facilitator should work with the project leader in properly opening meetings and closing meetings.

The best facilitators are

- Process experts
- Excellent monitors of team behaviors

- Objective and unbiased

- Great listeners

- Able to ask assertive, open-ended questions, such as, "How does the team feel about rearranging the agenda?" "What more can we do to make our discussions more productive?" and "What questions do you have about this process?"

- Able to bring a discussion to a close and sense when a team is ready to make a decision

Timekeeper   This is a team meeting support role. The timekeeper manages the team's meeting time. The role entails confirming the agenda time allocations, monitoring the time spent on each agenda item, and alerting the team when time is running out. The timekeeper should also monitor when the team needs a break and herd people back from breaks as needed. A preassigned volunteer works better than rotating the responsibility. People who are forced into this role do a poor job of managing the team's time.

Knowledge Manager   This person manages the team's handwritten and electronic documentation, shared files, and work products. The knowledge manager keeps the team's record current and creates processes for the team to share information. He or she provides information technology management skills to the team. Sometimes this role is also played by the facilitator. A person who is savvy with computing and organizing information is particularly valuable because the team's decisions are only as good as the information they used.

There are a number of documents that the knowledge manager coordinates:

- Team charter

- Team work plan, including time lines, flowcharts, and key deadlines

- Action register—a list of team actions, owners, and deadlines

- Issue bin—a list of deferred team issues

- Data files

- Data analysis and summaries

- Correspondence

- Decision support packages—the collection of information that supports the team's recommendations, which includes all relevant summaries and analysis with direct bearing on the team's recommendations and conclusions
- Team presentations—slides, handouts, notes, feedback, and so forth

Specialist   This support person provides unique knowledge, expertise, and skills to the team. This can be an accountant, attorney, technical expert, trainer, part-time facilitator, or business analyst, for example. Often the role is only part time.

Team Member   Each team participant represents the interest and knowledge of his or her organization. All provide timely communications to their management and home organization regarding the project. They are held accountable to the team for their project responsibilities and commitments. Their personal success is tied to the success of the team.

Work Distribution   One of the biggest issues facing a team is the fair distribution of work. Inequities in the workload are common complaints for a team. As early as possible, all of the administrative tasks should be identified and split among the team members as evenly as possible. When people are uncertain about the amount of the work required on a task, they may be inclined to undercommit and not volunteer for it. Teams can mitigate this issue by agreeing to periodically revisit the work distribution and rebalance the workload as needed. Some tasks, such as scribing and facilitating, are best rotated among the team members.

Communications

First impressions are lasting impressions, so the first meeting is important for bringing out the talents and positive feelings of people. Speaking to the significance of the project and the challenges ahead is a good way to instill interest and energy. It is not the time to begin dividing up the work or dividing people into subteams. The key is to build a team, not divide it.

If possible, it is best to issue a meeting agenda and a draft team charter in advance of the meeting. Also, before the first meeting, the project leader should take the time to welcome each team member to the team and express appreciation for his or her participation. This gives the project leader an opportunity to catch any initial conflicts in terms of having the right people, identifying any personal issues, previewing any individual concerns, and hearing about any other issues that may bear on the team's first meeting.

The first meeting provides an opportunity for people to meet and allay any concerns. It is common for people to have anxieties about a new project—for example:

"Whom will I be working with, and who will be in charge?"

"What work will I be expected to do, and will it be a good fit for my skills and interests?"

"How much time will this project really require?"

"What benefits am I going to get from this effort? What's in it for me?"

Anxieties can stem from uncertainties about the workload, its potential impact on others, and what roles and responsibilities they will be assigned. People may worry about whether the team will accept them, fully use them, and value their work and knowledge.

All of these anxieties and uncertainties create a nervous tension around the first meeting. Anything that can be done to relieve this tension and put people at ease will go a long way to creating a functional team.

To address the first worry about people, give the team a chance to meet each other. For example, make the first meeting a late-morning meeting, followed by a casual team lunch. This gives everyone some initial contact time to learn about the others in a relaxed setting. Moreover, you can learn a lot about a person by sharing a meal together. The more open and relaxed the setting is, the more likely people will talk openly and honestly.

Never underestimate the importance of this initial contact period for team building. People will draw conclusions about others based on that initial meeting, so establishing positive working relationships should be the top priority. This does not mean team members have to emotionally bond to each other. Some people prefer to learn about each other and build a good team relationship through the work itself rather than through team-building events.

For the worries about workload and time, expectations need to be clear so that everyone has an idea of the work required, the time frame of the project, and the level of effort required. This is information that the project leader can obtain in advance from the sponsors. Individual team members need to confirm their time commitment from their supervisors. For many projects, time requirements are uncertain until the work is fully defined. People expect that everyone will put in their fair share of time to the project, but where teams often fail is not getting clarity on exactly what each person is expected to put in. The key is to reach agreement on time commitments early.

In regard to the concern on the benefits to individual team members, the team should try to take an inventory of people's preferences on what type of work they enjoy the most, what skill sets they possess, and their personal expectations. Knowing what people want and expect from the project will relieve a lot of tension and anxiety. Giving people a chance to express their concerns and needs is a way of giving them a sense of control. In terms of personal benefit, it is best for employees to speak with their supervisor to determine how this experience will help their development and career in the organization. Being selected for a team project should be viewed as a vote of confidence. Having the opportunity to be exposed to a broader team of people and learn from others are inherent benefits of working on a team.

Team Roundtable   One process that is recommended up front is to go around the table and ask each person, "What concerns or issues do you have about the project or team?" Give each person two or three minutes to respond, with no discussion. Questions may be asked for clarification only. The scribe captures these issues on a display that everyone can easily see in the room (a whiteboard, flip chart, or projection from a computer). This process gives everyone a chance to share what is on their minds, sets the tone for openness and transparency, helps to flush out any hidden agendas, and acknowledges everyone's opinions and feelings about the project. By revealing concerns, this initial process helps bring the team together and supports the behavior of sharing information.

Communications Overload   The right size for a project team depends on the size and scope of the project, the number and type of stakeholders, the project time line, and the skill sets required. It is important to have the right number of people on the team. Having too small a team will overburden everybody, and too large a team will require more coordination and communications. As the number of team members increases, the number of communication channels also increases. The number of channels equals $[N \times (N-1)]/2$, where N equals the number of team members (Figure 4.1).

Creating a Safe Zone for the Team   To maximize participation, a team needs to create a safe zone for open and honest discussions. This means that team mem-

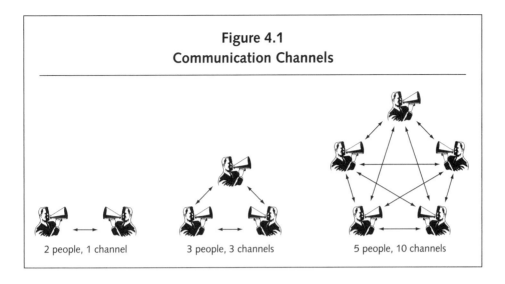

Figure 4.1
Communication Channels

2 people, 1 channel   3 people, 3 channels   5 people, 10 channels

bers must feel free to express their opinions and give feedback to others without fear of criticism, reprisals, and judgment. High-performing teams build a safe zone by creating an atmosphere of trust, respect, and interdependence. And individuals create a safe zone in the following ways:

- Express confidence in others and in their ability to do the job well.
- Do not assign blame to others.
- Ensure their actions are consistent with spoken words, do what they say they were going to do, and keep promises to others.
- Do a fair share of the remedial work.
- Freely share their knowledge.
- Take action to support others.
- Give credit and recognition to others.
- Explain their thinking and decision making and thereby give the whole story.
- Always accept accountability and admit to mistakes.
- Seek to understand first, then to be understood.
- Ask for feedback and suggestions from others.
- Honor team agreements.

A good place to institute these behaviors is in the team ground rules, which should be reinforced during the project. During these review periods, take the time to recognize and reward team members who have demonstrated these behaviors. A good indicator of whether a team has created a safe zone is the frequency with which people give feedback, positive and negative, to the team. For example, when someone is put down for presenting a contrarian view, will others speak up to correct that behavior? When people take risks in challenging the status quo, are they reinforced or punished? How often are people recognized for their ideas and contributions? Are people making the effort to recognize and acknowledge good behaviors? Are quiet team members being invited to speak?

Human Factors and E-Mail   For project teams, the most popular and universal system of communication is e-mail, especially for global teams. E-mails can be issued with a touch of a button and stored electronically for ease of access and archiving. E-mailing enables teams to share information instantly and dialogue on issues outside meetings. In addition to speed and convenience, e-mailing is low cost, high capacity, efficient, and accessible. Because of these attributes, e-mailing has become a significant factor in daily communications.

The biggest drawback to e-mail is the impersonal nature of the technology: e-mail does not accurately transmit human emotions and intentions. Comic icons are used sometimes to give feelings to the message but are usually distracting and not acceptable in business communications. In the workplace, e-mails are usually a cold string of words and information. Yet these electronic words can have a powerful impact on people's feelings. Moreover, too often people misinterpret the content of an e-mail, and e-mails are notorious for causing conflict among users. Even someone who writes a detailed e-mail or uses an unusual font can annoy others. I had a colleague once whose e-mails were transmitted in a light-green fluorescent font that annoyed everyone. I also had a friend who wrote rambling two- to three-page e-mails that contained questions to me in every paragraph. His e-mails were exhausting to read. People dreaded getting e-mail from him. To avoid these problems, team members should be sensitive to how others might perceive their e-mails and balance their e-mailing with telephone calls and in-person contacts.

Too little e-mailing can cause friction too. If a recipient does not respond to an e-mail, the sender wonders, "Did she not like my e-mail?" "Maybe she is out of the office on a trip." "Maybe she is too busy to answer." "Maybe she forgot about it." A nonresponse can irk people. When an e-mail is left unanswered, the sender will often view the recipient as rude, impolite, and inconsiderate.

E-Mail Tips   The purpose of e-mailing is to communicate information. Merely sending e-mails is not communicating. Communication occurs when a message is sent, and the recipient reads it. A key goal of e-mailing is to get a human response—an acknowledgment of the content or a response to the intent of the e-mail (such as a decision, help in editing or reviewing messages). Noncommunicative e-mailing occurs when no reply is intended, such as sending out meeting materials or simply sharing information. These are instances of distributing information, not communicating.

Teams typically distribute and communicate information. Communicating by e-mailing is much more challenging than sending out information. It takes crisp, clear, and compelling language and techniques. To make your e-mails more readable and reply-friendly, follow these e-mailing tips.

First, the shorter, the better. The key is to keep e-mails short and concise. A long e-mail should be organized into short bullet statements. Paragraph titles are also helpful in indexing a long e-mail for the reader.

Second, state what you want. It helps to state what you want up front and specify if there are any actions and deadlines requested. It is even better when the action requested is embedded in the title of the e-mail.

Finally, start positive and end positive. Sandwiching is a good technique for structuring e-mails: start positive, state your message, and then end positive. Start the e-mail with a positive greeting and acknowledging the other person's e-mail. This is nothing more than two to four words: "Thanks for writing," "Good hearing from you," "Hope things are well," "Thanks for sharing this," "Good job!" "Thanks for asking," and so on. These simple words go a long way in maintaining a good e-mail relationship. A short, positive acknowledgment and greeting helps prepare the reader. After this positive opener, present the content of the message in a brief and concise note. Then end by closing with a positive and genuine remark: "Thanks for considering my note," "Appreciate your support," "Thanks for your time," "Let me thank you in advance."

Everyone appreciates good e-mail manners. Even a critical message can be better communicated when it is framed in a positive and genuine way. This is the easiest and most effective piece of advice for polishing e-mails. People enjoy reading a positive e-mail among their sea of messages, especially when the e-mailer praises their behaviors. It is a win-win situation. They look forward to receiving your e-mails, and you have a good chance that they will read it. And remember that everyone always reads their happy e-mails first.

In general, e-mailing is an effective and fast way of recognizing and praising others. A written recognition is a keepsake that the recipient can read again and again. E-mailing is a quick and easy way to help motivate others. How many recognitions do you receive in your e-mail each day? People should try to make it a habit to make their first e-mail of the day a positive one that acknowledges and praises someone. It sets a good tone for the rest of the day.

E-Mail Ground Rules   Teams need to establish some ground rules on e-mailing. Otherwise e-mailing can get out of control and create frustration and miscommunication. It is too easy to copy and send an e-mail or hit the "Reply to All" button. Before long, the process becomes a massive electronic circus. Some common options are to control what everyone gets, put everything in a shared folder, or priority-code team e-mails. A good practice is to be selective in what gets distributed and store common electronic documents in a folder on a shared drive.

Appointing a Moderator   On many projects, the team may be quite large, and the work may be short term but intensive. In this situation, it works best to assign a moderator who will review and coordinate all incoming documents and help manage what everyone needs to see. The person can direct the traffic flow of e-mails by consolidating e-mails and putting them into subject files, or collecting and summarizing everyone's input on a given issue. Having someone available to help coordinate e-mail communications is a much better choice than having each person try to handle all of their e-mail individually.

Other Electronic Team Tools   In-person meetings are expensive when they involve distant travel. As an alternative, numerous online tools, such as NetMeeting, WebEx, Acrobat Connect, Microsoft Live Meeting, and MeetingPlace, allow teams to meet and collaborate virtually from their personal locations. With Web technology and telecommunication speeds, teleconferences are now cheaper than ever before and the broadcast quality much improved. With the focus on costs and travel time, Web-based teleconferencing systems will become more popular alternatives to in-person meetings. This technology will enable more people to connect to one another and increase worker productivity.

Decision Making

In evaluating autocratic-based teams (leader rules), democratic-based teams (majority rules), and consensus-based teams (team rules), it is clear that consensus is the preferred method of decision making by the vast majority of teams. Consensus means that everyone works together to reach a team decision. It does not mean that every team member is happy with the decision. Team consensus is not 100 percent agreement, and not everyone is going to be 100 percent satisfied. Consensus means all team members can live with the decision and will openly support the decision outside the team. Consensus is not necessarily a faster decision process. Being able to live with a decision is still a challenge at times.

Autocratic decision making works better when fast decisions are needed, when the decision is arbitrary (for example, selecting a conference room for the team meeting), or when the team cannot reach consensus. A democratic decision-making process works better when a large number of people are involved, across-the-board buy-in is not critical, or the goal is to see where the team stands on an issue to guide the discussion.

Team consensus is the most common decision-making process for teams. Because it gives everyone an equal stake on the decisions of the team, it feels collaborative and fair and reinforces the idea of no rank in the room. This decision-making method gives people some comfort knowing that power will be distributed among the team and that it will help to eliminate any power struggles within the team.

In reality, team consensus sounds good but is challenging to do. Too often teams get stuck around a decision point, which can lead to drawn-out discussions, resistance to compromise, and conflicts in behaviors.

Consensus decision making can fail when:

- Consensus is not defined, and everyone assumes people know what it means.
- Teams do not have a specific method for reaching consensus.
- Consensus is assumed because no opposition was voiced.
- No processes are in place to resolve stalemates.
- Team members falsely agree with the team in order to avoid further conflict, so there is no true commitment to the decision.

In their quest to reach consensus, teams sometimes fall into a dialogue trap: they believe that if they talk long and hard enough, somehow consensus will appear, and the team will somehow hit on the right answer sooner or later. It is like an act of faith. Unfortunately, long discussions create more team frustration than unity. In reality, consensus requires a foundation of mutual respect, willingness to compromise, and good team communications. These behaviors need to be established before team consensus can work.

Here are some useful techniques for building team consensus.

Know Where Everybody Stands   With any team, some team members talk more than others. It does not mean that nonparticipants do not have opinions. Rather, they are processing information and shaping their opinions internally while others need to verbalize it to understand it. These are just two different ways of processing information. However, without actively checking in with quiet members, the team may be in disagreement without even knowing it. The team may be building gaps in its beliefs and assumptions. To avoid this, a good team invites feedback and input from all team members and does not allow members to sit out. It is important for team consensus to keep everyone actively engaged.

Develop a Straw Model   If a team is pressed for time or is struggling to reach agreement, a good technique is to develop a straw model prior to the team meeting. Basically, a straw model is a proposed solution or position developed by a team member to help the team move toward reaching a decision. It can be a middle-of-the-road solution or a majority position. It provides the team with something to work from rather than starting from scratch.

It is called a "straw" model because it is designed to be easily challenged, changed, or rejected by the team. Although it may be drafted by one or more team members, no strong individual ownership is taken. By using a common document, the team is working together to improve a proposal that has no personal ties. The straw model then becomes a team product.

Identify Pinch Points   When disagreements occur, effective teams try to pinpoint and narrow the disagreements and do not allow them to escalate into a conflict. These specific points of disagreement, called pinch points, allow a team to focus on resolving specific differences rather than talking continuously about general areas of disagreement. Also, pinch points help clarify the basis for the disagreement among team members. The keys to finding "pinch points" are to actively listen, ask clarifying questions, and focus on narrowing the problem down. It requires inquiring, supportive behaviors. Team debate is healthy only when it serves to highlight specific differences. Advocacy needs to be balanced against listening in order for the team to reach mutual understanding.

The Silent Yes   A silent yes occurs when no one voices any opposition to a proposed action or decision. For example, a silent yes would commonly follow questions such as, "Are we okay to move on?" or "Does this solution sound okay?" In other words, "If you don't agree, speak up; otherwise I'm going to take your silence as a vote of approval." This is not a good way to make decisions. Silence does not mean agreement. It just means no one felt strong enough about it to speak up.

A silent yes does not fit the definition of team consensus, yet it happens regularly. Sometimes this silent decision-making behavior is nonconsequential, but many times, it comes back to haunt the team. A silent yes is a weak yes and may not hold up. It is always worth the time to confirm team agreements.

The silent yes is common because it expedites the process, people do not like confrontation, and it avoids conflict. It is a win-win situation: the team gets what it wants (to move on) and the person gets what he or she wants (avoidance of conflict). The team is taking a risk when it accepts a silent yes as a convenience to move forward.

A silent yes is acceptable when it is properly posed as a question: "Who cannot live with this decision?" or "Who is not a firm yes on this?" If one or two team members are not a firm yes, then the team can decide to continue discussing it, defer it, or look for other compromises. Do not use "Okay to move on?" unless you are just hoping to end the discussion. A silent yes should be avoided when making high-impact decisions, when the issues are emotional, or in coming to agreement on work assignments and deadlines.

Fist of Five   One highly effective technique to pinpoint disagreements and avoid the silent yes is the fist of five (Figure 4.2). It is a fast voting method whereby each team member is asked to show his or her level of agreement or disagreement by holding up one hand and displaying one to five fingers. Five fingers mean, "I support it and would be willing to champion it"; four fingers mean, "I support it"; three mean, "I'm not 100 percent, but I can live with it"; two mean, "I need more discussion"; and one means, "I can't support it."

The advantage of this method is that it forces everyone to show where they stand on the issue, thereby literally showing their hand. It gives everyone equal power and gives a voice to any silent dissenters. This method is revealing and can

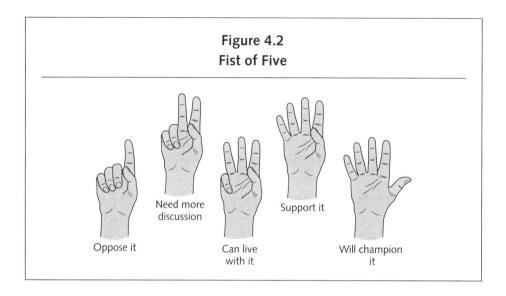

Figure 4.2
Fist of Five

Oppose it

Need more
discussion

Can live
with it

Support it

Will champion
it

strengthen trust and teamwork. It can also save time. I have been in meetings where everyone was already a four or a five, and if we had not called for a fist, we would have kept on talking. And there were times when we thought we had consensus, only to find that one or two people were actually "ones" and were holding back their disagreement. Sometimes people hang back because they are reluctant to voice a minority view. This method helps teams become more transparent and quickly pinpoints where more discussion is needed.

When a team member raises two fingers or only one, this is a good opportunity to find out why individuals are not on board. My favorite follow-up question is not, "Why are you a one or two?" but, "What is holding you back from being a three or higher?" or "What will it take to get you to a three?" Try to avoid asking "why" questions, which are accusatory and provoke defensive behaviors.

The fist of five is quick, easy, and graded on a scale. Everyone participates, and it promotes good dialogue and identifies points of disagreements.

Stake in the Ground   Teams need to be disciplined in adhering to team decisions. Reworking past decisions is a dreaded behavior for teams. A stake in the ground is a concept of committing to a team decision. It should be a team agreement that all stake-in-the-ground decisions will be honored and not recycled (or recycled only when absolutely required). In other words, it is a firm decision that will not be revisited. Too often teams rework issues because team members want to reassess and test past decisions. They assume that decisions can be revisited and revised as needed. This casual attitude around decisions results in weak decisions. A stake in the ground is an excellent way to nail down team decisions. Stakes in the ground should be reviewed at the end of each meeting and posted for reference in future meetings.

Measuring Performance

Metrics are highly effective for building teamwork and ensuring individual alignment to team goals. Defining goals without a method of measuring the team's progress often leads to unfulfilled goals. Three well-proven methods for tracking progress are action register, milestones, and team scorecard.

Action Register   The most common performance tracking tool is the team's action register (Table 4.1), a running list of actions that the team needs to take. The action register is reviewed and updated during each team meeting. The knowledge manager is usually responsible for keeping the list current. Each action item is numbered to enable the team to track and reference it during team meetings. Each action should have an owner before closing the meeting.

As action items are completed, they should not be removed from the active register until they are reviewed and then closed out by the team. Once they are

		Table 4.1				
		Team Action Register				
Number	Date Opened	What	Who	Date Due	Date Completed	Status
1	6/25	Finalize team charter	Greg	7/12	Open	Draft completed
2	6/25	Fill out team contact list	All	7/12	Open	Shared spreadsheet available
3	7/01	Draft work plan	Diane	8/01	Open	50% completed
4	7/01	Locate a room for next meeting	Matt	7/05	7/02	Done

closed out, these items should be saved in an archived file in case they need to be retrieved later.

Milestones   For long-term or complex projects, charting the team's critical work outputs and decisions is a good way of systematically dividing the project into manageable goals (Table 4.2). Some projects may not end for several months or years, so it is important to identify the key steps along the way. These key steps, called milestones, are interim goals and accomplishments that are critical for achieving the project's overall objective. They are mini-goals with deadlines. Project-level goals are too big and action items are too small; milestones are just the right size for tracking a team's progress.

Team Scorecard   One of the more elusive aspects of performance is measuring success. How does a team know if it is successful? What does success look like? Is the picture of success the same for everyone?

Success is probably a little different for each team member. If it is left as a judgment call by management, as it has been in the past, it becomes an external process, not a team process. Some people prefer not to know how they are doing and hate being measured, but in today's team-based environment, success needs to be explicit to the team.

The team scorecard is a reliable and objective way of measuring success (Table 4.3). It lists the key metrics of the team and quantifies what success means for each

---

Table 4.2
Examples of Milestones

Number	Milestone	Target Date
1	Complete team charter	February 2
2	Approve work plan	March 20
3	Project gets funding approval	April 15
4	Meet midyear budget target	June 15
5	Complete decision support package	September 29
6	Team recommendations receive management endorsement	December 1

Table 4.3
Team Scorecard

	Metric		Point range						Percentage Weight	Points × weight = score
			Minimum		Target			Stretch Goal		
			8	9	10	11	12			
Content	Project deliverables, meet interim goals	Completion of milestones	3 of 14 milestones on time	5 of 14 milestones on time	7 of 14 milestones on time	12 of 14 milestones on time	14 of 14 milestones on time	30	270
Process	Ground rules	Adherence to ground rules	4 of 8	5 of 8	6 of 8	7 of 8	8 of 8	30	300
Behavior	Satisfied team members: fun, team cooperation	Percentage of team satisfied	60%	70%	80%	90%	95%	40	440
					1,000 Hits All Targets			1,200 Maximum Score	100	1,010

metric. The metric can be a process, content, or behavior. Success is a complex end point that can be difficult to describe. It is multidimensional and rarely an all-or-none outcome. It can also change over time. A scorecard helps to focus the team on a series of key targets. It enables a team to break success down into measurable end points that they can accomplish. For example, if safety is a key success metric, then success may be the number of consecutive days without an injury (content metric), the number of safety training courses completed (process metric), or the number of individual safety actions taken to eliminate workplace hazards (behavior metric). The key is to define success in bite-size pieces. Ideally, if a particular end point is critical, it should have a content, process, and behavioral metric.

Success also needs to carry relevance for both the team and individuals. The scorecard helps people see their role in the success of the team. If they cannot see themselves in the scorecard, then the scorecard is not a good one. The set of success metrics may be tied to the deliverables of the team, to team behaviors as defined in the ground rules, or tied to the completion of specific team processes. Often the key metrics are sourced from the team's charter. As shown in Table 4.3, these key metrics are listed in the first column of the scorecard. It is best not to have a long list of key metrics—three to eight are desirable. Fewer than three is probably too broad and more than eight dilutes the focus. A critical few is the best approach. The team should brainstorm a list and then use a narrowing technique (described in Chapter Eight) to derive the critical three to eight metrics. For large and complex projects with large teams, ten to fifteen metrics may be needed. The best scorecards are ones that are simple and have a good mix of both leading and lagging indicators for content, process, and behavior metrics. These are called balanced scorecards. For example, a leading indicator for content would be completing action items on time, while a lagging indicator is completing a milestone.

For each metric, the team defines what success means. Cliff-type metrics, which are all-or-none type of end points, are ineffective. Instead, use a graded scale. Each metric should have at least a minimum goal, a target goal, and a stretch goal. An example of a graded scale is shown in Table 4.3. Under "Content," the team defined a performance range for completing project milestones—completing three out of fourteen milestones earns a score of eight points, and hitting all fourteen milestones earns twelve points. For each row on the scorecard, the team will have a success metric and at least three goals listed alongside each metric.

Since each success metric may have a different level of impact on the final outcome, a team can assign different weights to its metrics based on relative importance (percentage weighting). This would be a weighted scorecard. This scorecard process usually requires more debate and time than expected. It probably stems from the fact that some people are results- and bottom-line-oriented, while others are more process focused. It is not uncommon for teams to reach consensus quickly on project objectives yet struggle with drafting a scorecard. This struggle helps to uncover underlying differences in people's interpretation of the objectives. The scorecard is an excellent check of the team's understanding of its objectives and success factors. It forces the team to define its critical determinants of success. Importantly, success metrics serve as a behavioral antecedent because what gets measured gets done.

The biggest barrier to developing an effective scorecard is fear. Nothing focuses a person's mind more than being graded. It is like a flashback to school and bad grades. A scorecard is the team's report card, and getting agreement on grading criteria is not an easy process. The team will have risk takers and risk avoiders. Some will like to shoot high and push themselves, while others prefer to make sure the team gets a good grade. To avoid biases, the team's scorecard should be reviewed by management, peers, stakeholders, and the team's sponsors.

The scorecard in Table 4.3 lists three team metrics: a content metric on deliverables, a process metric on ground rules, and a behavioral metric on team satisfaction. For each metric, five levels of success are defined: a poor result is given a low score, and an outstanding result earns a high score. For example, under "content," successfully completing three out fourteen milestones earns the team eight points, and completing all fourteen milestones on time gives twelve points. Intermediate scores range from nine to eleven. Any results that fall between levels are given the lower score: completing eight of the fourteen milestones gets a score of ten. If fewer than eight milestones are achieved, the score is zero points. The point range does not have to be eight to twelve. Scorecards can range from six to fourteen points, or simply have only three targets: low (six points), medium (ten points), and high (twelve points). A low, medium (target), and high scale makes scoring easy and uncomplicated. Another option is to use scoring labels such as bronze, silver, and gold.

Hitting the target performance level earns the team a score of ten. Then each metric is assigned a relative weighting based on importance, with a composite total of 100 percent. In this example, deliverables are given a weighting of 30 percent, adherence to ground rules is also given a 30 percent weighting, and the remaining 40 percent is assigned to behaviors.

To calculate a total score, each performance level is multiplied by its weight. For deliverables, the team completed five of fourteen deliverables so far and thus earned 9 points. Nine points multiplied by the weighting of 30 percent equals 270 total points. The same calculation is done for the other two metrics, and the three subtotals are added together for a grand total score. In the example, the first metric earned 270 points, the second 300, and the third 440 points, for a grand total of 1,010 points. Hitting all targets for each metric would earn a total of 1,000 points. Overall, the team exceeded its target. A total of 1,000 does not necessarily mean that the team hit all of its targets since a team can earn an 11 or 12 for each metric. A team can exceed one target and fall short for another and still total 1,000 points or more.

Scorecards are also useful for rewarding performance. Rewards and celebrations should be tied to the scorecard: the higher the score, the higher the reward. A team can tie rewards to the scores in each category or overall scores. A team should avoid waiting until the end of the year to determine success. It is important to celebrate successes as soon as they occur. When the team hits a certain threshold in total points, such as 500, a celebration with awards and recognitions should take place.

In summary, scorecards have numerous benefits:

- The scorecard can be tied to the team's work plan or business plan.
- The team's level of success is specifically defined.
- Success is measured and quantified.
- Each metric is weighted according to degree of importance.
- The team earns a cumulative performance score.
- The scorecard provides flexibility to use different types of metrics: process, content, and behavior.

Team Feedback

The scorecard provides a big picture of the team's performance, but processes are also needed to assess the team's day-to-day interactions and individual satisfaction. High-performing teams use process checks to solicit team feedback. This feedback can be built into the team's meeting agenda or gathered outside the meeting using a written or an e-mail questionnaire. There are several effective tools for taking quick snapshots of the team's well-being: plus/delta, meeting monitors, smile index, and spider diagram.

Plus/Delta   At the end of team meetings and key project phases, conduct a team survey on what is working and what is not working. The plus/delta process is an excellent self-assessment tool for critiquing team meetings or project reviews. "Pluses" are things that have worked well so far and should continue, and the "deltas" are things that need improvement. The facilitator scribes a vertical line down the middle of a flip chart or whiteboard, then writes a plus at the top of the left side and a delta at the top of the right side of the sheet (see Table 4.4). The team can go around the table or use a free-for-all process to ask for pluses and deltas. The feedback is recorded with no embellishments or rebuttals from team members. The only exception is when clarification is needed. The plus/delta tool is a pulse check, not a discussion technique. The proper way to ask for feedback is, "What pluses or deltas do you have for the meeting?" rather than a yes-no question: "Do you have any pluses or deltas?" If people are tired, they will dismiss it with a quick no.

Table 4.4
A Plus/Delta from a Team Meeting

+	▲
• Balanced participation; no one dominated	• Not enough breaks
• Excellent advance reading materials	• No coffee in the afternoon
• Well-designed agenda	• Room too warm
• Met objective: Completed outline of team work plan	• Some team members did not attend
• Good facilitation: Kept us on time, asked good questions, kept us focused, did not digress too much	• Send out advance reading earlier next time
• Team enthusiasm and energy despite long day	
• Collected some key issues for team to work on	
• Finished on time	

These guidelines are useful for conducting a plus/delta:

- Give people a moment to think; then ask for their feedback.
- Keep the feedback short, with no speeches.
- Capture each thought as concisely as possible without discussion. Ask for clarity only.
- Thank all contributors.

If the team is inexperienced with this tool, the facilitator should first define a plus and delta and then explain the process with examples. If a team is reluctant to offer any deltas, the facilitator should offer one to break the ice. A plus/delta takes about five minutes to complete and is highly effective because it gives voice to team problems that would otherwise not be expressed. When feedback is provided, a good facilitator will make sure the feedback is clear and pinpointed. For example, if a person says he liked the facilitation, the facilitator should ask for more clarification: "What did you like about the facilitation?" In the example in Table 4.4, the response was: "Kept us on time, asked good questions, kept us focused, and did not allow us to digress too much." The reason clarifications are important is that they serve to reinforce what the team liked and pinpoint what behaviors they want repeated. A behavior that is recognized will likely be repeated. Getting clarification on the feedback is the key to a good plus/delta.

Without a feedback mechanism, small annoyances and problems can fester and grow into larger issues, manifesting themselves in other destructive ways. The most effective plus/deltas are ones that capture content, process, and behavior. Feedback on behaviors is the toughest to get, so a good facilitator should try to encourage behavioral observations or identify some for the team.

A plus/delta gives people an opportunity to praise and recognize others. This verbal recognition gives them an emotional lift, especially after a long, hard meeting. In this way, the meeting closes on a positive note.

Many teams make the mistake of just stopping there and doing nothing with the feedback. Instead, the team leader and facilitator should address every delta and then report back to the team at the next meeting. The plus/delta is a method to improve teamwork and team dynamics.

Meeting Monitors   Meeting monitors are team observers. They are preassigned volunteers who observe the meeting and give feedback to the team at the end. The meeting monitors give a verbal plus/delta about what they thought went well and what could be improved next time.

There are three advantages of this technique:

- The team has one or two people observing the meeting full time, which gives strong attention to team interactions and processes.
- It gets more people involved with meeting processes and team behaviors.
- People tend to demonstrate good behaviors when peers are watching them.

The downsides are that the observers may be less engaged in the content of the discussion. Most of the time, however, the advantages outweigh the disadvantages. This role is best rotated among team members to give everyone a chance to participate.

Smile Index   While working as a manager of a team with members scattered over wide geographical areas, I found I needed a quick, anonymous feedback tool to gauge our team's level of employee satisfaction. I wanted something simple that took only a few minutes to complete and was self-explanatory. I came up with a smile index: a survey tool using five faces of varying degrees of happiness (Figure 4.3). I asked each team member to select the face that best describes his or her personal level of happiness about his or her job. This was a check on how people felt that day, week, or month. For our team, this survey was sent out by e-mail at the end of each quarter. In addition to the five faces, two additional questions were asked: "What things contributed most to your smile over the past quarter?" and

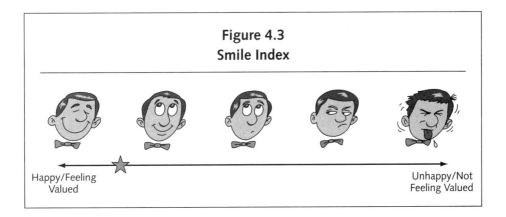

**Figure 4.3
Smile Index**

Happy/Feeling
Valued

Unhappy/Not
Feeling Valued

"What could you or the team do to widen your smile?" The index was the average of all responses (indicated with a star in the figure), and all comments were shared anonymously with the team. Trends and common themes were identified and acted on by the leadership team.

Spider Diagram Another quick tool for getting team feedback is a spider diagram, a visual status report on how well the team feels it is performing on its key metrics. The diagram is a polygon with spokes on it—lines drawn from the center to the outside points of the polygon. Each spoke represents one key metric, which may be a content, process, or behavior metric. If a team has seven key metrics, the diagram would have seven spokes. Within the polygon, the diagram contains a graded scale such as 0 to 5. The intent is to place a mark on each spoke that corresponds to where the team is performing. With the diagram displayed in front of the room, the facilitator selects a metric and asks the team where they feel they are performing. A mark near the center means the team is doing poorly, and a mark on the outside point of the spoke means the team is exceeding expectations. A mark in between means intermediate performance.

The way to establish the mark is to have the facilitator start with a pen in the center and move it outward until a person says "stop." The facilitator then asks for consensus on that spot. If the team agrees, the facilitator marks the spot and moves to the next spoke. If the team disagrees, the scribe continues moving the pen outward until team consensus is reached. It should take less than a minute to reach consensus on the spot for each metric. One metric is done at a time until the entire polygon or wheel is completed. Then the points are connected with a line forming a weblike tracing (Figure 4.4).

In the spider diagram, points near the center hub may mean that the team is struggling or has not worked on that item yet. A point on the outside usually means the team is performing at a very high level. The spider diagram gives a snapshot of the team's performance level. This picture may change over time; some items may drop, and some may move higher on the wheel. Typically teams start in the center and then continue to move outward as their work progresses.

The spider diagram helps a team maintain focus on its key measures and provides a quick check on how well it is doing. Marks on items near the hub help identify potential problems and barriers. Marks on the edge deserve recognition and celebration. This tool also can help reveal differences of opinion on some end points, leading to some healthy dialogue and improvement ideas.

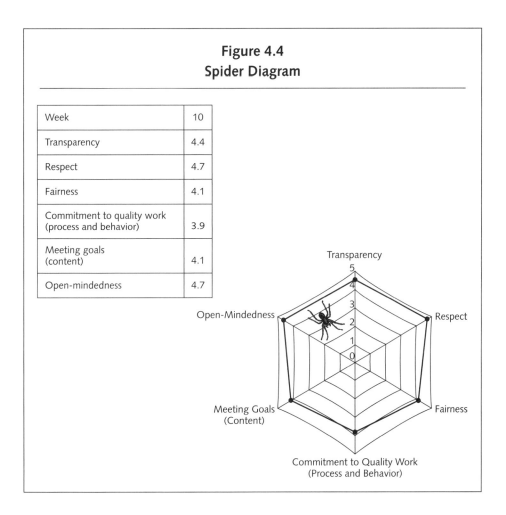

Figure 4.4
Spider Diagram

Week	10
Transparency	4.4
Respect	4.7
Fairness	4.1
Commitment to quality work (process and behavior)	3.9
Meeting goals (content)	4.1
Open-mindedness	4.7

SUMMARY

Process overlaps with content and behavior and plays three roles:

- Converts the team's charter and work plan into actions
- Influences individual and team behaviors
- Helps to reveal the intent behind behaviors

Effective team processes help motivate people to share their thoughts, feelings, agreements, and disagreements. They help to level the playing field, foster more balanced participation, reduce conflicts, uncover hidden agendas, and reinforce desired behaviors. Processes support the execution of team charters and work plans by putting words to actions. In sharing common team processes, the work is better coordinated, and people are working in alignment with each other.

Good processes drive good behaviors; bad processes drive bad behaviors. Using the right processes will help reduce and resolve problems that a team may encounter, and bad processes increase the probability of conflicts. Good processes enable a team to move more quickly.

The key processes for effective team interactions are meeting processes, communications, roles and responsibilities, decision making, measuring performance, and feedback. The tools and techniques that work best depend on the size, maturity, diversity, experience, and complexity of the project team. Regardless, a team needs to have clear processes in each of these areas to be successful.

These key processes need to be established up front instead of waiting until there is a conflict to try to agree on a process.

Key Elements
of Team Performance
Behavior

The third key element of team performance is behavior. Behaviors are what we see and hear. They reflect who we are, what we believe in, and how we feel. In teams, behaviors are shaped by team processes and are critical for the execution of the team's objectives and strategies. Team behaviors are the collective interactions among people, and these behaviors shape the dynamics and culture of a team.

The mission and objectives of an organization are fairly easy to understand; the strategies and processes supporting those objectives are easily seen, but the deployment of these strategies depends on people's behaviors. Behaviors are less obvious and the most challenging to manage. The reasons organizations fail to meet their goals are due not to content or process but to a breakdown in team collaboration and behaviors. Interpersonal discontents, misunderstandings, and

miscommunications are responsible for most of the stress, reduced effectiveness, and conflict that teams encounter. Because of that, successful organizations spend considerable time and resources to train and motivate people to possess consistent and collaborative behaviors.

HOW TEAM BEHAVIORS AND PROCESSES ARE RELATED

Processes are the tools, techniques, and procedures used to get work done. They are the infrastructure, rules, and methods that a team needs in order to operate smoothly and effectively. A clear decision-making process enables a team to make fair, consistent, and logical decisions, while minimizing personal biases, dissent, and personality conflicts. Processes are the mechanics of the system.

In contrast, behaviors are the human actions and interpersonal dynamics behind the execution of these processes. A team can have excellent decision-making process, yet if people do not trust and value each other, its decisions will be weak and uncommitted. A team leader can successfully track and score team performance, but if the team does not feel accountable for the results, its performance will be sub-par. Team communication processes may be in place and operating well, but if people do not feel interdependent about their work, communications will suffer.

Processes help guide behaviors by establishing rules and procedures on how work will be done. Team interactions, collaborative behaviors, and the relationships are built not on process but on mutual trust, transparency, respect, interdependency, team learning, and accountability. Process is how people apply themselves to the work, while behavior is how people interact with each other. Effective team behaviors require conscious effort. Unfortunately, once the team launches into work, the focus is typically on meeting deadlines and completing milestones. Behavioral modifications are more difficult to address since team members are more focused on improving content and process than behaviors.

People tend to treat process and behaviors as the same. Many believe that if the process is right, the right behaviors will follow. This is not always true. Processes are defined by the team, which are externally driven and intellectually based, while behaviors are individually defined, internally driven, and emotionally based. For example, showing trust is not a process but a feeling one person has for another. There can be processes to help build trust, but trust is still an individual feeling. In addition, a given process is the same for everyone, but behaviors are much more varied and dynamic. For example, meeting your work deadlines may be enough for someone to trust you, but others may take more convincing. Also, different people demonstrate trust differently. I know many people who say that they trust me, but I do not always feel that trust; it is not transparent to me. I need more visible validation of that trust in the form of friendship and mutual support.

To achieve teamwork and team synergy, the collective behavior of the team needs to be in sync. Team sports such as football, baseball, and soccer require trained players, equipment, a playing field, and game rules. But how well a team performs within the game depends not only on the skills and talents of the players but also on the mutual behaviors that exist within the team. It is often referred to as team chemistry. A team member's willingness to give discretionary effort and inspire others is generated not from process but from mutual trust, respect, transparency, and accountability. When the team successfully executes a process, it is due to team learning and interdependency.

Processes guide and support desired behaviors, and behaviors determine the success of processes. Both behaviors and processes are needed to have a successful team.

TOP SIX TEAM BEHAVIORS

Six key behaviors are needed for team success. They create an open, honest, and productive work environment and generate feelings of mutual respect and motivation:

- Mutual trust
- Interdependency
- Accountability
- Valuing individual differences
- Transparency
- Learning and recognition

Mutual Trust

Building trust is one of the most desired behaviors for successful teams. It is the core of any relationship. Trust is a personal belief and faith that people have in each other. Trust is the belief that team members can count on each other to perform and support the common goals of the team. It is the inherent confidence that people have in each other based on shared values, demonstrated behaviors, and mutual experiences. Therefore, trust is earned through the interactions and behaviors of people on the team.

Mutual team trust is about

- Believing in each other's abilities and commitments
- Doing what you said you were going to do
- Having faith that you will keep the interests of the team ahead of your own and if not, have the faith that others will speak up when you are unable to do so
- Recognizing others for their contributions
- Freely sharing information and knowledge
- Giving authority to others to make decisions on behalf of the team
- A willingness to forgive others
- Seeking solutions rather than seeking blame
- Standing by the decisions and actions of the team

Trust is a core belief that develops first between two or three people and grows within a team. For team trust to occur, a critical mass of people must feel that way. People feel safe to speak up, take actions, share information and feelings, and consistently work hard for each other. Trust elevates a team to perform at a higher level. One of the best things that a team can do to build trust is to get to know each other as individuals. Believing in people takes a deeper understanding of who they are, what motivates and demotivates them, and how they like to be treated. Individualism needs to be respected in order to operate well as a team.

Mutual trust diminishes when any team members show low accountability or commitment to the team. There are remedies that teams can take when trust issues occur:

- Case example: The project team feels slighted when one team member takes independent actions without the team's knowledge or consent. The individual is criticized for this behavior by the team. As a result, the team feels less trust for this individual, and the individual feels less trust for the team.

Solution: The team needs to clearly define as a ground rule what decisions and actions team members are free to take when doing assignments. The authority level must be clear. Without clear guidance, team members will assume their own level of independence, which may not be acceptable to the team. The team needs to agree on what requires team review and approval.

• Case example: A team member is not completing his assignments on time and misses some meetings. The team feels they cannot trust him anymore and decide to give him only noncritical assignments. He feels demoted and distrusted.

Solution: Instead of dismissing this team member, the better response is first to understand what is preventing him from meeting his commitments. It may be due to cultural differences, a misunderstanding of expectations, lack of information, schedule conflicts, work overload, or a miscommunication on deadlines. Nevertheless, the focus should be on identifying the cause and then seeking possible solutions. Ask, "What can I do to help this person perform better?" Make sure expectations are clear and realistic. People are not mind readers, and you need to show people what you want. What is clear to you may not be clear to others.

Interdependency

The most committed team members are those who have something significant to gain or lose from the team's output. Everyone needs to have a stake in the game. A team member who is not committed usually has little or no stake in the outcome. The level of commitment by team members is an important factor to assess early. One of the first processes that a team should address is to describe their stake in the project, their reasons for being on the team, and the level of time and effort they are willing to commit. This feedback can be used to gauge if sufficient people are committed to do the project.

When everyone has a personal stake in the team's success and the work requires a broad effort, people will depend on each other and support each other to do the best job possible. The bigger the stake is, the greater the motivation will be to work on the project. People who have a stake in the game will contribute greater energy and enthusiasm to the effort. This energy has a positive, uplifting effect on the team, influencing others to perform at a higher level too. Energy begets energy and builds team synergy. Synergy means that the overall output of the team is greater than the sum of the individual efforts. Interdependency has a bonding effect among teammates. The secrets to building strong interdependency are to understand that working together will yield better results than working alone, empower each other to make judgments, and hold each other accountable.

Several tools and processes can be effective in maintaining a strong team focus. A team charter, team milestones, team scorecard, decision-making criteria, team assessments and feedback, rotation of team roles, and spider diagrams are all designed to increase team interdependency behaviors (see Chapter Four). These tools and processes create interdependency by establishing joint ownership of the team's charter, mutual dependency on performance through the team's milestones and scorecard, mutual responsibility in performing team roles, and meeting team expectations by using team assessments and feedback processes. Interdependency supports inclusive team behaviors. As these behaviors are reinforced by the team, interdependency and trust grow within the team. Individual work still needs to be done; however, the praise and recognition delivered to the individual work should always be placed in the context of supporting team goals and objectives. Teamwork is not about dividing up the work to reach a common goal; it is about managing the work in an interdependent way to achieve efficiency and maximum output.

Forming subteams can greatly improve interdependency. For example, a work team of four employees—Sam, Veronica, Wilbert, and Ann—was assembled to develop new health plan options for the company. Each team member represents one of the company's four geographical business units and 100 to 150 employees per unit. Each member had both personal and business interests at stake. The team's work plan consisted of evaluating current company health benefits, surveying employees and families, meeting with health plan providers, gathering customer satisfaction data, working with outside consultants, and benchmarking competitors. The work was done by forming four cross-member subteams: Sam and Veronica worked on the benchmarking and surveying as a subteam; Wilbert and Ann interviewed and collected information on health plan providers; Veronica and Ann put together the current health benefits; and Wilbert and Sam gathered the customer satisfaction data. Instead of dividing one area for each person, pairs of cross-subteams were created to enable each person to be more involved, more knowledgeable, and also more interdependent. Each person had an opportunity to work with another team member, which created camaraderie and interpersonal connection. Also, each subteam had a backup person for each area in case one person was out. Instead of everyone working on everything, the team had mutual trust, empowerment, and interdependency. The team also knew they needed data from all four subteams to produce their work outputs. This was a high-performing team.

Interdependency fails when individual needs take priority over team needs. It takes great strength and loyalty to relinquish personal ownership of ideas and individual preferences in support of the team. These are behaviors that support interdependency:

• *Concept of team ownership.* Ideas may be generated by individuals, but once presented, they should be viewed as team property rather than individual property. People should be motivated to contribute ideas, not compete with others for credit. Individual expectations need to be met, but not at the expense of the team. The attitude should be that everything that is individually produced is contributed to the team. What goes in may be individual; what comes out belongs to the team.

• *Concept of team loyalty.* The most important interdependent behavior is the mutual trust and expectation that the team will stand together on all key decisions. Behind closed doors, the team may vigorously disagree and debate issues, but when a team decision has been reached, those decisions are always honored outside the team. The team as a whole, not individuals, is held accountable for the decisions of the team. External dissension and negative gossip significantly undermine the trust and interdependency behaviors of teams. Individual loyalty to team decisions strengthens interdependency and teamwork.

Accountability

In ancient Rome, the law held that an engineer who had just completed building a new archway had to stand squarely beneath it when the scaffolding was removed. If the structure collapsed, the engineer responsible for it would bear the painful consequences firsthand. That is true accountability.

Most people think of accountability as a punishment for poor performance. You hear all the time that people need to be held accountable for their actions. Accountability has been associated with assigning blame for a failure. Indeed, it is analogous to standing beneath a newly built archway. These negative connotations of accountability have been sown in our thinking for centuries.

Accountability in fact is about being responsible and taking ownership of a task, project, or activity. It means that a person is willing to bear the consequences (good or bad) of his or her actions. Accountability should not be viewed solely as a punishing behavior. People should be rewarded for taking the responsibility of doing something well.

The team concept works well in today's organizations because people enjoy working on teams. Teams provide the opportunity to be intellectually challenged, make an impact, meet other people, and broaden their knowledge and skill set. The team is empowered to look for positive change and to have influence on the direction of the organization. Also, the team provides protection from individual accountability. This safety in numbers lowers the element of personal risk for people. However, this sharing of personal responsibility and accountability has both positive and negative consequences. The upside is that a person working together with a diverse team will likely generate better solutions than working alone. On the downside, the motivation and commitment of an individual may be lower in a team with shared accountability. This is especially true for independent, self-centered workers who prefer to be accountable for only what they can control: their own work and performance. Self-centered behaviors can be tolerated to a certain extent, but in many cases, they will have a negative impact on the team.

Accountability is a behavior that all team members should bear equally as individuals and as a team. On my daughter's soccer team, everyone understands that each player must play her position well to compete. But winning takes a collective team effort. No one can win a soccer game alone, regardless of her skills. A player can personally play the best game of her life, and the team can still lose. Project teams, like soccer teams, need both individual and team performance and accountability to win.

What is unique about team accountability is that the team mutually shares in the responsibility of the project; if one person is unable to complete his portion of the archway, others step in to fill that gap. This is common in soccer games as offensive players hustle back to help out on defense and defensive players back up the goalie. It happens seamlessly, and no blame game occurs. Team players stand together beneath the archway not because they have to but because they want to stand together and bear the consequences, good or bad.

Accountability is about stepping up to help out when a fellow team member is struggling and staying constructive and supportive when things fail. The team should also come together and celebrate successes and achievement and recognize what has been accomplished as a team. Accountability cuts both ways.

Accountability is about accepting personal and team responsibilities and creating a safe and positive environment for problem solving:

• *Team acceptance of responsibility.* Good teams create a safe environment to openly admit mistakes, address problems, and constructively discuss team breakdowns. The focus is on learning and continuous improvement rather than personal blame. Team responsibility means looking beyond personal interests and being willing to take action to fill gaps in the performance of others.

• *Positive accountability.* Good teams recognize individuals for their contributions to the team effort and for helping to meet team expectations. It is important to give credit when credit is deserved and to recognize it immediately.

Valuing Individual Differences

There is an old saying that people like people who are like themselves. This is certainly a truism: people who are alike culturally, professionally, educationally, in gender, in age, and in personality are likely to get along and build good relationships. When people have different backgrounds and thinking styles, building trust and establishing relationships takes more time. To accelerate this process, experienced teams create opportunities for different people to work together, share ownership on project deliverables, and socialize during lunches and breaks. The team should try to reserve some time during its initial meetings to learn about the diverse backgrounds and experiences of each other. It is helpful to ask people what their strengths are and what they like working on. These types of inquiries serve a dual purpose: they get people talking, and others learn about their work preferences. People like talking about themselves. When team members get to know each other, the natural tendency of judging and assuming things about people fades. In the absence of real information, people make assumptions based on limited impressions. Good teamwork relies on knowing, understanding, and appreciating people as individuals.

Understanding and managing individual differences enhances teamwork and the quality of the decisions and work products. The following actions can increase a team's awareness of individual differences:

• Selecting people with the right mix of backgrounds and skill sets.

• Adopting a flexible interpersonal style.

• Making a point to learn something new about a team member.

• Positively recognizing a person for sharing a cultural perspective.

• Recognizing that there are many right ways to get the job done.

• Treating differing viewpoints as a learning opportunity, not as a conflict.

• Admitting biases.

- Taking the extra time to get everyone's thoughts and buy-in on key issues and decisions.
- Not playing favorites. This is critical for team leaders and project managers. All of us may naturally enjoy working with some team members over others; however, do not let your behaviors become exclusionary. Be inclusive with your behaviors, especially your nonverbal communications because people will pick up your hidden meaning.

Teams lose when individuality is ignored or discounted. Common mistakes that teams make include failure in understanding people's strengths and treating everyone the same way:

• *Failure to understand the strengths of individual team members and assuming that people will naturally gravitate to things they prefer.* People seek challenge and growth in their careers. They want to make a difference and be recognized for their contributions to teams. To help them achieve these expectations, conduct periodic checks on their level of satisfaction and how things can be improved for them. This can be done openly with the team, one-on-one by the team leader, or anonymously using a written survey. High-performing teams are effective in matching people's skills and interests to the work required.

• *The blind-eye philosophy, which supports treating everyone the same and not valuing diversity.* Treating people fairly does not mean treating everyone in the same way. A common and misguided mind-set is to try not to see people as different and in that way preserve objectivity. This blind eye to diversity and different cultures is a lost opportunity for those who carry this view. Gaining insights into the similarities and differences of others offers endless opportunities.

Transparency

Transparency means being able to see the motivation and intentions behind people's words and actions. We see people's behaviors, but can only perceive their intentions or surmise them through our own feelings. We judge others based on our own experiences and relationships with them. People's ability to communicate their feelings and intentions vary widely and is based on their culture, personality, communication skills, and thinking styles. Some people are open and direct about their intentions and share their thoughts freely; others are reticent and prefer not to show their feelings. Good leaders and team players are transparent in their communications and are not afraid to show themselves. There are numerous personal barriers to transparent behaviors. Most people prefer to keep their intentions to themselves, not necessarily because they want to but because they have internal factors that preclude them from expressing their honest thoughts to others, especially people on a project team. Their personal barriers may be cultural (speak only when spoken to), personality related (not comfortable speaking about self), or risk aversion (afraid of saying something wrong or out of line with the team). Generally people refrain from showing themselves for fear of causing conflict. This usually stems from a lack of confidence and trust. As we will learn in Chapter Thirteen, the lack of transparency is often a defense mechanism. This behavior is intended to hide themselves from others.

Fear is the biggest demotivator for transparent behaviors. People fear conflict, embarrassment, ridicule, failure, inferiority, and rejection. In response, they hide, withdraw, retaliate, defend, or argue.

Fearless team players are highly transparent and are not afraid to show their genuine intent, knowledge, and feelings. People who are good communicators are more transparent and trusted. As a result, this behavior motivates others to be transparent too and builds mutual trust. Transparency does not mean explaining yourself for every behavior. But if you feel strongly about an issue, say so, and explain why you feel that way. More often than not, others probably share your feelings. A team member who expresses his thoughts and feelings is doing the team a favor. You will find that people may refute your opinions but will rarely refute your feelings. Your intentions and feelings are solely yours. It is ironic that people fear showing their feelings when in fact feelings are the most honored and safest thing to express.

It takes courage and confidence to adopt a transparent communication style. Transparency is about showing yourself, conveying the honest thinking and feelings behind your words. Allowing people to guess what you are thinking is a barrier for good teamwork. One of the key causes of conflict is the lack of transparency on the part of the team. Trust is shallow when transparency is low. Promoting transparency leads to greater teamwork, trust, and understanding. Transparency makes you a better manager, leader, and team player.

A lack of transparency leads to poor team communications. The best remedy is to engage others and encourage people to challenge each other. There are three common signs of poor team transparency:

- *Team members do not speak up.* This hampers team progress because assumptions and decisions will be made without everyone's thoughts and opinions. In a respectful manner, ask people periodically for their opinions and thoughts. When quieter members speak up, listen with great patience, and positively reinforce their participation. Encouragement and positive reinforcement are team-building behaviors.

- *Team members are afraid to challenge each other.* They are too polite and tolerant. Lack of disagreement and challenges are not necessarily a good sign. Use processes that force people to take different views. For example, do a force field analysis (Chapter Eight), ask the team to play devil's advocate for a few minutes, ask for other options, and ask "what if" questions, such as, "What if this idea doesn't work?"

- *Team members have difficulty understanding each other.* Ask for more information: Make it a practice to ask for each other's thinking behind their statements before responding. Try to ask more clarifying questions. Asking questions honors the ideas and opinions of others. Always seek to understand before responding.

Learning and Recognition

The rate at which the team learns together will determine the speed of success. Team learning takes place in many different ways: learning to work together as a team, learning to adjust work plans in response to new information and changes, and learning to reach team conclusions and decisions.

Learning to Work Together as a Team   The first step in learning to work together is to recognize different learning styles in people. There are three primary learning styles.

Visual learners learn best by seeing a picture, figure, or graphic of the concept. They like to see the interrelationships of different pieces and how they all fit together to form a picture. These visual images are easier for them to remember. Also, color and texture can enhance these images for them.

Auditory learners learn best by hearing the information. It is easier for them to internalize a concept by hearing it discussed or read aloud. They do problem-solving better through dialogue and iterations, and they prefer to take verbal directions over written directions.

Kinesthetic learners learn by doing. Pictures or verbal explanations are helpful to them, but they need to get their hands on it before it becomes real to them. Direct involvement is necessary for them to stay engaged on a topic. Expressions through body movements and gestures help to instill their understanding and feelings. Materials and equipment such as computers and board games provide good feedback for learning. Kinesthetic learners are attracted to interactive situations, role playing, and live demonstrations.

In working content, process, and behaviors, the learning styles of individuals on the team will have an impact on team dynamics. The majority of people are visual learners; they like to see something to fully understand it. My older daughter is an auditory learner; she prefers to hear information. For example, when she studies, she likes to read aloud and listen to lecture tapes. Kinesthetic learners are better taught by doing and physically feeling the work. Learning style is individual; it is all about what accelerates each person's understanding the most. For most teams, there is a strong preference for both visual and auditory learning. However, in some disciplines, such as the performing arts, the preference is for kinesthetic learning.

Learning to Adjust Work Plans in Response to New Information and Changes

What differentiates a good team from a great team is the ability to recognize when a change is needed and to take prompt action. One of the common mistakes of project teams is waiting too long to make needed changes. The inertia required to make significant course corrections is difficult in a large team (it is like steering the *Titanic*). People are usually reluctant to admit mistakes and tend to stick to original plans too long. As circumstances change, the team needs to learn to adapt and make changes quickly.

Learning to Reach Team Conclusions and Decisions   Learning as a team entails

- Gathering information efficiently and accurately
- Evaluating and analyzing the information
- Understanding what the team has and what additional data it must collect
- Interpreting the information and drawing conclusions
- Using that information to shape future actions and recommendations

Bringing all these pieces together to reach a decision is a critical process for any project team. People know how to process and interpret information as individuals; doing it as a team is much more challenging. Some individuals require more time than others to evaluate information and may rely on their feelings more in drawing conclusions; others are more analytical and systematic in deriving conclusions and want the team's conclusions to be technically correct. These types of individual preferences can have an impact on decision-making processes and affect how fast the team can reach consensus on issues.

These are the best team practices to increase team learning:

- Use team assessment and feedback processes.
- Freely share information and learning.
- Actively facilitate discussions.
- Take time to learn from mistakes.
- Invite different opinions and points of views.
- Ensure that results and analyses are owned by the team, not by individuals.
- Always develop alternative solutions and trade-offs.
- Welcome proposed changes and challenges.
- Agree to a criterion for important team decisions.
- Document the team's rationale for its key decisions and recommendations.
- Review and reinforce team ground rules.
- Give feedback.

One common obstacle to team learning is when individual team members hoard or withhold information from the team. Hoarding information is a form of power and protection for some people; it gives them a competitive edge over others. It might stem from mistrust: that other team members will take ownership of the person's idea and the person will be denied credit. Or a team member might withhold information for fear it may not be valued by the team. All of these possible psychological explanations may be understandable, but it is the role of the team to drive this kind of fear out of the system. Hoarding is a selfish behavior that high-performing teams spurn.

Learning Through Feedback: Techniques in Giving Positive and Negative Feedback A good general strategy for giving constructive feedback to the team is to be transparent about any concerns, be specific about the problem, and frame the problem in a positive and forward-looking context. For example, perhaps you like the way the team is working together but think that the meetings are running too long with too many topics. As a result, you have had to leave meetings early in order to make other appointments and you feel badly about it. You might say in the next meeting: "Before we begin, may I say something regarding our meetings? I have really enjoyed our team discussions, but our meetings have run late. It's good that we have lots to say, but it does frustrate me at times. I would like to see if we can better manage our agenda so that we can finish on time and I don't have to rush out. I have some suggestions and would like to see if others have some too."

Asking a question before presenting an issue is a good way to get the others' attention. Then framing the problem engages everyone with the issue. It works well to personalize the problem by stating how the problem affects you and then suggest some solutions and invite other ideas too. Exploring root causes for the problem is constructive, but seeking blame is destructive. Remarks should always be honest and inclusive.

Giving Feedback on Individual Behavior Few people are skilled in giving individual feedback. The most common feedback process is the employee performance review. But even then the process is often not done well. The feedback is not communicated well and is often vague. Feedback is difficult because it deals with feelings and judgments about behaviors. Giving feedback to others—peer, subordinate, or supervisor—is much different from dealing with process and content issues. People have a hard time giving constructive (negative) feedback. No one likes to be critical of others, and giving bad news is never pleasant. It is a fear of conflict and a concern for the person's feelings. Also, it is a fear of not doing it well. But there comes a time when someone's behavior warrants constructive feedback, regardless of the risk of conflict.

For some people, giving positive feedback is also hard to do. Fear is not the reason in this case. It is a natural reluctance in many people. What holds a person back from giving positive feedback? In the traditional business culture, praising and recognizing others can be seen as a weak behavior. Some people shun recognition. Also, compliments that are not done well might appear patronizing and insincere. Some people do not feel comfortable giving positive feedback. Others have such a high threshold for giving a positive comment that they require something extraordinary before they recognize others. But in fact, giving positive, pinpointed feedback is an unselfish, giving act when done sincerely. Positive feedback is a thoughtful expression of appreciation. Praise motivates and reinforces desired behaviors. Having the ability to give meaningful feedback is a personal strength, not a sign of weakness.

There are also behavioral issues on the receiving end. People seem to struggle to respond smoothly to positive comments. The right response when receiving positive feedback is, "Thank you"—nothing more or less. It is also acceptable to recognize the giver ("Thank you for your kind gesture") or include others in the recognition ("Jay was a big help to me, and he deserves recognition too"). It is best not to try to deny it, downplay it, or brag about it. Long recognitions are fine, but long acceptances are irritating.

Anonymous Feedback Is Better Than No Feedback at All   If the comfort level is too low for in-person feedback, the team should try an anonymous feedback process to provide constructive feedback to people. Examples of anonymous processes include suggestion boxes, team surveys, upward feedback from employees, and 360-degree feedback processes (a person receives anonymous feedback from peers, supervisors, and direct reports).

Delivering Feedback   It takes good training and experience to deliver positive feedback. Here are some guidelines:

• Be sincere and genuine. Good feedback is pinpointing what the person did well. Instead of saying, "Nice job on the report," be specific: "I really like your report. It is clear, concise, creative, thorough, and very well written." The more pinpointed the comments, the more sincere they are. Also, this reinforces the things that you liked about the report, increasing the probability of its recurrence.

• Give timely feedback. Timeliness means giving praise promptly when the desired behavior occurs. How appreciative are you if you wait months to tell someone that she did a good job?

• Tailor it to the person. Praise to one person may be an insult to another. The type of recognition should be tailored to the person's preferences. To find out these preferences, ask the person how she likes to be recognized and rewarded. The best time to ask that question is when the person joins the organization. This is not an awkward question, and you will find that the person is flattered that you asked. It shows that you care and want to value the person's contributions in a way that is meaningful to her.

It also takes good training and experience to deliver constructive, or negative, feedback. Here are some guidelines:

• Sandwich the constructive feedback with positive remarks. Start with a positive remark, give the constructive feedback, and then end on a positive note. If the goal is to be constructive and motivating, positive comments help to keep things in a balanced perspective. Even if the person's response is hostile, defensive, or argumentative, keep a positive frame of mind even if the other person chooses not to. (I discuss these positive techniques in Chapters Thirteen and Fourteen.)

• A little constructive feedback goes a long way. People do not appreciate a long dissertation on what they did wrong. It is best to be specific and concise, and let the person ask for more feedback if the initial comments are unclear. A good rule of thumb is the harder the news, the shorter the delivery time. When delivering feedback, give time for the person to absorb it. You may get silence as the person internalizes your negative message. Silence is okay. Do not try to fill that silence with elaboration and overwork the process. People are usually harder on themselves than you think. Also, they get overwhelmed if they get too much negative input. It is better to stick with one or two critical points.

• Express the desired behavior, not the undesirable behavior. In most cases, you will have a choice to present feedback in a negative or positive way. Always choose the positive path. It is best to state what you desire ("I like it when you keep me informed of your progress") rather than what you do not want ("You never keep me advised of your progress"), which can be demeaning and hurtful. Some people believe that a strong remark can motivate a person to shape up, but it rarely does. Putting a person down only triggers negative feelings.

• Avoid giving negative feedback in public. Regardless of how justified you are in correcting someone's behavior, avoid giving negative feedback in front of others. Unless it is an emergency situation, find an appropriate time and a private place for this conversation. If appropriate, it can be done as a formal team process with the right support systems.

Negative feedback does not just mean verbal criticism; it could be a disgusted look, a groan, a laugh, a sarcastic remark, a negative response to a person's idea, a put-down comment, ignoring a person's comment, talking over someone else, or even a negative tone in your voice. It may not seem negative to you, but it can be negative to the other party. A sarcastic remark can be demeaning to others. In most cultures, giving criticism in public is an embarrassment to the person and his family. (Chapters Ten and Eleven discuss the impact of negative behaviors on individual and team performance.)

Judgments are interpretations of behaviors and usually are not accurate and not well received by the other party. Also, personal judgments often provoke a negative reaction. For example, it may be okay to say, "This report was submitted late," rather than, "Obviously you didn't care about this report since I received it so late." Avoid using "you" or "why" in feedback to describe a problem, such as, "You didn't get this right," "Why didn't you do it the way I told you to?" or "Why did you turn in this report so late?" Constructive feedback works best by sticking to the facts and expressing how the person's performance affected you and the project: "Because the report was late, we lost an important sale. I'm very disappointed because our department had worked hard to develop this opportunity. Reports need to be completed on time."

Summary Points on Giving Negative Feedback   Giving negative feedback is a difficult task but can be made easier by sticking to some simple rules:

- Focus on how the person's behavior has affected you.
- Use facts and observations rather than judgments.
- Avoid telling the person what to do.
- Avoid giving negative feedback in public.
- Be clear and concise, and allow the person some time to consider what you have said.
- Start positive and end positive.

Recognition   Positive feedback and recognition are the most powerful human factors for shaping and reinforcing desired behaviors. They tell the person that she is accepted, valued, and appreciated. These are the messages that everyone yearns for and works for. Deep inside, everyone wants acknowledgment of their work in some way. This is an area of great opportunity for all organizations and teams.

All recognitions, formal and informal, have a positive impact. Direct recognitions may be awards, money, promotions, and written commendations. Recognitions are not restricted to awards, trinkets, and monetary rewards. A smile, a positive remark in a meeting, a thank-you on the phone or in an e-mail, or a handshake can be just as uplifting as, or more so, than any award certificate. It is the sincerity, timing, and personal appreciation that make recognitions special. The best recognitions at work are those that come from people closest to you: your peers, supervisor, or people who work for you. Successful teams take the time to celebrate and recognize individual contributions to the team's success. They take time at the beginning of team meetings to recognize individuals for their team efforts. They set a positive tone and demonstrate that the team cares about its members.

It is inevitable that a team will encounter highs and lows during their period together. They will experience success in completing assignments, meeting deadlines, collaborating on solving problems, generating positive results, and achieving project expectations. And they will also face conflicts and problems. The key is to recognize the strengths and work styles of team members, hold periodic team assessments and feedback sessions to evaluate how well the team is working together, and promptly address and resolve any emerging team problems and conflicts.

THE TRUE TEST: INCLUSIVE TEAM BEHAVIORS

High-performing teams follow the six key team behaviors and maintain an inclusive team environment. A highly inclusive team develops a circle of trust and communications around the team. The team performs as a single interdependent unit, valuing the strengths and contributions of each team member. Individual weaknesses are offset by the strengths of others. Positive feedback and recognition keep people in the common circle. Good teams have a sixth sense and take action to retrieve team members who are in danger of being excluded.

Here are some key indicators of inclusive team behaviors:

- Equal authority: Team members are respected and accorded equal influence. Power is shared—everyone gets an equal vote in team decisions.

- No barriers: All team members are actively involved and contributing. The team is sensitive to any barriers, such as culture, language, gender, or work style, that may hold people back from engaging in team activities. The team makes an effort to ensure that these barriers do not exist or are minimized.

- Good team communications: Information is freely shared among team members. Everyone feels well informed and is given opportunities to work on things that they enjoy most. People are not afraid to speak their mind.

- Standing together: It is easy to show good teamwork when things are going well; it is when things seem to fall apart that team behaviors are tested. Inclusive teams do not punish and exclude team members who run into problems. Instead, they draw them closer and stand together, not push them away. As a result, team members feel safe to bring up problems when they arise.

SUMMARY

Behaviors reflect who we are, what we believe in, and how we feel, and they affect team performance more than content or process does. Project failures are most often caused by a breakdown in team collaboration and behaviors, which leads to poor project execution. The six keys to preventing team breakdowns are to build behaviors in mutual trust, transparency, accepting individual differences, interdependency, accountability, and learning and recognition. These behavioral strategies help create a positive, inclusive environment that enables people to work at their best. We perform best when we feel good about ourselves and what we are contributing to the team. For any relationship, positive feelings are generated from being trusted, valued, needed, and recognized. When the right behaviors are demonstrated, along with effective team processes (Table 5.1), the chances of team success greatly increase.

Processes are the tools, techniques, and procedures that the team uses to get its work done. Behaviors are the human actions and interpersonal dynamics behind the execution of these processes. Processes help guide behaviors by establishing rules and procedures on how things will be done. Team interactions, collabora-

Table 5.1
Summary of the Six Key Team Behaviors and Processes

Key Team Behaviors	Key Team Processes
1. Mutual trust	1. Team meetings
2. Interdependency	2. Roles and responsibilities
3. Accountability	3. Communications
4. Valuing individual differences	4. Decision making
5. Transparency	5. Measuring performance
6. Learning and recognition	6. Team feedback

tions, and team relationships are built not on process but on mutual trust, transparency, respect, interdependency, team learning, and accountability. A highly inclusive team will develop a circle of trust around the team. The team performs as a single interdependent unit. High-performing teams care about each other and value the strengths that each person brings. Inclusive behaviors are essential for team success.

Take the time during team processes to recognize individual team members. Positive feedback and recognition are powerful methods for shaping and reinforcing desired behaviors.

Secrets of Managing the Three Key Elements

The three key elements for team success are content, process, and behaviors. Content defines the purpose and intent, process is the "how" and set of procedures, and behaviors are the observable human actions and team dynamics. Besides helping to structure a team, these three elements are critical for managing team interactions and interpersonal conflicts. When team conflicts occur, most likely there has been a breakdown in one or more of these key elements. The key is being able to recognize and separate content, process, and behaviors. This chapter contains fifteen short stories that help reveal the secrets of the three elements.

SEPARATING CONTENT, PROCESS, AND BEHAVIOR

All three elements play important roles in team dynamics. Knowing how to recognize the interplay of these three elements in human interactions is a powerful skill for diagnosing problems and motivating people.

The Manager's Business Planning Meeting

In a meeting I attended as a young supervisor, our manager was facilitating a planning session to develop a list of improvement ideas with the staff. The meeting was well attended, and the group looked forward to the discussion. The manager

encouraged everyone to speak up and to think broadly, and he would record every-one's ideas. One staff member started the discussion by raising the issue of "too much bureaucracy" and delays in getting simple things approved internally, like travel and invoices. She expressed concern that the level of administrative work was taking away from the "real work." The manager responded right away by say-ing that these administrative procedures were dictated by company policies, that he was surprised to hear that a person at her level was spending valuable time pro-cessing invoices, and suggested better time management as a solution. He then asked if anyone else had similar problems.

Needless to say, few additional suggestions followed. This is a classic example where the manager's poor reaction to content (idea) negatively reinforced in oth-ers the desired behavior (speaking up with suggestions) and failed to honor the process of capturing ideas. The behavior was exactly what the manager wanted and the process was working, but it all went out the window together. This is a classic case of shooting the messenger.

Here is what went wrong:

- The manager reacted negatively to the content of the suggestion and at the same time unknowingly punished both the behavior and the process.

- Two processes were in play at the same time. Instead of the process of hearing and capturing ideas, the manager started a second process: giving feedback on the ideas.

- To make matters worse, the manager's behavior hurt the feelings of the staff member, who will remember that interchange for a long time.

The three key elements should have been better managed. First, the staff mem-ber's behavior of offering a suggestion should be praised; second, the process should be honored by writing the idea down on a board or flip chart; and finally, no judgment should be made on the content of the idea. The focus should be on understanding, not judging, the input. When the manager commented on the idea, he was starting a second process. Unfortunately, people always seem to react to content first. It is a learned behavior.

Here are some rules on managing the three elements:

- Separate content, process, and behavior.
- Make sure content, process, and behaviors are consistent and not in conflict.
- Always look for behavior first, because it affects people's feelings the most, both negatively and positively. In this case, the manager should have recognized the good behavior of the staff member by saying, "Thank you for speaking up" or "Thank you for raising your concern." The proper response is to acknowledge the behavior first and then move on to either process (for example, capturing the thought on a flip chart) or content (for example, repeating the staff member's comment to confirm understanding).
- Try to make positive comments on one or more of these three factors when you see it demonstrated. For example, one can be recognized for following a process or sticking to the subject of the discussion.
- Admit mistakes in your behavior.
- Always personalize behavioral reinforcement by using the person's first name and making eye contact with the person you are addressing.

Too often, when disagreements, frustrations, and conflicts occur, people become very content focused in trying to solve the problem instead of listening for verbal and nonverbal cues. They try to persuade others when they have a poor understanding of where other people stand. Too much may be hidden to talk productively. People hide their feelings and information in the absence of trust. Perhaps this happens because people do not have enough experience with one another to talk frankly and openly. These are human factors that impede communications in the workplace. It is important to know how to separate content, process, and behaviors and understand the underlying human factors in effect.

The Contract Offer

A few years ago, I needed to purchase some consulting services from a small firm. It was going to be a fairly large, long-term contract, and the contracting firm was considered one of the best in the state. I had other options, but I knew I wanted to go with this firm based on its performance record and references. I offered to pay

$250,000 per year for two years, with a renewal option for the third year at the same rate. They said they would consider it and get back to me within three days. After three days, the company called me as promised and said that they would need more time to consider my offer since they were considering a competing offer for the same resources. They indicated that I could improve my position by making a bigger offer. I was not very pleased to hear that, but what could I do? I was not in a strong position but nevertheless felt I should be the one in control. The playing field certainly was hidden from me. Knowing the power of separating content from process and behaviors, I knew content (that is, bidding higher for their services) was my weak suit. The contractor had the advantage here. I decided to gain advantage by switching to process.

I said, "Gee, I'm sorry you feel you need to ask for a higher bid. I was hoping we could do business together. It's a great opportunity for both of us. No problem. Just send me a written note that states you reject my offer, and I will go through the process of considering a revised offer."

The person quickly said, "Oh, no. I don't reject your offer. I was just wondering if you could sweeten the offer. I have another one that I'm comparing it to."

I replied, "I'm a bit confused. I thought you wanted a higher price."

The person replied, "Yes. Could you go higher?"

I responded, "Well, to go higher or not, our process is for you to reject the offer, return it to me, and I will take it through the channels again. That's our process. I will tell my company management that you rejected our offer."

The person finally said, "Boy, it sounds like a hassle. Let me go forward with what you sent me, and I'll get back to you." Two days later, the person called me to accept our proposed contract.

This strategy of separating content from process revealed four important things:

1. The reluctance of the person to reject it revealed to me that the person probably did not have a bona-fide competing offer or had a weak one and was playing me off.

2. Focusing on process provided objectivity and prevented me from making it a personal matter.

3. Instead of a conflict between me and the other person, I was working with the other party. By referring to the company process, the message I sent was, "I understand your request, and I'm not going to debate it with you. But here's what we need to do if you want a revised offer."

4. Unlike a minute ago when the other person was driving, I was now driving, using process and gaining a strength position. It is always better to drive than to be driven by someone else.

Had the person rejected the offer, the process would tell me that the person had a strong competing offer. In that case, I would shift to content and ask the person to explain to me in more detail where the gap was between my offer and the other person's offer. Asking the person to pinpoint the content enables me to get an understanding of the seriousness of the competing offer and allows me to consider other alternatives to make a successful offer. If the person refuses to discuss gaps and I was still intent to do business, then I would move to behaviors and meet personally with the other party. We could then explore where we could work together to secure a contract. It could turn out that the gap was too wide. Either way, I would gain an advantage in making the right decision for my company.

Always try to gain an advantage in content, process, or behavior (or some combination of these). As we will discuss in Chapter Fourteen, whenever you run into a conflict over content, process, or behavior, recognize your position, and switch the conversation to the element of your greatest strength and control. If you do not have one, work to establish one. The more elements you control, the greater leverage and influence you will gain. However, having control over all three may be a disadvantage depending on your position and circumstances. For example, when you want partnership, you do not want total control of all three elements. One partner being totally dominant is likely destined for failure. This technique can be used in relationships also.

The Slippery Glass

One day when my daughter Amy was six years old, I was in the kitchen preparing lunch. My hands were wet, and as I was reaching for a glass, it slipped from my hand and crashed to the floor. Amy heard it from the adjoining family room and came running into the kitchen. She asked if I was okay and then at the same moment started to reach down to help pick up the broken pieces of glass. That is when I yelled at her to stop and sharply told her never to pick up broken glass. I told her she could cut herself very badly by picking up jagged pieces of glass. Startled, she said, "Sorry," in a frightened voice and left quickly.

Right away, I realized that I had just punished her, even though she had acted in kindness and with good intent. I had scolded her "bad" behavior along with her "good" intent to help me. I neglected to tell her that her intent, or content behind her behavior, was caring and positive, and I want her to continue that behavior in life. Because her safety was at risk, my reaction was right, but I had left her with a completely negative feeling. I learned that I needed to recognize both behavior and the underlying intent in people. Also, I learned that in the absence of process, people will revert to their instincts and values. If I had taught her how (process) to handle broken glass, it would have prevented my daughter's undesired behavior. Process was missing.

Separating Content, Process, and Behavior Provides Advantages

Learning how to separate content, process, and behaviors enables us to improve our performance and interactions with others. Recognizing where your strengths and weaknesses lie among these three elements gives you great influence and maximal negotiating position. Also, this technique helps you stay objective and avoid making the situation personal. Conflict and misunderstandings occur when people are addressing different elements and mix them in discussion. When that occurs, communications can quickly become frustrating. This will be illustrated in further examples of differentiating the three elements of team performance.

BEHAVIOR VERSUS CONTENT

Of the three elements, people do not naturally differentiate content from behavior. Typically they are too focused on one, usually content, and fail to appreciate or understand the other. Such a disconnect can often lead to conflicts.

The Vice President's Call

One important leadership behavior is to model the behaviors that you want repeated. Whether it is complying with company policies or following through on promises, the leader sets the bar for the organization.

I remember a time when our organization received word of a product contamination in a shipment of goods that was sold to a small county in the state. It was a minor contamination, and our experts felt that its performance could be slightly affected but probably no one would notice any differences in the product. The problem was quickly identified as a one-time product blending error, and there were no indications of widespread effects.

Without hesitation, the vice president of the business issued a recall of the contaminated product, authorized compensation of any claims from customers, and ordered an immediate incident investigation with deadlines for correcting the problem and sharing the findings widely in the organization. The cost was modest, but the leadership behavior sent a loud message to the organization and our customers that product integrity and stewardship were core beliefs (content) and the company's reputation was not to be compromised. The vice president recognized that the organization's content had little meaning unless its behaviors supported it.

It is inevitable that all organizations and teams, large or small, will be tested to see if behaviors stay true to content. To support content, behaviors must be visible and consistent with stated values and objectives.

The Bike Trip

Sometimes we mistakenly treat behaviors and content as the same.

Many years ago, I had an experience with my daughter Sarah, then eight years old, during a bike trip to the store. The shopping area from our house is only about a mile away, but to get there, we had to bike down a busy street. The bike lane is narrow, and it is easy to swerve into the traffic. Fortunately, the street had a wide sidewalk, which we rode on instead. Sarah was riding ahead of me so that I could keep an eye on her.

Sarah was a strong-willed child and got distracted very easily. We rode down the street quite a distance without incident, when suddenly Sarah rode off the sidewalk to the bike lane alongside the busy traffic. I yelled out right away for her to get back onto the sidewalk, but she apparently did not hear me over the traffic noise. I yelled out again, and she answered back, "No!" So I quickly biked up to her, stopped her bike, and forced her back onto the sidewalk.

We rode a couple of minutes more until we reached the shopping area. That is where we stopped, and I told her that she had frightened me with her move to the street. I asked her why she disobeyed my instructions and scolded her for not listening to me. She was getting a little tearful when she finally spoke up: "Dad, I was being safe. When I came up to the part that was over the canal, it freaked me out, and I was afraid I was going to hit the railing and fall into the canal. I was really scared, Dad!"

I looked back and saw she was correct: the railing was not high enough to prevent someone from going over the top of it. Her intent was consistent with the safety behavior that I had taught her. I was making a judgment through my eyes that she was being defiant and unsafe when in fact she was reacting exactly as I had wanted: safety comes first. I gave her a big hug and told her I was sorry and that she had done the right thing.

I misread this situation because I misunderstood the intent behind her behaviors. Also, when an unexpected change occurred, there was no process to address it. In the absence of process, people revert to their personal values, and conflicts may arise. This happens all the time with team and work relationships.

Shooting the Supervisor

The department manager e-mailed the company's business plan and annual goals, which turned out to be difficult to read and understand. A supervisor then met with the department manager and informed him that the employees were confused about the new business plan and suggested a meeting with employees to help answer questions. The manager responded that he had written most of the plan himself, did not understand why there was any confusion, and reminded the supervisor that he expected the supervisor to support the plan, not criticize it. He advised the supervisor to hold his own meeting, and if there were still any confusion, he would consider a meeting.

The supervisor, dejected over the response, left the manager's office and dropped the issue.

By focusing only on content, the supervisor missed an opportunity to praise the supervisor's behavior by thanking the supervisor for raising the issue and suggesting a solution. Instead, the manager had rejected the content, ignored the suggestion, and berated the supervisor.

The Hard-Working Office Assistant

The boss needed a rush report completed for his meeting the next day and called on his office assistant to get it done. The office assistant worked until 9:00 P.M. to complete the assignment and proudly left the report on her boss's desk. The boss drifted in at 11:00 A.M. the next day and became upset when he saw that the document was missing page numbers. He called in the office assistant, who showed up at the boss's door expecting thanks for a job well done, but instead was greeted by, "What happened to the page numbers? This is going to make me late for the meeting. Could you please correct this as soon as you can. This is urgent!" The office assistant was crushed and hurried to reprint the document with page numbers.

In assessing the behavior of the boss, the question is, What was more important: pointing out the lack of page numbers (content) or recognizing the effort and timeliness (behavior) of the office assistant? The boss should have recognized the good behavior first instead of admonishing her about the missing page numbers. He was too focused on content to care about the office assistant's behaviors.

Waiting in the Drugstore

One day I was in the drugstore buying a few things for a trip. I went to the checkout line to find six other people waiting. It was lunchtime, and a lot of other people were running errands too. The person in front of me appeared impatient that the store had not provided more cashiers during the busy lunch period and remarked aloud, "I don't think these people know what customer service means." Just at that point, an attractive young woman rushed by us in line, hurried to the front, and was allowed to pay for a small item quickly in cash. In seeing that, the person in front of me was angry, said a few nasty things, and remarked, "That's not fair! I'm going to talk to the manager." No one looked pleased.

As he took off, a couple of people turned back to me and said that the young woman had a child in her car having an asthma attack and she was rushing to buy an inhaler. Everyone in line was suddenly more sympathetic and concerned for the mother than angry. People had been angry based on the young woman's behavior, but once they understood the content behind her behavior, everyone's mood changed dramatically. In fact, I think we all felt a bit guilty for judging the woman so harshly. I do not know what happened to the customer ahead of me; he may have left. This was a lesson in interpreting behaviors without knowing the genuine circumstances and content behind the behavior.

Recognize Behaviors First

When people react too quickly and negatively to the content of an idea, they unintentionally shut down a desired behavior. The person may be bringing up an issue to stimulate a discussion or to speak frankly on a personal point of view.

Instead of acknowledging the validity of the point, people quickly judge the content instead of honoring the person's good communication behavior. By recognizing and praising people's behavior first, the discussion will stay at a higher level. In putting down a valued behavior, the team shoots the messenger and risks lowering the team's behaviors.

Use Content to Change Behaviors

When we are confronted by bad behaviors, our first reaction is to react negatively to it. Such a response is nonproductive. Giving a negative response to a bad behavior rarely leads to a positive result. For example, when two team members are caught in a loud side conversation and you wish it to stop, a common reaction is, "Excuse me, but do you mind?" or "Excuse me, but I can't hear the discussion when you two are talking like that." This negative feedback may temporarily shut down the behavior but does nothing in building a positive relationship. A better response to this negative behavior is to switch to content, not behavior, by using an inquiry technique: "Excuse me. It sounds as if you're engaged in an important point [content]. Is it something we need to discuss?" or "Do you have another issue or question [content]?" This is a neutral, not a critical, remark in response to an undesirable behavior. It is always better to neutralize a behavior than to fight it.

PROCESS VERSUS CONTENT

Process can be used to uncover content. When problems arise, too often people leap to solutions instead of seeking to understand the problem first. Another common mistake is confusing process and content.

A New Database System

Last year I had a project meeting to discuss a better way of keeping training records for regulatory compliance. We had worked two months to narrow our recommendation to two options: a centralized corporate electronic database or a locally

managed database. The first option was two and half times more expensive but well controlled and better secured. The second option allowed each business unit to manage its own records. The latter choice was a bit riskier but less expensive to operate. After two hours of lively discussion on the pros and cons of each, two people wanted local control, two others liked central control, and two members were absent. Seeing that our time was up, the facilitator suggested that we close the discussion by going around the table and have each person state, in two minutes or less, his or her position on the issue. We would capture everyone's thoughts, summarize them, and make a decision the next morning when the entire team would be present. This was a closing process to the meeting.

The first person stated that he was concerned about costs and preferred the local option. The second person agreed. The third person strongly supported a centralized system to ensure better compliance. He did not feel that the cost difference was important. At that point, another person countered that the costs were substantially higher and would likely inflate over time. The third person was annoyed by that remark and indicated that the database already existed and the costs would likely go down, not up. The facilitator stepped in to control the discussion and said she would capture the point on the flip chart for follow-up tomorrow. As she was recording the point, both people continued the discussion. The facilitator felt trapped in trying to capture the opposing views, time was running way over, and the fourth person still had not spoken. When she finally finished scribing, twelve minutes had transpired. By the time she called on the fourth person to speak, one person had to leave, another was digging into some cost spreadsheets, and the last person felt insignificant. The meeting ended rushed and disorganized.

The team made four common errors:

1. The team did not separate process from content. As they went around the table in a process to close the meeting, they reverted to a content discussion midway despite agreeing to close.

2. The two individuals agreed to the process but could not let go of content.

3. The facilitator did not clearly explain what a closing process meant.

4. The team allowed the breakdown to happen and did not aid the facilitator.

The discussion had moved from an open discussion to a closing process. Instead of switching to process, content crept back into the process, and the team members restarted a discussion on the content. If the team had truly understood the closing process, the meeting would have ended on time. Instead, the team recycled the pros and cons of costs and ended on a frustrated note. Always separate content from process, and separate opening and closing in a given discussion.

The Manager's Noninvitation

A team leader wanted to invite her office assistant to a project strategy meeting. The manager rejected the idea because he did not think the office assistant would contribute any content to the discussions and would likely be bored. The office assistant was not invited.

What the manager failed to recognize was that the office assistant was responsible for preparing and organizing the meetings, transcribing everything afterward from the flip charts, and did the follow-up work on the team's action items. Although she was not directly involved with the content of the meeting, she was very much involved in the process. She would operate more effectively if she had a chance to hear the discussion, meet the people whom she would work with later, and felt included in the team's process. The office assistant had a process reason for attending the meeting, and she was also a member of the team. Unfortunately, the manager's behaviors did not make her feel that way. The manager was too focused on content and failed to appreciate the importance of process.

Having ownership in the process is important in high-performing teams. The manager also missed a good opportunity to promote teamwork and inclusive behaviors. The manager's right response would have been to say to the team leader, "I appreciate your thinking of your office assistant. I'm concerned about her time. What value do you see her adding to the meeting?" This approach recognizes the team leader's thoughtfulness and sets up his question in a positive way. Commenting about his concern on her time provides transparency. If he had asked directly, "Why does she need to be there?" the team leader may have reacted defensively.

Dinner at Lucia's Cafe

Another good example of confusing process and content happened one Friday night when my wife wanted to have a quiet dinner out to reconnect after a hectic week. Just as I arrived home after a horrendous commute, she greeted me by saying, "Hi, honey, how about you and I go out for a relaxing dinner at Lucia's Cafe and catch up on things?" I quickly responded, "I don't know, honey. I went by the place on the way home, and the traffic is bad. Who knows how long the wait for the table is going to be, and I'm not sure what the kids are going to eat."

This was the wrong answer. I gave a process-focused response when her focus was on content: having some relationship time. I was not hearing the content of her message but heard and reacted only to the process. Worse, she heard my negative process response as a negative content response to spending time with her. If I had listened better, I could have said, "That's a great idea. I would love to go out just the two of us. The traffic and parking may be tough at Lucia's, but I'm sure we can find a backup." This answer works much better because it acknowledged her content first, and I was able to express my process concern.

The learning is to respond to content with content first and then elaborate on any process issues. The way to prevent this type of conflict is always to respond in kind: process to process and content to content.

The same thing happens in teams when one person is trying to communicate content and someone else is talking about process, and they wonder why they are not communicating. Here is one more simple example of a process-content conflict in a team setting. Sometimes team members are reluctant to accept certain responsibilities because they feel they do not have authority and control over the content of the work. Many people feel that if they accept a responsibility such as leading a meeting, they will be held accountable for overseeing the work of the participants and the content of the meeting. People are more accepting when it is clarified that they are the process owner only and are not responsible for supervising others or producing all the content of the meeting. This type of uncertainty occurs when there is a lack of clarity around content and process.

The Helicopter Tour

When we become too process focused, we lose focus of the objective. I had an example of too much process during a mix-up on an excursion. I had signed up for a helicopter tour of a city with a local vendor and was instructed to assemble at its facility headquarters with my paid ticket at 1:45 P.M. I arrived about 1:15 P.M. and encountered a long line of people taking different excursions that day. When I finally made my way to the front of the line, I was given an excursion group number and told to wait with three other people on the same tour. We would be escorted out in a little while. It was about 2:00 P.M., and the trip was scheduled to depart at 2:15 P.M. The three of us waited patiently as 2:15 P.M. came and passed. At 2:30 P.M., I asked the attendant when we were going to start our trip. She responded, "Oh, you need to get outside and catch a bus to the helicopter pad right now." The three of us rushed to the bus area, only to find that the bus had left and we missed our trip. Of course, we were all very disappointed.

I headed back to the facility headquarters and asked to speak to the excursion manager. I told her what had happened, and she apologetically explained that there had been a mix-up in the organizing process. The escorts were new, and the time schedules were tight due to some scheduling changes. She went on and on about how their process worked and how essential it was to organize people in groups to ensure everyone got to the right place. She was engrossed in explaining the process to me, while my focus was elsewhere: I wanted to get compensated or rescheduled for another excursion. She was entirely focused on process and how the mishap occurred. I wanted to switch from process (which was not solving anything for me) to content as soon as I could, so I interrupted her and said, "Would you like to make me happy?" (content). She stopped talking and said, "Of course." I told her that I appreciated her explanations, that I was in town for only today, and that I wanted to be booked on the next excursion and given a discount for my trouble. She said, "How about if I give you a credit of 20 percent and a front-row seat on the next helicopter?" I said, "Thank you. That's very kind of you." I had a late but a great excursion at a lower price.

This example illustrates that process was not a strength of mine in negotiating what I wanted. My strength was my satisfaction as a customer: my content. I moved to my strength and came away satisfied. The key is to recognize the element of the dialogue (content, process, or behavior) and then move to the element that gives you greatest strength.

PROCESS VERSUS BEHAVIOR

Just as with content, process also takes priority over behaviors in team dynamics. However, unlike content, process is a powerful motivator of individual and team behaviors.

The Tower

In a popular team-building exercise called "The Tower," teams are challenged to build a free-standing tower in the classroom out of some paper, a cardboard sheet, tape, a coat hanger, and other sundry items. The class is divided into teams of six to ten members each. The teams are given ten minutes to plan and design their tower and then eight minutes to build it. The purpose of this exercise is to test the team's ability to work together under pressure. The team that builds the highest tower is given extra points, so there are tangible benefits at stake. Also, to make it more interesting, one or two team members are excluded from the team during the planning phase and are allowed to join the team only when the building starts. Another rule is that everyone has to build at least one part of the tower.

Invariably this process is dominated by a small group of competitive construction-eager individuals. Some debating typically occurs during the planning phase, but due to time limits, no one is ever satisfied with the final plan. When the building phase begins and the excluded members are allowed to rejoin their teams, the pace and activities are frantic. The teams are usually successful in building some kind of tower and meeting the deadline, but not everyone feels good about the experience and the team's behaviors. The process is ragged, and so are the behaviors. The feedback is usually that ideas were not discussed enough, changes were made by individuals on their own, work was done ad hoc, many people felt left out, and some simply backed off and withdrew from the process, among many others. By design, the exercise demonstrates that when pushed, people will drive to meet deadlines and work requirements, but usually at the expense of human behaviors and feelings. In other words, the process always takes priority over behaviors. It appears that highly aggressive and even rude behaviors are excusable and necessary to get the job done as the end justifies the means.

Under pressure, people who are aggressive or assertive take charge, dominate, and run the process, while people who are passive and conflict avoiders concede and are dependent on others to take the lead. Adrenaline and stress force people to take on a persona that enables them to cope with the situation. Coping behaviors are usually selfish and sometimes destructive. Some people do not see the point of competition and the need to run over people for the sake of meeting a deadline. Others believe that they were simply being aggressive and responsible for the good of the team. If their behaviors were a bit intense, it was not meant to be hurtful and should not be taken personally. Some forgive and forget, while others either resent the exercise or regret how they acted. The aggressive ones feel they were too competitive, and passives feel they lacked assertiveness. Either way, the exercise has a way of exposing team behaviors. The lesson is that we should never let the process override the feelings and respect of others. Towers come and go, but people and relationships remain long after the event. Human factors are not about building towers; they are about building personal capacity to have a positive influence on ourselves and our work environment.

The Annual Team Meeting

A good example of the linkage between process and behavior occurred at a large team meeting I attended at the end of the year. A team meeting was called to review business improvement suggestions that had been collected anonymously over the previous four weeks. These suggestions were compiled and summarized by the team's office assistant and sent out as advance reading three days before the meeting. Accompanying the results were a meeting agenda and instructions for people to review the data and come prepared to discuss and select the top priorities for action next year. The information was well formatted, easy to read, and concisely written.

The meeting started with a brief review of the purpose, the data collection process, and how the suggestions were consolidated and categorized. Also, the manager thanked everyone for attending the meeting and submitting their suggestions on time. She expressed how pleased she was with the response. Then each category with its various suggestions was reviewed, with time allowed for questions and clarification. Few questions were asked. The manager wanted to see people participate and take ownership of the content: that was the desired behavior.

It was clear from the start that interest was low. Although it was a late-morning meeting, people seemed modestly attentive and probably preferred to be elsewhere. Obviously the process was not generating the desired participative behaviors. The manager was focused on content, but the people needed a process. The manager thought that the content would motivate people to express opinions and participate in a lively discussion (process). With no questions, the facilitator proceeded to ask the team which suggestions they thought were priorities. Some discussion ensued, but it was very flat. The facilitator was trying to encourage dialogue, but none was forthcoming.

At that point, one of the senior members suggested a voting process to get everyone's input in the decision making: "We could give everyone five votes in a list of fifteen items and identify our top choices." The facilitator asked, "Is everyone clear about the choices before we start voting?" That triggered a series of clarifying questions and discussion about what they were voting on. This voting process triggered the desired behaviors that the manager was looking for. Someone then asked who was expected to do this work, and the manager responded that the team leaders would convene later and assign it to the right people. Right away, this stirred more discussion and participation on the items. The meeting ended successfully, participation was high, and the items were prioritized for action. Everyone left with good energy and a positive attitude about what was decided.

There are three important learnings from this story:

1. To get the desired participative behaviors, we needed to use the right process, not content.

2. To personalize the process and get personal engagement, we used a voting process to get people involved.

3. To increase ownership of an issue, clearly communicate expectations, consequences, and actions.

This is a good example of using the right process to drive the right behaviors. Most ineffective meetings are due to poor processes, not poor attitudes.

The Employee Survey

Here is an example of the process driving the wrong behavior. Performance metrics are valuable in helping teams set goals and measure success. "You can't improve what you don't measure," it is said. One performance metric that I like to measure is employee satisfaction.

In my first attempt, the process was to ask employees anonymously in an electronic survey to score their level of satisfaction about their jobs on a scale from 1 to 5, with 5 being "highly satisfied," 3 "satisfied," and 1 "highly unsatisfied." Average scores above 4 were considered excellent, and we would administer team rewards and recognitions based on hitting certain targets.

As you might have predicted, this process was a self-prophecy: each time we surveyed, the scores were always at or above the target. The employees were feeding back what was being rewarded, not their level of satisfaction. We had the wrong process: we were rewarding the process, not the behavior. The intent was to get open and honest feedback when in fact we were encouraging and rewarding the scoring process and not the behavior. If we wanted to shape honest feedback behaviors, we should have measured the number of people who responded with written comments. Of course, we cannot measure honesty, but we can measure the frequency of the behavior and take action to resolve employee problems.

The next year, we changed the metric to the percentage who responded and whether action was taken to address the problem. Measuring performance is a tricky process, and if without care, a faulty process may be used that results in the wrong behaviors. Metrics that are properly used are an effective way to change and shape new behaviors.

Using Processes to Reveal Behavioral Issues

Every team should have a defined process for raising behavioral issues in a safe and constructive way. Without a process to surface what may be bothering people, problems can fester and get worse. Small issues can quickly become big issues when it comes to behavioral problems. It becomes a source of stress that will lead to underperformance. The most common team feedback tool is the plus/delta, where the team is asked, "What have you observed that you like, and what things would you like to see changed?" It is important to listen closely to the feedback because behavioral conflicts can be subtle. It does not take a great deal of time but can save the team a lot of grief later. Another option is to collect the same feedback anonymously by doing it on slips of paper or entering feedback into a shared electronic file. With an electronic file, everyone has write access to it, but authors are not identified. The information is then compiled and discussed at the next team meeting. Anytime you ask for feedback, be committed to value all comments and be willing to take action as appropriate. Otherwise the participation and feedback will be poor next time.

SUMMARY

The power of human factors is embodied in the three elements of content, process, and behavior. Content, the purpose and intent, directs a person's actions. Process executes the purpose and shapes people's behaviors. Behaviors are what people say and do. These three elements represent the motivators and demotivators of people and will determine the level of success of the team. When teams struggle, the breakdown can usually be attributed to one or more of these elements.

You can greatly strengthen your abilities to manage, facilitate, and collaborate by using techniques to separate content, process, and behavior. Reinforcement motivates desired behaviors. We are too content focused as a culture, and too much focus on any one element weakens the power of the team. The goal is to achieve balance in content, process, and behavior.

The following key interpersonal concepts and techniques were covered in this chapter:

- To maximize negotiating power, establish an advantage in at least one of the three elements: content, process, or behavior. Effective negotiators always move to their element of greatest strength.

- To maximize problem solving, ensure parties are addressing the same element. Is the problem a content, process, or behavior issue? Are the two parties talking about the same element? Conflicts often occur when each party is speaking to different elements (such as "Dinner at Lucia's Cafe").

- When negative behaviors arise, it is best to switch to an inquiry process to help understand their motivations.

- Process should not drive content; it should support the content and help reveal and shape behaviors. The key is to select the right process to drive the right behaviors. Also, process can help neutralize interpersonal conflicts. In the absence of process, people will revert to their personal values and needs.

- Train yourself to recognize behavior first and then content, which will enhance your interpersonal skills and effectiveness. Look to make positive comments on one or more of the three key elements when you see it demonstrated. Always personalize behavioral reinforcement by using the person's first name and making eye contact with the person you are addressing.

Key Stages
of Team Development

As Bruce Tuckman reported in "Developmental Sequence in Small Groups" (1965), the four main stages of team development are forming, storming, norming, and performing. Forming is the start-up phase of a team. Storming is the stage for clarifying team objectives, building a work plan, and resolving conflicts. Norming occurs when the team successfully executes the team's work plan and actions. Performing is the final step in meeting the team's goals and objectives. I have extended this description to include one more stage in this model: reforming. Reforming, which occurs between norming and performing, is a stage where the team regroups and makes final adjustments before completing the final work outputs and decisions. As Figure 7.1 illustrates, these five stages occur sequentially, and each stage is characterized by a rise or drop in the level of collaboration and teamwork. Forming, norming, and performing stages build teamwork, while storming and reforming tend to result in lowering teamwork.

FORMING

The forming stage is the initial period of team formation when team members are assigned to the project. The start cycle is a period of strong forward momentum and energy as each team member is assigned to launch the new project. Being

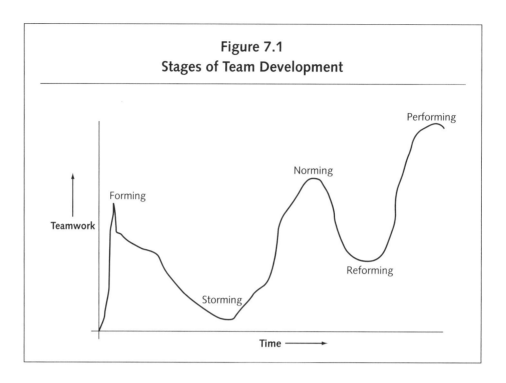

Figure 7.1
Stages of Team Development

Teamwork

Forming

Storming

Norming

Reforming

Performing

Time

assigned to a team is a form of recognition of the individual's knowledge and value. It may also be a unique development opportunity for people to show their talents; if they are successful, more opportunities and advancements may come their way.

Projects are usually sponsored by the company's management, which in itself bestows importance and prestige on the team and its members. Each team member may represent a different function or part of the organization. Also, announcements are made about the project, which reinforces the significance. The anticipation of doing something special has a motivating effect. Team members enter the first meeting with great anticipation, high hopes, and empowerment as they are introduced to this special workforce.

The first team meeting brings all team members together, in person or by teleconference, or a combination of the two. In-person meetings are always preferred, but in global organizations, this is not always possible. The first team meeting may be attended by management to ensure that the purpose of the project is clearly understood and to give the team an opportunity to ask questions. Having management participate in the team's first meeting infuses power into the process.

In the forming stage, the team talks about the significance of the project and the positive benefits and impact that this project may have on the organization. People have high hopes and look forward to learning more about what the project will entail and what roles they will have on the team. This honeymoon period is ripe for team agreements on ground rules, personal commitments, and building positive work relationships. There will be no better time to get volunteers and to reach team agreements than the forming stage. Like a first date, people are excited and positive, and they show their best side.

The key priority in the forming stage is team building: establish good working relationships and team behaviors.

Key Outputs from Forming

- Identification of project leader and sponsors
- Team objectives and goals
- Team charter
- Ground rules
- Roles and responsibilities
- High-level deliverables
- Personal work preferences and availability to work on the project

Common Pitfalls in Forming

- Not taking the time to get to know each other
- Hidden agendas
- Unvoiced personal issues and preferences
- Absent team members
- Failure to establish team ground rules and commitments
- No team-building processes
- Compelling business case is not well accepted by the team
- Missed opportunity to get volunteers during the initial meeting

STORMING

This initial burst of cooperativeness and newness during forming is soon replaced with a period of uncertainty, varying opinions, and differing assumptions about the specific purpose, expectations, and content of the project. In addition, the team is exploring and experimenting with processes, and discussions tend to generate more issues and questions than answers. This storming cycle is part of the normal process of projects, and team conflicts with the content of the project are expected. In fact, they should be welcomed. Some creative tension and conflict are healthy in developing a team's purpose and direction.

This is the time to challenge the purpose and expectations of the project and make assumptions explicit to the team. Teams that avoid the storming cycle will likely regret it later because fuzzy objectives and hidden assumptions eventually will surface and cause rework and much deeper team conflict. Teams that duck the storming phase inevitably face a longer, deeper, and more painful reforming stage later. It is not exactly a "pay me now or pay me later" scenario, but there is no substitute for good planning, and storming is nothing more than having a good planning session. This is the best time to propose different ideas and challenge each other on the goals of the team and how the team will accomplish those goals. Out of this spirited process will come a robust and sustainable plan.

Of course, too much storming can be bad too. Teams experience bad storming when people are not willing to talk freely anymore, disengage from the team, start taking things personally, or cannot make decisions.

The key during the storming phase is to use the right team tools and processes to facilitate team agreements. From my experience, teams that are unable to establish effective team processes to address and productively work together to resolve team conflicts and differences will remain bogged down. Teams that are able to self-facilitate, use effective decision-making processes, and reach compromises will storm more constructively and strengthen their resolve as a team. Teams that struggle to reach consensus are not using good narrowing behaviors and processes for decision making (see Chapter Eight).

The other human factor that contributes to storming is personality differences in communications and conflict styles. The aggressive, dominant personalities are often the toughest to deal with during storming and may tend to push forward without full team agreement. Moving ahead without buy-in from everyone will result in resentment and negative feelings, however. Success will be relegated to the outspoken few rather than to the team. Power struggles and competition will churn a team and exasperate the storm, while shared power will free people to collaborate and stand together through the storm. Shared power means everyone has an equal stake in the outcome, and everyone feels valued for their opinions. Dominant personalities compete for power, while collaborative personalities empower others. Dominant personalities take energy from the team; collaborative people generate energy for the team. How low (negative teamwork) a team falls during storming depends on the willingness of team members to listen, compromise, and accept different ideas.

The key priority in the storming stage is conflict management. The team has a constructive process to identify and debate issues, resolve conflicts, and make team decisions. Difficult behaviors are not accepted.

Key Outputs from Storming

- Team work plan and milestones
- Identification of people and resources to execute the plan
- Team metrics—how the team plans to track and measure success
- An accountability system

Common Pitfalls in Storming

The team

- Is not comfortable with storming, that is, it does not recognize that storming is part of the process
- Is unable to cope with conflict
- Develops an unrealistic work plan that exceeds its resources
- Fears confrontation and conflict, which leads to mediocre objectives and an inadequate work plan
- Fails to gain individual commitment from team members to do the work
- Proceeds without clear consensus and buy-in from everyone
- Leaves some team members feeling left out
- Has poor leadership
- Has weak facilitation, which leads to uneven participation and no closure on key decisions
- Has a poor or no decision-making process
- Has no documented team agreements
- Develops personal conflicts

- Has no clear accountability

- Has no team metrics

NORMING

Ideally all teams emerge from the storming stage with consensus and agreements concerning their charter, team processes, goals, strategies, and the team's work plan. Through the process, the shine of the team gets a bit tarnished from the storm, but team members are ready to get on with the work. Many details and assumptions are still uncertain, and some agreements are soft and will require rework as the team takes actions to implement them. Most important is that the team has achieved sufficient alignment and understanding to do work individually and in subteams. Action items are defined, deadlines are set, milestones are identified, and future meetings to review the work are scheduled. When the team is cut loose, a surge of teamwork occurs. People are ready to do some real work. Now it is a matter of execution and tactical adjustments.

As data and information are collected, people are engaged in their assignments, and their skills, experiences, and expertise are used. When people are working productively and are acknowledged for their contributions, tremendous work can be accomplished. People who are entrusted to do work for the team establish a strong sense of accountability and loyalty to the team. They want to show what they can do and prove their worth to the team. People who do not get recognized will seek validation of their value. This may come in the form of contacts, e-mails, analysis, and information flow to the team. As everyone engages, team productivity dramatically rises, and intrateam communications increase.

The key priority in the norming stage is team communications: processes are in place to hold regular team meetings, coordinate data collection and analyses, review status of work plan, and address problems and changes.

Key Outputs in Norming
- Data collection

- Data analysis and interpretation

- Data summaries

- Consensus on findings and conclusions

- Options and alternative solutions

Common Pitfalls in Norming

- Lack of consequences for good or poor performance by individual team members
- A sense by some team members of not feeling fully used and valued by others
- No clear method on how to process incoming information and data
- Inequality in workload among team members
- Team members who take independent actions without first consulting with the team
- Poor work coordination, leading to redundancies and missed assignments
- Confusion on roles and responsibilities
- No formal process checks and feedback

REFORMING

As the work and analyses flow in, the team begins assessing what they have done and what still needs to be done. Some amount of ambiguity and gaps in the work plan are expected. In addition, some elements in the work plan were successful, and some fell short or did not work as planned. The reforming stage calls on the team to do a process check on where they are with respect to their objectives and goals, determine what work is still outstanding, assess what new work needs to be done, rebalance the team's workload, and recalibrate the team's expectations.

Many years ago, I was on an asset management team that was chartered to sell off a portfolio of underperforming properties. The strategy was to package these properties from different regions, move quickly, and sell them as a big package. From experience, we knew that a large number of companies would be interested. We generated a lot of interest for our portfolio of properties, but when the initial bids came in, we had only four bidders, and all the bids were below our estimated fair market values. Fortunately, we stipulated that the seller had the right to cancel the sale or withdraw the properties if we did not get our desired price.

Instead of canceling the sale or selling the portfolio to the highest bidder, we reassessed what we were offering and determined that we had a mixture of poor properties that were encumbered with legal and environmental issues and other properties that were highly desirable but too expensive for many of the bargain hunters. We changed our strategy by reclassifying certain properties, taking some properties off the table that had little commercial value, and repackaging the offering so that we would have a separate bundle of properties for bargain hunters and a separate package for high-end investors. We went back to management to gain endorsement of our alternative strategy, and it was approved promptly. We knew we had to move ahead while the buyers were still engaged but not revamp the offering so much that it would scare them off. It was a risk, but the team did a good job of reforming its strategy to meet the objective. This strategy turned out to be highly successful, and we received top dollar for our entire portfolio. What caused us to reform was the poor outcome and the fact that we did not have all the facts about the market until we had moved into the sale process. Instead of accepting the results, we reformed, that is, developed alternative strategies to get fair value for the properties.

As smooth and logical as this case may seem, the team was not totally behind this reforming, and the process was taxing on the team. Some resisted the change. Some did not want to admit failure, and some thought it was just creating greater confusion. Reforming does not occur without some venting and rework because it involves change—not only change, but change in the middle of a team project that is under pressure to meet looming deadlines and objectives. Unlike conflict that occurs during the storming stage where different opinions surface on content, process, and behaviors, reforming involves change conflict. Change conflict is different from storming. It means disrupting the norming process, changing what people are doing, and asking for more energy when people are already weary. To get people to change requires team consensus, and that means more discussion, problem solving, decision making, and resolving disagreements.

People are reluctant to make changes at this stage. Change is a process that does not come easily. Some people feel they have put a great deal of effort and commitment in one direction and emotionally are not prepared to make a course change. Others want to live with original commitments and believe everything will work out. Some will accept tweaking but nothing dramatic. It takes significant energy to make changes. How much change conflict occurs at this stage can vary (as in the storming phase), but in most cases, some degree of reprioritization, rework of issues, and process checks are required to get the clarity the team needs to make the final push to completion.

How well a team reforms depends on how well relationships have developed within the team. Everything will get magnified in reforming. Good relationships will yield good collaborative behaviors in defining new changes, and bad relationships will likely result in more selfish behaviors where people will gauge change only in terms of the impact it will have on their personal workload, risks, and recognition. You may hear some "I told you so" types of comments, "we're not going to get it done" remarks, or even some finger pointing during this phase. People who have grown apart from the team due to personality differences will tend to do what is right for them. People who believe in the team and the objectives will rise above the fray, volunteer to commit to the change, help reform the path forward for the team, and champion the change management process. Good team players and high-performing teams will carry the extra weight of change to produce a superior team product. They will see change as an opportunity to learn from experience and make greater impact. This can-do attitude is the energy that the team uses to conquer change and the brief down cycle that comes in reforming.

Reforming is where good relationships and good team communications come into play. Teams that stay well connected, meet regularly, and conduct self-assessments are able to move smoothly through the reforming phase. Good team communications and feedback processes buffer against discontent, resentment, and exclusion. At this stage, teams should not be afraid to overcommunicate and ensure clarity and buy-in to the changes. There is a distinct difference between information overload and overcommunications. Information overload is exceeding the physical capacity of the team to process and analyze information. Communications is about listening to others, giving honest feedback, admitting mistakes, forgiving yourself and others, and staying connected with the team. High-performing teams do not let problems fester, and they work together to make final adjustments during reforming. For low-performing teams, reforming is when the personality issues will emerge. The process of change, weariness, and the mounting pressure of the project will uncover unresolved conflicts and emotions.

To manage reforming

- Prepare for reforming in advance during the norming phase by scheduling periodic process checks during the project so problems do not accumulate.

- Prepare for change by keeping a running log of team issues so that they do not fester in silence.

- Schedule an interim peer review, and invite other colleagues to do a peer assessment on what aspects can be improved.

- Conduct team assessments and feedback during the course of the project.
- Collect issues and change proposals prior to the meeting so no one gets unpleasantly surprised in the meeting.

The key priority in the reforming stage is change management. There is not enough time to do everything perfectly, so compromises need to be made. It is a matter of prioritization, rationalization of resources, and agreement on the critical few changes to catalyze the team to the finish line. People must be willing to accept compromises in order to meet project objectives.

Key Outputs from Reforming

- Team agreement on final deliverables and work products
- Amended work plan to complete critical final actions and deadlines
- Assigned roles and responsibilities in executing the final work plan and changes
- Securing additional resources to complete the project

Common Pitfalls in Reforming

- Resistance to change
- Poor listening
- Not allowing people to vent
- Jumping to solutions without fully understanding the problem
- Too much advocacy of one position and too little understanding of other points of view
- Not clearly separating content, process, and behaviors
- Not sustaining a positive, supportive, problem-solving outlook
- Lack of effective team facilitation to move the team forward
- Inability of the team to manage conflict
- Impatience
- Unwillingness to take on any additional work
- Denial or deferment of team problems
- Fear of taking risks and avoiding issues

- Lowering their standards and behaviors to meet a deadline
- Lack of process and teamwork to reach team consensus

PERFORMING

Performing is the most satisfying part of the journey. With successful forming, storming, norming, and reforming, the team knows exactly what to do, priorities are set, and everyone is working with great urgency to get the job done. The adrenaline rush is in full swing, and things are starting to make sense and come together. The reforming stage has allowed the team to shed its extra baggage and any lingering conflicts to lift the team to higher performance. There is a strong convergence of thinking, people are pulling together, and the focus is on finishing. Reforming enables the team to reach agreement on final adjustments and definition of its final work output. Each team member has a piece of the work, peer expectations are high, and deadlines and objectives must be met if the team hopes to succeed. This may look like a mad scramble at times as final gaps are filled and remaining tasks are completed.

If the team is behind schedule, the performing stage can be a time of high stress, which can result in impatience, anxiety, and aggressiveness. Nevertheless, team members are tolerating stress behaviors and forgiving each other in the interest of the final work. This type of constructive, directed stress can be an advantage. Stress that is directed to the work is different from stress consumed by interpersonal conflicts. Work-directed stress generates great energy and focus for the team. Processes are more efficient, conflicts are quickly resolved, and the team rallies around a common cause. The other phenomenon that is occurring is that the stress of the work is being relieved by the pride and satisfaction gained in the production of the final work products. The team can see the light at the end of the tunnel, and past conflicts now appear insignificant.

Performing is the act of executing a plan with grace, competence, and efficiency. The team is able to apply itself and work in synchrony to complete the project. By necessity, motivation, or inspiration, team members are able to set aside differences and distractions to put their focus on the most important tasks. The team will experience its highest level of productivity, collaboration, and motivation on the team. At this stage, final work products, such as reports, presentation materials, final team recommendations, and performance metrics, are energetically prepared.

Expectations are clear, and the team is working collaboratively to hit all targets and achieve their project goals. Successful performance means completing project deliverables and meeting the expectations of the team. It is getting the right things done and feeling good about it. This is characteristic of high-performing teams. Performing is achieving success as a team.

The key priority in the performing stage is completing the project deliverables on time and meeting team expectations.

Key Outputs from Performing

- Final team deliverables
- Project recommendations and decisions
- Awards and recognitions
- Team learnings
- Follow-up work required

Common Pitfalls in Performing

- Lack of active stress management
- Lack of individual praise
- No recognition for successful completion of outputs
- No team recognition or celebration
- Team learnings not well captured
- Poor management of time, resulting in incomplete products
- No formal hand-off process to the next team or organization

SUMMARY

It is normal for teams to go through stages of good and bad teamwork and productivity. There are five main stages: forming, storming, norming, reforming, and performing:

- Forming initiates team building.
- Storming requires conflict management.
- Norming depends on team communications.

- Reforming focuses on change management.
- Performing means meeting team expectations.

This up-and-down cycle exists as we develop and execute a team work plan. Forming is the initiation stage, where the team meets and learns about the project. The second stage, storming, is the roughest and most stressful stage for the team. The most important thing to remember is that storming is normal and that all teams go through this stage. Some apprehension and conflict will occur, and trying to avoid this stage is a mistake because it usually results in more headaches and heartaches later. When the team addresses early gaps and disagreements, the project runs better. The rewards coming out of storming are periods of productivity and teamwork called norming, a rebalancing and recalibrating step that occurs during reforming, and a final surge of team output, called performing. Each stage is unique and requires skills in teamwork, communications, conflict management, change management, and project management.

Moving the Team Forward

Facilitation Techniques

One important skill that project managers and team leaders need is the ability to facilitate a team. Facilitation is the art of leading effective team meetings. It involves designing and using meeting processes to enable a team to reach timely agreements through effective discussions and behaviors. Good facilitation requires knowledge of meeting tools and techniques, team dynamics, and human factors. Facilitation is about helping a team make good decisions. That often requires encouraging debate, hearing all sides of the issues, and stretching people to think differently. Highly effective facilitators have the ability to read people and situations and to apply the right processes at the right time.

For many people, running a good team meeting seems to center around a written agenda, a stated objective, preassigned discussion leaders, and a comfortable room. What are often overlooked are the processes that will be used to facilitate the meeting. The assumption is that people know how to facilitate themselves, and as long as they follow the agenda and behave themselves, there is little possibility of a bad meeting. This is a risky assumption. Bad meetings do not result from bad agendas or bad behaviors. They result from poor processes. Knowing how to position and operate team meetings is the key to good decision making and high team performance. Operating a team with poor processes is like building a house with the wrong tools. The house may turn out okay, but the process of getting there will be slow, frustrating, and error prone. Building a high-performing team requires the right tools.

Team leaders tend to spend too much time on formulating content and too little time on formulating team processes. Developing a process strategy to execute a team's work plan is critical. Here is a quote that I received from a team leader that captures the problem well: "I know the content of the meeting coming in and I know what I want coming out of it, but it's the stuff in between that's hard for me." The "stuff in between" is process. Process is how things get done. Unfortunately, many people are process averse. They offer all kinds of excuses for not using processes: "It takes too long," "We don't need it," "I prefer to do real work," "It's a waste of time," "It's boring stuff," and "I'm not good at it" are just a few of them. This resistance to process is likely due to past failures where process has been misused. Poor processes are indeed the silent killers of teams, leading to poor behaviors and negative memories. Nevertheless, it is no excuse for giving it up. Process is far too important for a team.

Process is a source of power for the team. It helps generate better ideas and solutions and maximizes output by organizing the team's thinking into a form that helps the team see and understand the right issues. Getting a team of people to agree and make decisions is a challenging process. The key is having the right facilitative processes to convert content into decisions and actions.

In team meetings, the facilitator is the process owner. This person's role is to focus on the process: (1) design processes to support meeting objectives, (2) explain and demonstrate the process to the team as needed, (3) implement the process, and (4) monitor how well the process is working. The project team owns the content. Behaviors are managed by the facilitator and team members. The secret to good facilitation is channeling the flow of information and energy toward a desired outcome. In most cases, the desired outcome is team consensus. Getting everyone to flow in a single direction is not an easy task.

SEVEN KEY FACILITATION CONCEPTS AND TECHNIQUES

Facilitation takes considerable experience and knowledge, particularly in dealing with people who are not accustomed to working in structured team environments or facilitation processes. A good facilitator does not control people but instead manages the flow of information and exchanges among people in a highly efficient and positive manner. Of the many facilitative tools and techniques that exist, here are the seven that I think are most effective:

1. Go slow to go fast. Take the time to get things organized and clear before launching into the project. This early investment will enable the team to move faster, not slower.

2. Work one process at a time. Close a process before beginning another.

3. Use process checks. Stop and check to see if the process is working.

4. Agree on the 80:20 rule: Do not spend 80 percent of the time trying to get the last 20 percent of a solution. A 100 percent solution is rarely required or achievable; 80 percent is close enough.

5. Learn to park issues. Ensure that the topic under discussion is relevant to the question at hand. If it is not, save it for a later discussion.

6. Know how to open and narrow thinking. Use the right opening and narrowing techniques to direct team discussions.

7. Break team stalemates. Know what to do if the team cannot make a decision.

GO SLOW TO GO FAST

Teams often make the mistake of not devoting enough time at the start of a new project to ensure mutual understanding of the team's content, process, and behavior. Being eager to start work is a natural reaction to those who prefer to work independently and are ready to get to the "real work." Unfortunately, all too often, the team as a whole is not ready to move forward. Checking for understanding using good facilitation processes is essential for team development.

One good practice is to ensure that all three key elements of team performance are in place:

- Getting clear agreement on project objectives and assumptions (content)
- Spending time to get to know each other and take inventory on people's level of commitment, strengths, and preferences (process)
- Identifying the team's ground rules and consequences (behaviors), which greatly increase a team's chances of success over the life of the project

These agreements will help the team avoid misunderstandings and conflicts. Experienced team players will spend extra time in the beginning of a project to cover these key elements. They know that poor framing and planning at the front end of a project will lead to greater problems, costs, and rework later. These early efforts may feel slow and time-consuming, but the investment is well worth it. "Go slow to go fast" is a well-proven facilitation strategy.

WORK ONE PROCESS AT A TIME

Another common mistake for teams is running too many processes at one time. Have you ever been in a meeting where the team starts with one process (for example, reviewing action items) and then suddenly begins chasing other issues and discussing new items? People have a tendency to lose focus and shift gears before properly closing a process.

This commonly occurs in problem-solving discussions. When a problem is opened for discussion, the team typically starts by discussing what the problem is and its impact on the project. People share their personal opinions and try to characterize it in different ways. Instead of closing in on what the problem is, part of the team will start a second process of discussing possible solutions on how to fix the problem. So part of the team is still trying to process what the problem is, while other team members have moved on to processing a solution. No one seems to notice that the team is operating two processes, which makes for a confusing and unproductive discussion.

How do you know when you have two processes operating?

- The discussion is hard to follow. People are talking about content, process, and behaviors at the same time.
- Different types of suggestions are being made that are unrelated.
- Two or more decisions are being processed at the same time. More than one topic is being discussed.

Here are examples of two processes operating at the same time:

- A team is brainstorming a list of ideas (first process). One person throws out a new idea, and a team member asks a clarifying question. This brief interlude grows into a team discussion about the merits of this one idea (a second process). The team's behavior has shifted from brainstorming ideas to evaluating an idea.

- The team is mapping out a project schedule, and it appears that the workload is greater than they thought it would be. A team member raises the question of outsourcing some of the work. Part of the team begins a discussion on the feasibility of outsourcing, and the remaining team continues to discuss the project schedule. Now people are talking about two different things and trying to decide on both the project schedule and the feasibility of outsourcing.

It is okay to begin a new process, but it helps to close one first before opening a new one. When a second process occurs, team members need to speak up and correct the problem: "Process check: I think we are moving to another topic. Can we close this discussion first?" Working one process at a time will make meetings much more productive and focused. (Techniques in opening and closing discussions are discussed later in this chapter.)

USE PROCESS CHECKS

Not all processes work as expected. Some people can become too committed to the process and lose focus on the objectives. They will push a team through a process even though it does not generate anything useful. Never let the process drive the content. Instead, decide on the content first, and then select a process that fits it. Good facilitators know when to increase, decrease, or change a team process. If you feel the process is breaking down and the energy level is waning, simply call for a process check and assess if a change in process is needed. Too often teams blindly follow a process to the bitter end or start drifting from process to process. Just say, "I feel the energy level is down" or "I feel we're losing focus. What can we do to improve our focus?" These simple inquiries will help restore energy and concentration.

"Do we need to solve this now?" is a good process check question if the team seems to be getting ahead of itself. This happens when people are concerned about what may happen and start asking hypothetical questions. Look out for "what-if" questions. People like to solve problems posed to them, but it is a wasteful use of team energy and time. Be sure to break this cycle by asking, "Do we need to solve this now?"

AGREE ON THE 80:20 RULE

Perfection is admirable but not practical. In the quest for excellence, teams have a tendency to overwork issues and overanalyze information, especially in the early storming phase of team development. A good rule for the team is to agree that an 80 percent solution or work product is okay. It is tough to get to a 100 percent answer on the first pass. Also, given limitations on time and resources, 80 percent may be all the team can afford to do. Most problems and issues do not require a 100 percent solution or 100 percent agreement; 80 percent is good enough. The 80 percent is an arbitrary number. The purpose is to establish a team mind-set that 100 percent is not the goal. Most problems are not 100 percent understood anyway and may change over time. The last 20 percent can be hammered out later. Many teams make the mistake of spending 80 percent of their time trying to chase down the last 20 percent of the answer. It is better not to do too much or be too exact; teams need to stay flexible and use their time wisely. For the 80:20 rule to be effective, it is important to get team agreement up front. It can be established as a team ground rule: "Let's not get bogged down in nailing down every detail and every process. Our goal is to reach 80 percent."

LEARN TO PARK ISSUES

It is inevitable that during the course of any team discussion, subjects will pop up that are off topic. For example, the team may be talking about operating budgets and a person may suddenly raise a secondary issue about capital project approvals. It may be an important issue that deserves discussion, but it takes the team into another topic area. When these topics come up in the discussion, teams may chase them and find themselves off track. Another problem is that they may identify an issue as something off topic and dismiss it. In the latter circumstance, the person who raised the issue may feel put down. As a result, the person may recycle the issue again and again until he feels heard.

When people take the initiative to bring up good points that may be off topic, acknowledge the behavior and content by having a process to capture these good issues: "park it" by recording it on a flip chart or a personal computer (Figure 8.1). These topics are captured in the team's "parking lot"; at the end of the meeting, they are reviewed and a course of action decided. This process ensures that the point does not get lost, the person feels recognized, and it avoids recycling behaviors.

Figure 8.1
Team Parking Lot

#	Priority	What Is the Issue?	Who Owns?	By When?	Status
1	HIGH	Need agreement on inquiry process	Joe	Mar 4	Done
2	Medium	Determine executive summary format	Mary	Mar 28	Inquiring
3	Low	Finalize team meeting schedule	Karen	Apr 15	On hold

HOT! HIGH priority	Medium priority	Low priority

KNOW HOW TO OPEN AND NARROW THINKING

Kenny Rogers's famous lyric, "Know when to hold them, know when to fold them," is a good analogy for a common pitfall: teams do not open and close discussions well. Most teams come up with a list of topics for an agenda, assign some approximate time to each item, and then start talking about them. Basically they engage in a free-wheeling discussion. In this exchange of views and opinions, somehow a decision will fall out. This process may seem reasonable, but in reality, the discussions are usually inefficient and indecisive. One of the biggest problems that occur in team discussions is the conflict between opening and closing. In a given discussion, some people are openers, and some are closers. Some people want to hear and analyze as much as possible, while others want to drive for a solution as soon as possible. The failure to differentiate between these two behaviors is the root cause of many poorly run meetings. Teams need to separate opening and closing.

How to Separate Opening and Closing

Before starting a discussion topic, state what the process is, and then close each process before starting another one. For example, open the discussion and state the purpose of the discussion: "The purpose of this discussion is to agree on what the problem is, not the solutions, and whether it is worth our time today to try to solve it." With team agreement, engage in the discussion, agree on the problem, and close on the discussion. Then move to the next process: "Now let's talk about possible solutions."

The key is not to narrow thinking until the team is ready to do so. Initially teams should aim to open minds and open the team's thinking to enable a good, informed decision. Too often people allow others to stifle and narrow the team's thinking too soon, robbing it of some creative thinking and ideas. If a team consciously agrees to have open discussion for a fixed time, the closers will not be frustrated. After the allotted time, ask the team if they want to spend more time or are ready to close the discussion and make a decision. If the team wants to close down, use one of the narrowing processes. Once you are closing, do not reopen the discussion. You can avoid this by explicitly stating, "We will close down now." Figure 8.2 lists some effective tools and techniques for opening and narrowing team thinking.

Opening Techniques

Opening techniques are valuable in inviting team participation. All too often, creative ideas are left unspoken because team members do not feel they have the opportunity to speak. Teams with balanced participation are likely to be happier, more productive, and highly creative. Managing and encouraging team participation is one of the key challenges for a team.

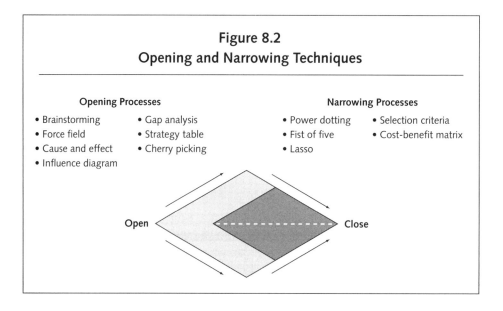

Figure 8.2
Opening and Narrowing Techniques

Opening Processes

- Brainstorming
- Force field
- Cause and effect
- Influence diagram
- Gap analysis
- Strategy table
- Cherry picking

Narrowing Processes

- Power dotting
- Fist of five
- Lasso
- Selection criteria
- Cost-benefit matrix

Open   Close

Brainstorming   This is the most commonly used method for opening a team to different ideas. The objective is to capture as many ideas as possible in a short amount of time.

Brainstorming can be done using one of three popular methods:

- A freewheeling process, where everyone is free to shout out their ideas and a facilitator captures them on a flip chart or personal computer

- A round-robin process, where everyone is given a few minutes to silently brainstorm a list of ideas, and then each person is asked to share one idea at a time until all ideas are captured

- A slip method, where each team member anonymously writes down ideas on separate slips of paper, sticky notes, or index cards that the facilitator collects, reads aloud, and clarifies for understanding

For all three methods, similar ideas can be combined. It is important to respect and capture all ideas whether they seem relevant or not. The list can be narrowed down later. The goal is to generate as many ideas as possible. Sometimes seemingly ridiculous ideas may foster great ideas. Before changing or deleting any ideas, it is best to seek permission from the owner first. Deleting someone's idea without his or her approval will result in feelings of rejection.

Freewheeling is well suited for situations where a team needs a fast, spontaneous, creative process where people can interact and build off each other's ideas. Round-robins are a bit more orderly, systematic, and participative. Any team member may choose to skip a round. The slip method is preferred for larger teams, when anonymity is desired, or when people need more thinking time.

Force Field   When a team faces a high-energy or controversial issue, the risk is that the discussion may be highly exhaustive, emotional, or divisive for the team. But the team needs to talk about it and make a decision. The goal is to have a discussion that is objective, open, thorough, balanced, and efficient. People are going to have lots of energy for these issues and will want to voice them and challenge each other. Nevertheless, the focus should be on the issues; not on the people who strongly support one view or another.

One excellent way to get all the views on the table without risking personal conflicts is to do a force field. This is a facilitative tool that involves capturing all the plausible reasons (the forces) that are driving the team to do one thing versus the forces that are compelling it to do the opposite (Table 8.1). The force field is a method for analyzing both sides of an issue. It is a formal way of capturing the pros and cons. What is motivating me to say yes, and what is motivating me to say no on a particular issue? What is compelling us to take an action versus not taking action? A force field requires a brainstorming process to generate the team's pros and cons, and a flip chart to capture all the information. A vertical line is drawn down the middle of the page, with pros on one side and cons on the other. Opposing arrows can be drawn on top of the page to designate two opposite views. The team can do pros first and then cons or do both simultaneously. This technique helps the team frame the issue, invites both points of view, and involves everyone on the team.

For large teams, two subteams can be used. One team can work on the pros and the other on the cons, and then they can swap roles. This process usually yields richer results than having a single large team. The force field is a fast process and gets everyone involved. This process works well for breaking groupthink and biases and getting a more balanced point of view. It is less likely that someone will

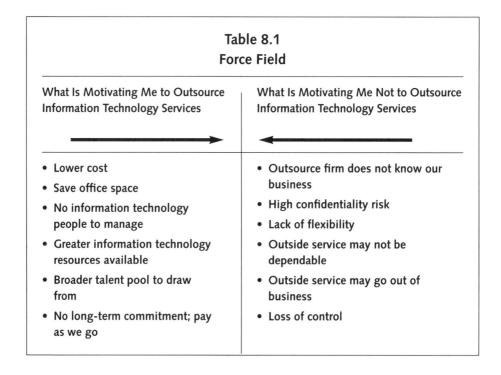

Table 8.1
Force Field

What Is Motivating Me to Outsource Information Technology Services	What Is Motivating Me Not to Outsource Information Technology Services
• Lower cost	• Outsource firm does not know our business
• Save office space	• High confidentiality risk
• No information technology people to manage	• Lack of flexibility
• Greater information technology resources available	• Outside service may not be dependable
• Broader talent pool to draw from	• Outside service may go out of business
• No long-term commitment; pay as we go	• Loss of control

dominate the discussion, and it captures a wide range of different views on a single page. From there, the team can clarify and narrow further.

The force field is an effective tool for getting opposing arguments on the table quickly. By doing the process together, the team creates a common product. Another good way to ground the team on an issue is to collect just the facts. Simply list what is known about this issue and what is not known about it. This method separates facts from perceptions and allows the team to get centered around the facts. It is okay to discuss assumptions and perceptions, but it works well to get the facts first. Facts have a way of bringing logic, reality, and objectivity to a discussion.

In summary, the force field helps to impersonalize the issue, invites both points of view, involves everyone on the team, and, best of all, is much faster than having an open, freewheeling discussion. By having all the pros and cons listed, the decision becomes more objective, thorough, and logical. People will feel satisfied that all sides of the issue were heard. It neutralizes dominant behaviors and is an excellent collaborative tool for handling hot issues.

Cause and Effect   Fishbone diagrams are commonly used to identify potential causes of a particular effect or outcome. The goal is to identify as many possible causes that could be contributing to a given effect. The first step is to define the goal. This is captured in a box on the right side of a board or sheet of paper. Then the team brainstorms all possible causes that may be contributing to the effect. These causes are grouped into broader categories and listed like fishbones under each category, as illustrated in Figure 8.3. The team can see, discuss, and decide on the major causes of the effect. Cause-and-effect diagrams help the team explore all of the factors contributing to a given problem.

Influence Diagram   An influence diagram is a team mapping process that opens the team's mind to the factors that are key to the project's success and how these factors relate to each other. The process involves brainstorming a list of factors that will determine success. It works best to do a silent brainstorming where each team member writes down his or her key factor on a large sticky note. These sticky notes are collected, read aloud to the team, clarified as needed, and any similar factors combined. Then the team is asked to arrange these various factors by order of their dependence on each other or, if applicable, their respective chronological order. For dependencies, if the success of factor X is dependent on the completion of factor Y, then factor X is physically placed on the board preceding factor Y and an

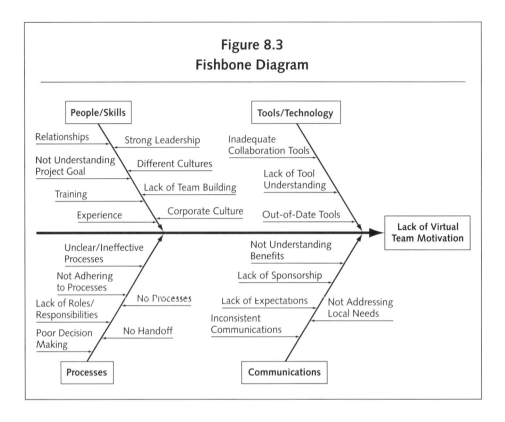

Figure 8.3
Fishbone Diagram

People/Skills

Relationships
Strong Leadership
Not Understanding Project Goal
Different Cultures
Training
Lack of Team Building
Experience
Corporate Culture

Tools/Technology

Inadequate Collaboration Tools
Lack of Tool Understanding
Out-of-Date Tools

Lack of Virtual Team Motivation

Unclear/Ineffective Processes
Not Understanding Benefits
Not Adhering to Processes
Lack of Sponsorship
Lack of Roles/ Responsibilities
No Processes
Lack of Expectations
Not Addressing Local Needs
Poor Decision Making
No Handoff
Inconsistent Communications

Processes

Communications

arrow is drawn from factor Y to factor X. A sample influence diagram is shown in Figure 8.4 for a project to improve safety performance: achieving zero injuries.

Influence diagrams help create a shared vision of the content and processes involved with the project. It is an inclusive activity that acknowledges everyone's ideas and perspectives. The physical process of doing an influence diagram creates team energy and discussion. A large majority of the population are visual and kinesthetic learners, so an influence diagram is a useful team learning tool. It also suits auditory learners because the act of mapping requires team discussion.

Influence diagrams promote team interaction and team learning and help to identify the success factors for the project. On the diagram, factors that have the largest number of arrows coming out of them will have the greatest impact on the project. In the example in Figure 8.4, management leadership would be a key driver. These are the biggest success drivers and deserve the most attention. The elements with the highest number of arrows pointing to them represent the proj-

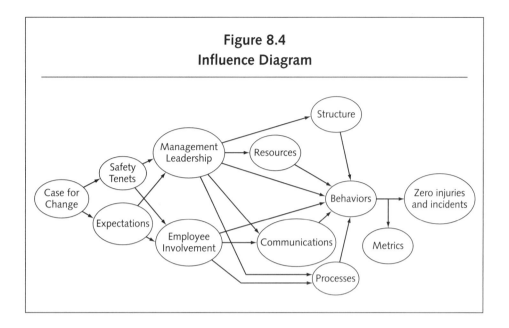

Figure 8.4
Influence Diagram

ect's major milestones, end points, or key work products. In the example, behavior is a key end point for the success of the project. Identifying the team's key factors helps set priorities, assign resources, and design a work plan from it.

Gap Analysis   Team success requires a shared vision of success and a clear road map to get there. An opening technique for developing a team vision and a conceptual work plan is to do a gap analysis to identify what actions will be required to change from the current state to a future desired state. For example, if a team's objective is to increase its production rate by 30 percent over the current rate, what needs to change in order to achieve this higher rate of output? What does the company need to do to close the gap between current and desired performance?

A gap analysis is basically a four-step process. Step 1 is to define the desired state. The purpose is to reach consensus on the team's vision of the desired state. Key questions are: What do we want to achieve? What does success look like? What are the benefits of the desired state? What is the payoff? For example, if the purpose of the team is to reduce customer delivery times for receiving mail orders, the vision of success may be to reduce delivery times by 50 percent by the end of the year, which reduces receivables, increases cash flow and profits, and increases the number of satisfied customers.

Step 2 entails understanding the who, what, where, when, and why behind the current state. Continuing the example on delivery times, the team would draw a picture of the current process, the various job tasks, data on delivery times, the customers and their locations, what delivery services are being used and their performance record, and benchmarking data from other companies that have shorter delivery times, for example. Gathering the facts on the current state may take a few hours to a few months depending on the scope and complexity of the delivery system. The team may need to conduct surveys, interview stakeholders, collect performance data, and capture best practices. With this information, the team can identify its gaps in terms of relative performance, delivery bottlenecks, barriers to faster delivery times, and opportunities to speed up the process. A root cause analysis can be used to pinpoint underlying sources for slow deliveries. The causes may be related to equipment, process, or behavior.

Step 3 is to determine where the gaps are. Having a good understanding of the desired and current states, the team can identify where the most important gaps are and agree on the root causes. In the example, the key gaps in delivery times may be in packaging, and the root cause may be embedded in the unreliability of the equipment or poor planning and scheduling between production and packaging.

Step 4 asks how to fill the gaps. What is it going to take to get from the current state to the desired state? With the key gaps and root causes defined, the team can proceed to develop ideas to fill gaps in performance and generate a range of options to improve delivery times. This method allows individuals on the team the flexibility to think forward or backward. The team can cast forward and think of what changes they can make to their current system to achieve their objectives, or they can cast backward and ask themselves what kind of delivery system they would build, if they started from scratch, to achieve their target delivery times. This forward- and back-casting produces a creative environment.

A gap analysis helps a team address the right problems in a process and focus on developing the right solutions for those gaps.

Strategy Table   Sometimes a team is faced with a complex issue that requires many different decisions. Within each decision are different options. In these situations, a strategy table can be used to break down the different decisions of the team and to determine various options.

The strategy table is a simple matrix of decision and options. In building a strategy table (Table 8.2), the first step is to define the project's objective. The objective

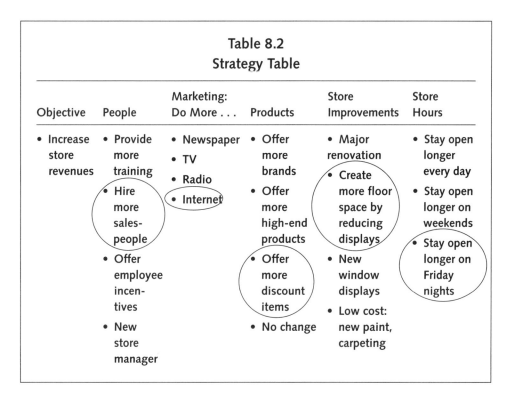

Table 8.2
Strategy Table

Objective	People	Marketing: Do More . . .	Products	Store Improvements	Store Hours
• Increase store revenues	• Provide more training	• Newspaper	• Offer more brands	• Major renovation	• Stay open longer every day
	• Hire more sales-people	• TV	• Offer more high-end products	• Create more floor space by reducing displays	• Stay open longer on weekends
		• Radio			• Stay open longer on Friday nights
	• Offer employee incen-tives	• Internet	• Offer more discount items	• New window displays	
	• New store manager		• No change	• Low cost: new paint, carpeting	

is placed in the first column. In this example, the objective is to increase store revenues. Second, all the key decisions to achieve that objective are identified and entered across the top of each column. In this example, there are several decisions: people, marketing, products, store improvements, and store hours. Underneath each decision, all potential options are entered. These options are usually selected from a separate brainstorming session. After the content of the table is complete, the team narrows and selects the best options among the choices in each column. The preferred option within each decision column is circled to highlight the preferred choices. In this example, the decisions were to hire more salespeople, do more Internet advertising, offer more discount items, create more floor space, and stay open longer on Fridays. A strategy table shows at a glance the combination of decisions that were made.

A strategy table has these advantages:

• The table organizes all key decisions into a single matrix and enables the team to work from a common understanding.

- The team works together to construct it, which promotes a shared ownership.
- It is a systematic way to stimulate different ideas and alternatives.
- The team will discover areas of agreement and disagreement as they fill out the strategy table.
- It identifies where more information or discussion is needed.
- The table documents the decisions and options that were considered.
- The table is both an opening and closing process.

Cherry Picking   Some of the best solutions and ideas are ones that are constructed from combining or expanding on many different ideas. A good technique for hybridizing ideas and generating additional ideas as a team is to use cherry picking, a process of discussing and selecting the best thoughts from an array of ideas. The team first brainstorms a list of solutions for a problem and then discusses which ideas they like and why. It is a good way to force the team to look at all of the ideas together, pick one or two that they like, and express their reasons behind the selection. It reveals people's thinking and forces the team to work together on identifying the positive aspects of the ideas. As people discuss the positives of various ideas, they will naturally start generating options or combinations of options that are even better. People will build on each other's thoughts and ideas. Cherry picking generates energy and puts people in a problem-solving mind-set, creating a strong team product. This is a real gem of a process: it is positive, productive, inclusive, and transparent.

Narrowing Techniques

Once a team has completed its opening process and has generated a long list of choices, the next step is to narrow the choices and make a decision. Focus on options, not people. The key is always to choose the best option, not the best advocate. Decisions should be objective. To help make that happen, there are several good techniques for systematically narrowing choices for a good team decision.

Power Dotting   Power dotting is a rapid voting method for narrowing a list of choices. Let us say a team has just completed a brainstorming process that created twenty-four items on a flip chart, and the team wants to reduce the list. First, they combine similar items and check them for team understanding. Each item is then assigned a unique number for reference. In the discussion period that follows, team members can share opinions on items that they especially like or dislike. After the discussion period, a vote is called. Each team member gets the same number of votes that is proportional to the total number of items on the voting list. The number of votes is calculated by dividing the total number of items by three. For twenty-four items, each team member is given eight votes (24/3), or dots, which are small, brightly colored self-adhering paper disks a half-inch in diameter that can be purchased at most stationery stores. The team is given a few minutes to silently consider which items they want to vote for. Team members then cast their votes by sticking their dots against their items on the flip chart. If dots are not available, people can use a broad-tip marker to check the ones they like.

Ground Rules for Power Dotting

- The person can stick only one dot per item (no ballot stuffing).

- Each dot may have equal weight, or each colored dot may have a different weighted value (for example, five points for a red dot, three points for a blue dot, and one point for a yellow dot). When each colored dot has a different value, the voter can place greater weight on some items. This helps to achieve a wider spread in the votes among the items.

- Items with the highest number of dots are selected. Typically, there will be a distinct break between those receiving a relatively high number of votes from those receiving fewer.

- If one round of voting does not reduce the list far enough, continue for another round or two with the most popular items, and then narrow to the desired number.

- After two rounds, any ties will be decided by the team leader. Items selected may not be clear. It is not unusual to discover that the top dot getters are not clearly understood by all.

Power dotting is quick, easy, and fun, and everyone has an equal vote. Moreover, the process keeps everyone moving around, and it forces people to make decisions.

Off-Line Voting   Off-line voting is a good narrowing technique to use when the team cannot meet in person. It works the same as power dotting except an e-mail survey is used. Each team member is still given N/3 votes (where N equals the total number of ideas), and they submit their choices to a facilitator. If desired, the votes can be handled anonymously by the facilitator. The facilitator counts the votes and sends out a summary of the results. Unless there is a clear winner, the same survey is sent out again. The purpose of the second survey is to allow the team to maintain, change, or adjust their votes based on the first round of results. Having an opportunity to see how the team voted in the first survey is an effective way of building consensus. A team can have a conference call to discuss the results between the two rounds, and this second round can help converge the team's thinking.

Fist of Five   The fist of five, described in Chapter Four, is a quick team voting process that asks each team member to express agreement on a scale of one to five fingers. Team consensus is reached when everyone is at least a three or higher. The fist of five gives the team explicit consensus before moving forward, and when consensus is not achieved, the team knows who is not in agreement and what dissenting issues need resolution.

Lasso   Trying to compose a team statement or document during a team meeting is very difficult, especially when the team is large. The energy level is usually mixed for this type of activity, and the end product is rarely satisfactory. Yet team input and consensus are required for the written statement. Lasso is a simple technique for getting everyone's input for a written team statement but without engaging the team in a tedious writing exercise.

Lasso starts with a team brainstorm on what the statement should say. The brainstorm is a quick, shout-it-out, freewheeling process. Short statements, sentences, or even key words are acceptable. These ideas are captured on a whiteboard or flip chart and checked for clarity. Team members are then asked what key words or phrases they like. With a broad-tip marker, the scribe draws a bold circle around each key word or phrase (the lasso) that the team likes. The team is not composing, just identifying key words and phrases that everyone likes. This usually takes only a few minutes. Congruent thinking occurs as the thoughts and words go up on the board. From there, the scribe has enough words to draft the team statement. Focusing on the message (content) rather than the process of editing a statement saves a tremendous amount of time and is consistent with the 80:20 rule. People walk away feeling satisfied that the key messages were decided. The final drafting can be done outside the meeting. Most important, the team does just enough work to move forward and avoids wasting time editing a document.

Selection Criteria   Having a narrowing process is no guarantee that a team will reach a decision. What if the vote is called, and there is no consensus? The team needs more explicit decision making for these situations. One effective narrowing method is to build a selection criteria table (Table 8.3) that then serves as the team's basis for making a decision. It is a list of critical factors that serves as the basis for making a selection among different alternatives.

Selection criteria is an excellent tool for revealing what is motivating people to choose one alternative over another. The reason for the lack of consensus may be due to differences in what people believe are the most important factors in making a selection. Once these unspoken drivers are expressed, the team can work together to develop a balanced criteria to make the decision. The criteria table is effective because it supports an objective decision and creates a shared basis for decision making. With a criteria table, people do not have to take sides on an issue. It helps to remove any personal biases. People will see a side of the story that they may not have recognized. Also, the team may find that they are in 80 percent agreement and that the indecision was being driven by only one or two factors. The selection criteria table is an effective tool for breaking stalemates and revealing underlying differences.

Table 8.3
Criteria Table: Choosing Among Alternatives

Number	Criterion	Weighting	Team Alternatives			
			A	B	C	D
1	Economic benefit	50%	2	3	4	5
2	Cost-effective	25%	3	3	4	5
3	Ability to mitigate risks	10%	2	2	3	2
4	Level of impact	10%	2	2	3	2
5	Ease of implementation	5%	5	3	4	2
		Total	14	13	18	16

Note: **Scoring is on a scale of 1 (low) to 5 (high).**

Typically a criteria table is set up as a matrix table, with criteria defined on the first vertical column and the list of alternatives along the top row. Each alternative is given a label (A, B, C, D) and described in more detail on a separate sheet. Each criterion can be weighted if needed, and each option can be scored on a graded scale, like 1 to 5. In the scoring example in Table 8.3, alternative C received the highest overall score (18) and alternative B the lowest (13). Total scores for some alternatives can be very close in some cases, especially if the list of criteria is short.

In case of ties or close calls on your selection criteria, some additional measures can be taken:

- Run the table again using only the top alternatives.

- Expand the list of criteria, and conduct the analysis again with all or a narrow list of alternatives.

- Run the table again, but assign different weights to each criterion—in this example, economic benefit = 50 percent, cost-effective = 25 percent, ability to mitigate risks = 10 percent, level of impact = 10 percent, and ease of implementation = 5 percent. To get a weighted score for an alternative, multiply each score against the weighted percent, and then sum all of the weighted scores in the column for each alternative. In the example, the sum for alternative A = (50 $\times$ 2) + (25 $\times$ 3) + (10 $\times$ 2) + (10 $\times$ 2) + (5 $\times$ 5) or 240 points. Applying a weighted scoring system, alternative D received the highest overall score and alternative A the lowest. With weighted scoring, assigning a value to each criterion can change the rank order of the alternatives.

Cost-Benefit Matrix   Another criteria-based narrowing tool is the cost-benefit matrix (Figure 8.5). When there are several viable solutions to a problem, the one that provides the greatest benefit may not necessarily be the best solution. For example, the one with the greatest benefit may also be the most costly to implement. The desired solution is more likely the one that offers the greatest return for the required effort.

The cost-benefit matrix is a simple plot of the various options (depicted as letters in the bubbles in Figure 8.5) of its estimated cost against its expected level of benefit. It is a relative ranking of all options in a single visual. If we wanted to capture a third factor (for example, strategic value, size of market, or size of current investment), we could also vary the size of each bubble proportionately.

In Figure 8.5, alternatives that have high benefit and low effort are "low hanging fruit," such as options G and I. Based on this matrix, option D would be the

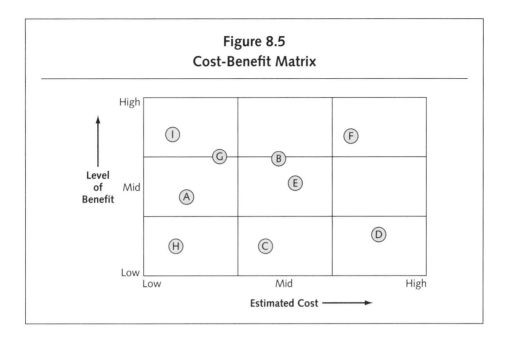

Figure 8.5
Cost-Benefit Matrix

least desirable. One can also substitute "cost" with "level of effort" or "risk." Also, benefit can mean different things, such as profit, earnings, productivity, morale, or quality of life. With this tool, it would be important to define the terms being used: benefit, cost, effort, and risk. Also, the low, mid, and high levels of efforts need to be defined, but broadly enough to get separation among the options. This matrix is an excellent tool for narrowing and screening a wide range of ideas.

BREAK TEAM STALEMATES

If the project team constantly struggles to reach consensus, people will begin feeling stressed, confused, and frustrated. These impasses tend to carry over to other aspects of the project and bog down teamwork. How well teams are able to overcome stalemates is a sign of a high-performing team. Here are seven methods to help break stalemates:

• Seek higher authority for a decision. This means going to the project's sponsor or management for a decision that will break the stalemate and enable the team to move forward. This works best when the team is far apart on an issue and has exhausted all other means for reaching a team decision. The downside is that the team will see this as a failure. If this is a concern and the team does not want to appear inept, the team could seek management "guidance" or "clarification" instead of a "decision" on the issue.

• Minority report. If only a small minority disagrees, the team can propose to go with the majority position but include the dissenting opinion in their report. In turn, the minority group agrees to support the majority decision. When minority opinions are captured in the team report, the team is demonstrating inclusive team behaviors and respect for the opinions of the team.

• Form a subteam. There comes a point when everything has been said and people are simply recycling. It is time to say that the team has covered it well and there appears to be no merit in further discussions, so "let's just take it off-line, and let a couple of people work on it." Usually it is far easier to work an issue off-line (apart from the team) as a subteam. It allows people to cool off, take a renewed look at the issue, and discuss it in a less contentious climate. Also, a change in venue can spur compromise. The team leader can appoint or solicit volunteers for the subteam. Volunteers will be more committed and usually have more energy for the topic. The subteam would be expected to produce a recommendation for the rest of the team.

• Pinpoint the disagreement. Go around the table and ask people, "What is keeping you from living with the other decision?" When the issue is framed that way, people tend to get more specific, minor points drop off, and more commonalities are revealed than expected. If nothing else, the team is at least able to identify the gaps and can move forward to address them through more discussion to reach a compromise. At least it moves the team from a contentious mode into a problem-solving one. With this information, a team can choose to work on this further, take it off-line, or put it in the parking lot.

• Agree on next steps. Sometimes teams are in stalemate because the decision covers too much ground and uncertainty. A good fallback is to identify only the next one or two steps and revisit the broader decision later. For tough cases, the next step may be to meet again. Regardless, it is important to leave in agreement.

• Empower the team leader. This method empowers the project leader (or the issue owner) to make the decision off-line and consult with others as needed. At the next team meeting, the decision is shared with the team. This enables the team to move forward when there is limited time for additional debate.

• Recap the discussion. When a team is stuck, it helps to call for a break and then recap the discussion. By taking a break, the team has a chance to reflect on the issue. For example, I attended a meeting where people were getting a bit tired of discussing an item and could not reach consensus. I simply said, "I sense we are all a bit drained from the discussion. Why don't we take a break and get refreshed. I'll throw up the key points that I heard on the flip chart, and then we can take a quick vote when we return." When they returned and looked at the points, the team was able to reach a compromise and move on.

• Switch elements to reset the discussion. As an alternative to taking a break, switch the discussion to another key element (content, process, or behavior). If a team is stymied on content, switch the discussion to process for awhile. This shift to another element provides a change of perspective, which breaks the team freeze. When the team returns to the content issue later, people are often pleasantly surprised to find agreement.

SUMMARY

Teams are prone to being too content focused. They tend to spend too much time discussing and developing goals, milestones, and deadlines and too little time on process. Process is the heart of the three key elements of team performance. It takes good processes to execute content, and processes are the actions that convert content and information into decisions.

Good team leaders are good facilitators of process. Facilitation is the art of using the right processes to enable a team to reach timely agreements through effective discussions and behaviors. It guides the team in focusing on the right things. Facilitation helps channel energy into the things that really count. To achieve good facilitation, a team leader needs to be knowledgeable about useful techniques and tools, experience in applying them in team meetings, and knowing which tools to use for the situation.

This chapter covered a number of well-proven processes and techniques. The processes create an inclusive work environment, accelerate project execution, and help in making quality decisions. A fundamental skill is to understand how to open and close discussions and how to facilitate team consensus. Process tools are critical for moving teams forward and breaking stalemates. People who know how to convert information and judgments into actionable decisions are the stars of the organization. People who ignore process are missing out on a huge opportunity to become better leaders and managers.

Personal Space

The goal of project management is to meet the project's objectives. It usually means completing the project on time, on spec, and within budget, the old mantra of project management. We have been taught that getting to that point requires strong skills in planning, execution, and control. Yet in today's competitive environment, getting results is not good enough. Superior project management is about getting desired results over and over again to sustain high performance over the long run. To be successful over the long term, organizations must be successful in meeting people's goals. It is the inspiration, motivation, and human energy of people who make or break projects, not plans, process, or control. We have learned from Chapters Three to Eight that content, process, and behavior are essential ingredients for good teamwork. However, individual motivation and inspiration require much more than that. We need to understand people's expectations and give them hope and confidence that their expectations can be met or exceeded. After all, we all want the same things in life: to feel needed, valued, and fulfilled. Believing that those desires can come true is a powerful force that motivates and inspires all of us. Knowing what our desires are and how to fulfill those desires reside in our third space of human factors: personal space.

Personal space is the most complex and least transparent of the three spaces. It is a space that defines who you are and what you do. I have defined personal space as the inner self, a place where internal interactive thinking occurs and human factors are formed. External information is internalized in personal space and intellectually and emotionally processed through internal dialogue. Internal dialogue occurs as people mentally process new information, interpret its meaning against their human factors, and express those perceptions in their behaviors. Personal space can generate enormous desire and human energy. Deep inside, it contains the things that people believe in: their personal values. Personal values guide their thinking, judgment, feelings, and behaviors. Values are at the core of human factors.

How people act with others may seem like spontaneous events, but they are actually a set of acquired responses driven by individual values. Every day people make value judgments about their environment, distinguishing what is good from bad, acceptable and unacceptable, and right and wrong. Some values are derived from genetics (personality type), while others are developed from culture and life experiences (Figure 9.1). Regardless of origin, values are inherent in human behaviors. They are engrained in how people think, learn, communicate, and work with others.

Because values are formed by a combination of genetics and environment, no two people are alike. A diversity of values exists within populations, organizations, and teams. Each of us acts and responds differently to situations, because we possess different individual values. In fact, all dimensions of individual diversity can be related to the three factors of genetics, culture, and experiences. Whether diversity is attributed to race, gender, ethnicity, family, sexual orientation, religion, education, profession, or abilities, they all help determine individual value systems and

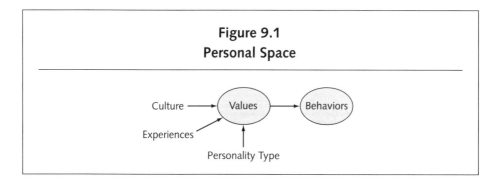

Figure 9.1
Personal Space

Culture ⟶ Values ⟶ Behaviors

Experiences

Personality Type

set of behaviors. This is our personal space, which defines who we are and what we believe in. For some people, values are defined largely by their family, religion, and ethnicity. For others, they may be driven by internal beliefs of fairness, justice, and compassion for others. And the values of some people have been greatly influenced by childhood experiences, tragedies, and historic events, such as wars and natural disasters. Regardless of diversity and background, behavior flows from a developed set of values based on culture, life experiences, and inborn personality type.

Behaviors come from values. This is an important concept: truly understanding others' intentions and the basis for team behaviors requires fully understanding individual values. Values are powerful human factors that carry much emotional meaning. A good test of whether something is a personal value to you is to ask yourself, "What types of behaviors or circumstances set me off emotionally?" or "What things excite me or upset me the most?" These are things that you care most about—that stir your inner soul and trigger emotional reactions. Because values are unique to you, what may upset you may not upset others. Undoubtedly you have encountered a situation where someone was upset over an event that you did not find upsetting at all. For example, some people find it upsetting when someone cuts in line, yet others find it not offending at all. In fact, they could not care less. For many, cutting in line is considered a rude and offensive behavior because it violates personal values of honesty and fairness. Another strong value is financial security, which motivates saving first and spending later. People with this value are more motivated by employee benefits and a steady income than by professional impact and prestige.

If an organization's goals are to bring out the best in people, maximize performance, and build high-performing teams, then they must respect and understand individual differences in personal values. These values are the underlying human factors of behaviors, the hidden truths inside everyone and not apparent to other people. In some cases, they may not be even apparent to ourselves. A good visual image of values is the floating iceberg where we see only the behavior that appears on top and not the massive volume of values that exist underneath. Regardless of how well you know another person, his or her behavior is only the tip of the iceberg. Much lies beneath it.

The following sections discuss what personal space contains and how values relate to team space and then organizational space. We begin by looking at the three key components of personal values: culture, experiences, and personality type.

CULTURE

Culture is a key human factor in determining individual values and behaviors. It is defined as the shared ways in which groups of people understand and interpret the world. Culture consists of ideas, values, attitudes, traditions, beliefs, morals, and customs. Together, these act to drive personal behaviors and serve as filters to determine what form of behavior each of us considers normal to us. We interpret the environment from our own cultural viewpoint. Our cultural diversity comes from things that we grew up accepting from our family, friends, and community.

Culture is a reflection of our environment. We learn a language, a way of interacting with others, and our personal values. We learn very early in life what is right and wrong, and these early learnings stay with us for the rest of our lives. They become second nature to us. We do not fully appreciate how deep our culture is ingrained in each of us until we visit a different country or interact with people of different ethnicity. What is perfectly normal for an American driving on the right side of the road is perfectly abnormal to a British driver. Our culture defines who we are and how we behave. Let us review some cultural elements that teams frequently encounter.

Language

English may be the predominant global language, but often it is not the predominant native language for the people on a team. According to 2002 U.S. Census Bureau estimates, the nation's foreign-born population numbered 32.5 million, or 11.5 percent of the total U.S. population. Among this population, 52 percent were born in Latin America, 26 percent in Asia, 14 percent in Europe, and the remaining 8 percent from Africa and other countries. It is projected that Hispanics will become the nation's largest minority group and rise to 24 percent of the U.S. population by 2050.

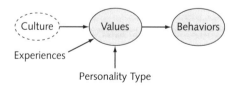

With these changes in demographics, there will be a greater need to learn and understand different languages and cultures. Private industry and school systems alike will need to adapt to a population of professional workers who need broader language skills. Globalization demands greater fluency in languages.

One cultural feature of language is the use of idioms or slang in communications. Idioms are well-accepted expressions in a culture that have a different meaning from the literal words, so they can be confusing to people outside that culture. Idioms are most often used in verbal communications, but they can find their way into written communications too. The U.S. business culture freely uses idioms in their speech, and they frequently pertain to animals, the body, and sports, such as "chasing rabbits," "fox guarding the hen house," "tongue in cheek," "shake a leg," "gut check," "time to punt," "slam dunk," and "ball's in your court."

Besides idioms, we need to be careful in how we use terms across cultures. There are numerous words that are culturally shunned such as referring to clothing as costumes, ethnic groups as tribes, Asians as Orientals, African Americans as colored, a group of men and women as guys, women as gals and chicks, and southerners as rednecks. In Europe, formal titles (doctor, sir, honorable) are commonly used. In Japan, san is added to the end of names, and in China, the family name is said first.

Being loud and boisterous are turnoffs for most cultures. A mild speaking tone is preferred, which shows modesty and respect for the other party. Self-aggrandizement is seen as selfish. In Asian and Middle Eastern cultures, communications are more contextual, indirect, and respectful. In contrast, the American culture admires people who speak directly, even bluntly. In many countries, conversations normally begin with a personal greeting or family inquiry. It is customary to start each day in the office with an exchange of polite and cheerful greetings, whereas in the United States, a family inquiry may be taken as an invasion of privacy. For most of the rest of the world, personal exchange should precede any business talk. Small talk is actually big talk in certain cultures. Having a personal interest in people can carry much more weight than the work.

Individual versus Community Orientation

American culture is built on individualism and independence. The strength of the U.S. business culture is derived from individual initiative, entrepreneurship, and freedom. Privacy is highly valued. People are recruited to serve on teams based on their individual skill sets and their ability to work with others on a team. Nevertheless, the drive for individuality remains strong. In contrast, for most other cultures in the world, community and interdependence are more important than the individual. The interest of the community is valued much higher than the interest of individuals. The greater good should always prevail. On teams, the workload is expected to be equally shared. Someone from a community-based culture is more comfortable with team actions versus individual actions and would seek to understand how his or her work contributes to the team as a whole. Also, it may be more important to conform to the ways of the team rather than take an independent approach. Team loyalty and unity are traits that are highly valued by those who were raised in a community belief system. As such, they expect their organizations to reward team achievements over individual successes.

Respect for Authority

Many cultures have a deep respect for elders, status, and authority, such as governmental officials, military officers, teachers, law enforcement, senior colleagues, and company management. Some people may feel uncomfortable challenging the status quo for fear of disorder, punishment, or conflict. One does not openly disagree with a superior. Respect is reflected in their greeting, dress, position at the table, speaking style, and meeting protocol, such as elders being greeted or introduced first, and it is important to maintain formal behavior and rank within the hierarchy in the meeting. In teams, the norm is not to speak up unless spoken to, respect the authority of the team leader, await permission to talk, and expect work to be defined for them. Hierarchy is seen as necessary for maintaining order.

This respect for authority can bear on team decision making. For example, a silent yes may indicate respect rather than agreement. Some people may prefer to stay silent on their positions until they have had a chance to hear from a senior member of the organization. A team may not reach full commitment until there is endorsement from management.

Relationship with Peers

In most cultures, mutual trust and respect are held in highest regard, and any personal disagreements should be disclosed only in private. Relationships are highly valued, so no one should openly criticize or interrupt another person in a meeting. Public criticism, in fact, is a show of disrespect and dishonor. A Kazakh once said to me, "Never make someone look silly or stupid in front of others." Causing someone to lose face is an ultimate insult. No one should ever point out shortfalls in others to make a point. The first priority is to protect others, even if it means a personal sacrifice. How one looks in front of peers may be much more important than how the person looks to management. Interrupting a speaker, especially someone more senior, is regarded as extremely rude, and questions are reserved until the end. Sometimes questions are raised not in public but only in private settings.

Relationships are valued, and open conflict with peers is to be avoided. In fact, maintaining good relationships may be more important than project goals. In many cultures, people on work teams are also considered friends at work and home. Work colleagues are expected to socialize away from work; families, for example, get together to eat, drink, and have fun. So with this value, it is not surprising that a colleague may choose to change or withhold information in order to protect a friend. Protecting relationships is an important cultural value that may underlie certain behaviors. There is a common proverb in West Africa that says, "Always select the neighbors before you select the house."

Nonverbal Communications

Body language and gestures can be just as important as verbal communications. For example, not looking people in the eye may be considered a weakness in one culture but a sign of respect in another. Back-slapping, tickling, and arm squeezing may be considered offensive behaviors. Physical affections like hugging and kissing may be acceptable in some cultures but inappropriate in others, especially across genders. In some countries, men do not initiate handshakes with women or even take pictures of women. Westerners tend to stand apart when speaking; in the Middle East, close exchanges are more common, and backing away may be a sign of disrespect. Hand gestures, thumbs up, and use of the left hand may be offensive. In many cultures, it is common to eat with the fingers. Also, in certain cultures, it is disrespectful to show your feet or the soles of your shoes to others.

With all of these don'ts, it may seem that anything we do can be potentially offensive to somebody. Fortunately, globalization has raised awareness and understanding across cultures, and people are showing more sensitivity to their own behaviors and greater tolerance of that of others. The way to minimize behavioral risks in different cultures is to be a good observer.

Here are three ways to improve your nonverbal communications:

- Pace others. Watch the behaviors of the other party, and use a manner consistent with it. If the person tends to speak softly, you should speak softly; if he or she stands apart when speaking, give some space too. Being on an equal level with someone else sends a subtle but positive message to the other party.

- Look for cues. Watch how people react in certain situations, and adjust your behavior accordingly. For example, if you notice a person is uncomfortable speaking in front of a crowd, you may want to make an encouraging remark early in the talk to help the person relax, or if you noticed a person does not approach others well in social settings, you may want to accompany that person next time and introduce him or her to others.

- Be yourself. Pacing and adjusting your behaviors are good techniques, but you still need to be yourself.

I once attended a special concert in a small, lavish hotel. It was an audience of senior citizens from Europe and America, and the entertainer was a country singer from Tennessee. In the beginning, she tried to get the audience excited by speaking loudly (almost screaming), prancing around the stage, singing a couple of stale tunes, and telling people to "get excited." She generated little excitement in that crowd. In fact, people were getting a bit annoyed. Her failure was trying to bring the audience up to her emotional level through physical and verbal cajoling that was common in her culture, but it was not motivating to this audience. You just cannot tell people to "get excited." More important, she was too out of pace with the audience. Halfway into her performance, she suddenly switched to her natural talent of singing country western songs, and the crowd came alive. They started clapping and smiling, and by the second song, the clapping turned into cheering and loud applause. The performer was aglow. What I believe she realized was that this audience got excited by her genuine talent and passion for the music she enjoyed most, and it was also in pace with the emotional state of the audience. They just wanted to hear good, genuine music.

Openness

Establishing a team ground rule to speak openly and honestly may be culturally challenging to some people who have strong cultural beliefs against someone speaking out. These common beliefs include

- Speak only when spoken to.
- Always respect rather than oppose authority.
- Never impose your personal feelings or opinions on others.

- Keep your feelings to yourself.

- Expressing how you sincerely feel is a sign of weakness.

A strong preference in many cultures is to express opinions in an indirect manner, especially when conveying negative news. Indirect communications are meant to maintain group harmony. A person may be reluctant to speak up in a team setting but will open up in the safety of a private setting. Also, embellishments may be seen as dishonest and superficial. In many cultures, bragging is considered a dishonorable behavior. Modesty and humbleness are taught at a very early age.

The Value of Time

Westerners are seen as more time dependent compared to Asians, Africans, and Latin Americans, who view time as being more fluid. The American culture is fast paced: Americans eat fast, drink fast, and work fast. Most countries enjoy a more leisurely pace.

Being punctual has its virtues, but in many cultures being late is a common and accepted behavior. People who attend social parties and meetings on time may be seen as anxious, selfish, competitive, greedy, and hungry. In many Asian cultures, people are expected to arrive late. This same behavior is seen as extremely inconsiderate in the United States and Europe.

Having a highly structured, time-driven agenda may not be culturally favored. Being flexible and open with topics can send a better message. Many people are quite comfortable with a more spontaneous, subjective flow of the agenda. Some cultures expect meetings to start and end later than scheduled. In some countries, it is not unusual for people to wander in and out of the meetings.

Decision Making

In decision making, trust and relationships may be more important than content. It is important to respect how people make decisions. Pressuring for a decision does not demonstrate good relationships. It may be customary to have several discussions and meetings before decisions are made. Cultural superstitions can come into play and can pervade one's thinking, including beliefs in luck, fate, and bad omens, which are outside one's control. These behaviors can be read as avoiding risks and not taking responsibility for one's actions. Putting off a decision to gather more opinions may be commonplace in some cultures.

How to Value Cultural Diversity on Teams

There are a number of ways teams can show they value cultural diversity.

Create an Inclusive Team Environment   Teams need to make a conscious effort to involve everyone as much as possible at meetings, presentations, teleconferences, planning sessions, and team communications. Everyone, not just the project leader or a handful of people, should feel success and mutual respect. It is too easy to let assertive individuals take control of the core project and allow the others to fade into the background. Cultural values and behaviors can be barriers for balanced participation on team projects. Always assigning the critical work to the most experienced person is a missed opportunity to stretch and develop others. Often people rise to the occasion and perform in ways that they thought were out of their reach. A large part of team success is allowing individuals to experience personal growth and achieve higher self-confidence and respect within the team structure.

Give Appropriate Recognition   Nothing makes a person feel more valued than sincere praise and recognition. A high-performing team takes the time to recognize good behaviors. More important, it gives recognitions that are meaningful to the recipients. A public recognition may be a true honor for some but an embarrassment for others. A trinket may be a symbol of appreciation to certain people but an insult to others. To know what is appropriate, a good practice is to ask each person in joining the organization or team how he or she wishes to be recognized.

Make Your Intentions Transparent   With so many different cultures represented on teams, words can be often misinterpreted. It helps to clarify the intent behind words. If you are kidding, make sure the person knows it. If you are being facetious, say so. Never assume everyone knows your intent. A misunderstood joke can quickly ruin a good relationship. Check for understanding, clarity, and buy-in, and watch for nonverbal indicators of disagreement or puzzlement.

Use Visuals   Visuals increase the effectiveness of the communication. People of all cultures are aided by visuals, which usually speak louder than words. Also, we tend to remember pictures and visual stories much longer than we do verbal or written discussions. Visuals help convey abstract information more easily. People like road maps, graphics, diagrams, and images to help them see the bigger picture. Integrating complex information is always a special challenge for diverse teams.

Avoid the Rush   Americans are known to be fast talkers, fast movers, and fast consumers. In a gathering of people representing different cultures, it is best not to rush the process and get down to business too quickly. This is considered impolite in many cultures. The process of greeting and socializing is just as important as any topic on the meeting agenda.

Do Not Assume that Silence Means Agreement   In Asian and African cultures, saying no is a sign of disharmony and disrespect. It is best to use methods that make it safe to say no, such as the fist of five and off-line voting (see Chapters Four and Eight). Good communicators are skilled in picking up verbal and nonverbal cues.

Inquire into a Person's Underlying Values and Thinking   Some people are naturally inclined to let others speak first and wait for the right moment to speak. This is often a cultural behavior that demonstrates respect and cooperation. The challenge for the team is to avoid discriminating against these types of passive behaviors. Being quiet does not mean an individual is uninterested or incapable. Good teams seek out opinions in a positive way that builds trust. Balanced team participation does not just happen. It requires a conscious effort of talkers to switch off and listeners to speak up. Unbalanced participation can be avoided by taking the time to query others and invite participation. Quiet people can be the best listeners on the team and can pick up points that others miss. Team ground rules are a place to state that the team will seek balanced participation in its discussions and activities.

EXPERIENCES: GENERATIONAL DIVERSITY

Our values are also shaped by our life experiences. One of the most significant human factors affecting people's values is the generation that we grew up with and the experiences that we shared (Lancaster and Stillman, 2002). The generations

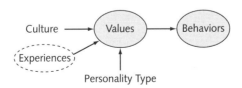

can be divided into five major periods: traditionalist (born between 1900 and 1945), baby boomer (born between 1946 and 1964), generation X (born between 1965 and 1980), millennial (born between 1981 and 1999), and generation Z (born between 2000 and the present). Each of these generations is united by the events and emotions of their times: wars, politics, economics, civil rights, technology, art, music, and people. What gets retained are the indelible memories of conflict, human tragedies, social change, industrial conquest, and technological growth.

Traditionalists

The traditionalists represent a population of people who lived through the Great Depression, World War II, the Korean War, and the cold war and witnessed the greatest period of invention and industrial expansion in the history of the world. They have also been referred to as the greatest generation.

As a subculture, traditionalists can be described as the no-nonsense, get-the-job-done generation. Their behaviors reflect their faith and loyalty to authority, hierarchy, and institutions. They believe in the system, the establishment, and top-down authority. Social order means stability and safety, and security is always high on their minds.

Working on a self-directed, cross-functional team is not a natural environment for traditionalists. They were raised in a chain-of-command structure, and their behaviors are based on compliance, loyalty, and delayed gratification. They learned their job, stayed obedient, and earned their way up. On teams, traditionalists want leadership, well-defined roles and responsibilities, governance, goals, and respect. Motivation comes from their desire for security, money, rank, and seniority. They want the work completed on time and on spec. A team project is a mission for traditionalists. Their goal is to develop and execute a game plan that will satisfy management.

Traditionalists have a strong faith in their country, company, and social institutions. They do not challenge authority. They believe that rules are needed to maintain order and discipline; otherwise the system breaks down, and the mission will fail. Traditionalists believe people should pull their own weight, work within the rules, and take pride in a job well done. They were raised to conform to the system, not to reform the system. The system works by fitting the person to the system, not the system to the person.

Traditionalists enjoy working with people who respect them for their know-how and experience. They need to be recognized for their wealth of knowledge and respected for their hard-won successes. They have a strong work ethic and respect others who work hard too. Traditionalists are concerned about content and solutions, not process and behaviors. This generation is not known as a touchy-feely generation. "Getting in touch with their feelings" is not high on their list.

Traditionalists grew up in a magical technological age, witnessing the invention of the radio, television, spaceships, and the computer. Yet they may not be current in digital and Web-based technologies. Do not assume that everyone is Internet savvy, can merge electronic files, and build PowerPoint presentations. Traditionalists are great at fixing things that are broken but are reluctant to "break things" for the sake of innovation. They behave to the adages of "let sleeping dogs lie," and "if it ain't broke, don't fix it."

Baby Boomers

Baby boomers represent by far the largest proportion of the population and therefore have had the greatest impact on the workplace. Baby boomers are self-driven, ambitious, materialistic, and achievement oriented. Unlike traditionalists, they believe that the status quo needs to be challenged. Baby boomers grew up in the age of great movements: the civil rights movement, the environmental movement, the antiwar movement, and the women's movement. On teams, they have an optimistic attitude and believe they can make a difference. This population lived through the long struggle of the Vietnam War and the shame of Watergate.

As a subpopulation, baby boomers are highly educated and seek to make a difference in the world. Baby boomers are driven to succeed, driven to compete, driven to make changes, and driven to make sure others know this about them. Life is a fierce competition and a zero-sum game. Boomers are much more process and change oriented than traditionalists, and with technology as an enabler, they actively use processes to facilitate their actions. They are obsessed by time: start time, cycle time, time management, down time, and, most of all, time is money. Because time is so important, they must work hard and play hard to get the most out of life. Their job defines who they are. This generation measures success by job title, professional status, and amount of wealth accrued. Where traditionalists want pride and security, boomers want wealth and prestige.

This push for financial success fueled the eighteen-year bull market that started in 1982 and was one of the greatest runs in stock market history. It was also the first time that the middle class participated so heavily in the stock market. Boomers are now approaching retirement age, and many are reevaluating their status and how they want to spend the rest of their working life. In their retirement years, they may continue to work part time, do volunteer work, or mentor others. They are now facing conflicts between a need to succeed and a growing desire to slow down, savor life, and contribute to their communities.

Baby boomers are valued for their great drive to succeed, willingness to challenge the status quo, and enthusiasm for lifelong learning. They are motivated by title, prestige, recognition, and rewards. Those who work with boomers must make sure the end game is clear: the deliverables, the value of the work to the organization, what they will get out of it, and the process for getting there. It is important to define the purpose, the goal, and the vision of success. Boomers need to understand the story behind the story. They want to know the objectives, strategies, milestones, key processes, success metrics, scorecards, and time lines. They want it all, and they want it done right away. Remember, that boomers have a title to live up to and a mortgage to pay down.

Generation X

Gen Xers are distinctive for their technological prowess, balanced view of work and personal life, and desire for career independence. The Xers follow in the shadows of the baby boomers and have inherited many good and bad lessons. Xers want success, money, and recognition but without the guilt of excessive materialism, ambition, and rebellion. They see baby boomers as a highly successful group but tainted in many ways by divorce, live-to-work syndrome, heart disease, stress, greed, and the high pace of life. They are not bent on a twenty-five-year corporate career with a corner office, an oak desk, a secretary, and country club privileges. The Xers have witnessed the elimination of the mutual commitment between employees and employer, where loyalty to the corporation is rewarded by the corporation's loyalty to workers. This unwritten agreement between employee and employer was broken in the late 1980s and 1990s by the chain of corporate downsizings, right sizings, rationalizing, and offshoring.

Where boomers learned to be skeptical about government, Xers have learned to be skeptical about corporate institutions. They have seen the desperation of older baby boomers trying to survive yet another round of layoffs. They do not want to put in twenty-five years and then hang on for company retirement. Xers want immunity from forced layoffs and seek strong control of their careers. Their success metric is always being in the position to go elsewhere if they choose to.

When I speak to Xers in corporations, the tell me that they do not expect to get retirement benefits such as lifetime health care, pensions, and social security. They accept the fact that they have to be responsible for their own well-being. They are not going to depend on their companies to take care of them.

The Xers shun fast food and the competitive lifestyle of the boomers and seek a more balanced lifestyle between work and family life and between materialism and spiritualism. They desire personal growth and want to grow in their skills, knowledge, and experiences. In a way, they shadow boomers in their drive to prove themselves and set a high bar in their careers. Xers want to establish a career that is invulnerable to corporate breakdowns. They want to be able to control their own careers, know where they are going, and choose their own paths where possible, and they are not in a mad rush to get there. They can wait to get married, wait to have a family, and wait for a big house. Xers want to be self-sufficient, self-assured, and self-managed.

The self-confidence of Xers stems from their broad reach. They are well connected to the world around them, have a network of colleagues and contacts, are Internet savvy and can access information instantly, and have the technology know-how to get smart quickly on any subject. While traditionalists are grateful for a stable job and boomers are happy with their competitive achievements, Xers take pride in knowing that they are mobile and have fungible skills that can take them into other sectors of business, government, or academia. They like to keep their options open. Because they have transferable skills, they feel less intellectually and emotionally attached to their current employer. They value freedom more highly than money or prestige.

Xers are motivated by personal growth, challenging assignments, and advancements. They shun the baby boomer mentality of working sixty hours per week and want work and family life effectiveness. They care deeply about their career track and wish to be recognized for the quality of their work. They have very little tolerance for people who are just putting in time and giving minimal effort. Job selections based on seniority or rank irk the Xers. Like all other generations, Xers seek recognition for their work. What sets them apart is their anxiety and assertiveness in seeking what they want. If Xers are not given responsible roles, they are willing to move on without regrets. It is best not to impose limits and outdated values on Xers. Give Xers a chance to demonstrate their skills, and trust them to take part in roles that were traditionally limited to more senior people. In a way, they are much more impatient and relatively fearless compared to traditionalists and boomers. Basically generation X wants flexibility in what they do and how they do it.

The Millennials

This is the newest generation entering the workforce. It will be interesting to see what learnings they will carry forward from the boomers and Xers. The millennials arrived in a world where information is instantly available and have learned to seek instant gratification. This is the first generation that has grown up entirely with the Internet and can be called the Internet generation. These young people grew up with instant connectivity with the Internet, cell phones, PDAs, and iPods. Instant messaging, text messaging, video downloads, instant music, and e-mailing are part of the instant communications for millennials. Sophisticated video simulations such as the Xbox provide entertainment and immediate gratification. The work turnover rate is faster for millennials than for other generations. They are self-sufficient. The millennials have grown up in a rather sheltered, information-rich world. They have yet to establish a rich historical context.

In business, the millennials are tech savvy but also carry a demanding disposition that stems from their need for instant gratification. You may hear remarks like, "Why can't I be given greater responsibility in the company now?" or "I do not want to wait for people to leave in order to move up or wait for my turn. Please use me now for my talents." A consistent comment that I hear from millennials is that they find that their generation behaves as if the company owes them opportunities. I have heard terms such as "act spoiled," "feel owed to," and "expect entitlements" to describe their colleagues. The millennials bring speed, networking, and enormous capacity to the game, which will bring further changes to the workplace. Whereas Xers are well connected, millennials are multiconnected. They have a high-capacity, multitask view of life: they are able to use iPod, Wi-Fi, and videolinks all at the same time. They want a high-capacity work life and family life with a strong social network.

Due to the enabling force of technology, they have tremendous personal capacity to do more things and have an impact on others. This generation is more diverse in work, career, lifestyle, and family. The Xers broadened the pace of change, but the millennials will change the capabilities of society. It is possible that this generation will not only have the skills of Xers but perhaps even multiple careers. Like Xers, millennials assume responsibility for their own careers and manage their own skills development. Money is important to them, but they also want rich experiences. This generation will take communications and the rate of change to a higher level. Information is not only accessible and fast, it will also take on much more functional forms in terms of interchangeability, transferability from one media to another, and sharing real-time information on a global scale.

The millennial generation values information, speed, networking, technology, globalization, and self-determination. This generation has high expectations and demands attention. Like the Xers, they want flexibility in their careers. They want to be used and respected for their performance, technological prowess, high work capacity, and global thinking. They are natural collaborators, team players, and quick integrators of information. Millennials expect instant feedback. They want speed, efficiency, and fast turnover, yet their work must also have depth and long-term meaning. Millennials want to be heard and want their opinions honored. On teams, they want to be treated as an equal and a peer. Rank, seniority, and hierarchy are not important to them.

PERSONALITY TYPES

All of us have natural tendencies in the way we think, learn, process information, and communicate. These individual preferences are defined by our genetic composition and expression and manifested in our temperaments and personalities.

The best known characterization of these tendencies was derived from the early observations of Carl Jung (1923), the Swiss psychiatrist who observed that people have consistent patterns of human behavior. Jung identified four primary functions of experiencing the world: thought, feeling, sensation, and intuition. His most famous concept is that people are basically introverted or extroverted in their behaviors. The extrovert has an external orientation, finding meaning outside self, in the surrounding world, whereas the introvert is introspective and finds it within.

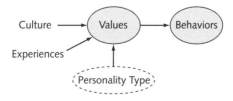

Jung believed that type preferences are inborn and not environmentally developed through interaction with family, culture, and other external influences.

Many years later, this theory of personality pattern was extended by Katharine Briggs and Isabel Briggs Myers, whose renowned work on the Myers-Briggs Type Indicators (MBTI) divided these basic patterns into sixteen types of people (Briggs and Myers, 1957). This work ignited great interest from all communities, and by the mid-1980s, over 1.5 million people had taken the MBTI. Since that time, MBTI and psychological typing have been applied to business, counseling, negotiations, matchmaking, diversity training, and team-building processes. On the surface, the subject appears almost too generalized, fitting the total human population into four main behavioral categories and sixteen subtypes. Nevertheless, these types have proven to be highly effective, being validated over many generations.

In his book *Please Understand Me II* (1984), David Keirsey discusses these different personality styles in sixteen temperament types within four basic temperaments. Keirsey's four main temperament types are Idealist, Guardian, Rational, and Artisan (Table 9.1). These types expanded the concepts of MBTI into a much broader and deeper view of temperament types. Keirsey believed each type has a unique behavioral predisposition in terms of values, orientation, interests, language, social role, leadership style, and vocational interests. Each type is distinct in how it learns, processes information, interacts with their external environment, commu-

Table 9.1
Team Player Styles by Temperament Types

Idealist ("Let's all work together")	Guardian ("Let's get the job done")	Rational ("Let's achieve our goals")	Artisan ("Let's go for it")
• Thoughtful	• Cooperative	• Analytical	• Persuasive
• Insightful	• Compliant	• Systematic	• Fun-loving
• Sensitive	• Well organized	• Strategic	• Risk taker
• Selfless	• Administrative	• Logical	• Performer
• Caring	• Strong work ethic	• Scientific	• Sensual
• Sympathetic	• Security minded	• Inquiring	• Artistic
		• Competent	• Adaptable

nicates, and works with others. (You can determine your temperament type by using the descriptions in the following pages or by taking various self-assessments that are available for free on the Internet. Search "personality type.")

In this book, I demonstrate how Keirsey's concepts of the four temperament types can be applied to a project team and how interpersonal styles affect teamwork. Not all people fit neatly into one type, although many have a predominant temperament type. People have natural tendencies in how they think, communicate, and interact with others. They have natural preferences in how they like to work and how they wish to be treated. Having characteristics in two different types is not uncommon, but most people should fit fairly well into one of the four types.

Characterizing people by their cultures, generations, or personality types runs the danger of stereotyping, discriminating, profiling, or even disrespecting people as individuals. Putting people in buckets for the sake of generalizing personality differences and similarities can have unintended effects of perpetuating biases and prejudices. Such generalizations are wrong when done to cause harm, exclusion, and discrimination. However, when generalizations are used to increase awareness and positive understanding of others, then we are honoring and respecting differences. Such insights into personality types, generations, and culture build greater understanding and acceptance of others and bring out the best in ourselves.

Besides the benefits of recognizing differences, people also take great comfort in knowing that there are others who struggle with the same things that they struggle with and who possess similar values and personality styles. Knowing that you are not alone can be a huge uplift for many people. Diversity is about valuing differences, but it is also about taking pride in self and recognizing rich commonalities shared with others.

All temperament types have strengths and weaknesses. Together, the four types offer tremendous advantages for a team. Since I will be using Keirsey's four basic temperaments (Idealist, Guardian, Rational, and Artisan) in the discussions ahead, knowing your predominant temperament type will help you get a deeper understanding of your personal behaviors. In this book, personality types and temperament types are used interchangeably.

The balance of this chapter discusses the human factors and team dynamics of each of the four temperament types, compares and contrasts the four types in a team setting, and discusses how to use these concepts to improve interpersonal behaviors. Each temperament type offers unique skills to a work team (Table 9.1). Rationals are planners, analysts, strategic thinkers, and achievers. They possess a strong drive to be exact and correct in everything they do. They are more goal oriented than people oriented and like to move efficiently and logically. Rationals are assertive, enduring, creative, scholastic, and highly dedicated. They judge themselves by their achievements, successes, subject matter expertise, and mastery. They are lifetime learners and prefer technical fields such as computer sciences, chemistry, physics, biology, engineering, and math.

Idealists are collaborators, relationship builders, and team players. They are simply nice people: thoughtful, kind, friendly, polite, sensitive, and sympathetic. In teams, they will do whatever it takes to avoid conflict. They are more relationship oriented than task oriented. They want to work with others and maintain positive relationships. Idealists are romantics who think with their hearts and want to be loved and admired by others: they judge themselves through the eyes of others. They are attracted by counseling, education, sociology, human resources, and health sciences.

Artisans are spontaneous, expressive, active, creative, and stimulating. They are attention getters who express to impress. They love freedom, are truly uninhibited, and provide spirit and fun to a team. They are great tactical thinkers. Artisans are not shy: they freely say what they think and feel. They are focused on everything that matters to them at the moment, which means they are highly observant, reactive, and spontaneous. They are performers who judge themselves by the impact they make on others. Artisans are athletes, artists, actors, marketers, and performers.

Guardians are reliable, trustworthy, accountable, responsible, and tireless implementers. They like to get the job done—on time and every time. They are more process focused than people focused and highly valued by others for their hard work, loyalty, and commitment. Guardians are doers. They are well organized, tidy, thorough, and unassuming. They judge themselves through the value and quality of their work. When duty calls, Guardians step up and tackle the work. They tend to work in government, institutions, corporations, schools, military, law enforcement, and business.

No style is more suitable for project management than others, although certain styles favor certain types of projects. For example, projects that involve team building, interpersonal relationships, or cross-functional collaborations are favored by Idealists, and highly technical, strategic projects have stronger appeal to Rationals.

Other than asking the person or using a skilled professional, there are no foolproof ways of determining a person's type. However, here are some classic characteristics that may help in distinguishing one type from another (Table 9.2). These

Table 9.2
Temperament Type Profiles

Idealists	Guardians	Rationals	Artisans
1. Preferred field: Humanities	1. Preferred Field: Commerce, institutions	1. Preferred field: Science and technology	1. Preferred field: Marketing, performing arts
2. Friendly, warm, reserved	2. Proper, neat appearance	2. Analytical in speech and thought, hard to read, cool, not emotional, may not be quick to respond	2. Engaging, active talker; speaks freely, very open
3. Sensitive to others, empathetic	3. Always well prepared and on time	3. Efficient in speech, does not speak out unless comments will add value	3. Colorful in words, dress, and speech
4. Inclusive behaviors	4. Not good with small talk but attentive	4. Witty; good sense of humor; may make sarcastic remarks	4. Excitable, high energy, fast
5. Shows feeling gestures and uses feeling words	5. Speaks concisely and properly	5. Skeptical and critical at times	5. May appear self-centered or selfish
6. Waits for cues (approval) from others before responding or speaking	6. Conservative, traditional views; reserved	6. Enjoys a good debate or weighty discussion	6. Multitasks easily
7. Shows concern for others, apologizes readily	7. Organized and cooperative	7. Busy thinking; may not be a good listener	7. Persuasive and may exaggerate things
8. Prefers to stay in the background	8. Respectful of rank and authority	8. Does not show or seek feelings of others	8. Very personable, lively
9. Good listener and conversationalist	9. Wants to fit in	9. Enjoys speaking of achievements or mastering things	9. Rapid speaker, animated, quickly changes subjects in conversation
10. Time orientation: Future	10. Time orientation: Past	10. Time orientation: None	10. Time orientation: At this moment

profiles are not 100 percent reliable but can serve as a basic guideline. Here are key questions to help identify the four personality types:

- What are your personal work values?
- What are your interpersonal strengths and weaknesses?
- How do you like to be treated at work?
- What team behaviors do you like and dislike?
- What motivates you? What demotivates you?
- How do you cope with interpersonal conflicts?
- How do you make important decisions?

The composites of these answers can be matched to one of the four types. For example, someone who is logical, systematic, linear, and objective in their thinking; likes to research issues, master techniques, and do problem solving; and enjoys the sciences is likely a Rational temperament type.

Rationals

Rationals like efficiency, analysis, productivity, and technical integrity. Things have to be done right, which to them means logical, supported by facts, and thoroughly analyzed.

Behaviors of Rationals on Teams   This temperament type performs especially well on technical projects. Rationals are powerful thinkers who enjoy debating issues because they process information and draw conclusions through analysis and discussion. Unfortunately, this can be quite a dissertation and taxing to others, but Rationals need to validate their own thinking through discussions, a way of testing themselves. This process enables them to feel better about where they are on issues and reaffirm that their thinking is correct. Sometimes they resort to argumentation to buttress their position on issues, which other team members may view as aggression, a power behavior to win over others with their strong opinions, and a desire to be right. Rationals constantly look for flaws in the system and make corrections. They will even correct people in midsentence when they spot a mistake. This behavior makes them feel valuable by keeping things accurate; however, it can also make others feel belittled. Rationals are known to shoot a messenger now and then, though that is rarely their intent.

Rationals may appear competitive and aggressive. They come across as unfeeling, defensive, and dominating on teams if their positions are challenged, but more often than not, their defensiveness is grounded in their basic fear of failure. An argumentative behavior by a Rational is usually a sign of insecurity, worry, or concern about their thinking. Rationals want to get it right in their minds in order to move forward with the team. Taken to extremes, Rationals may double- and triple-check things just to make sure they are right. On teams, Rationals may even hoard information to gain proprietary knowledge, a protective behavior for them. Also, letting go of an unsolved problem may be a challenge to them.

At times, Rationals may appear cold and arrogant. That is because they are preoccupied by their own internal thinking processes. They are constantly processing and testing what they hear and see and are often too withdrawn in their thinking to be effective listeners. They are so busy thinking that they can lose touch with others.

Rationals are competitive and hate to lose. This can-do attitude gives the team great energy and willpower. Those who do not like competition and this innate drive to win may be turned off. Also, people have a hard time quelling Rationals, who are committed to winning. Their drive and intellect make them great problem solvers.

In project teams, Rationals do well as project leaders and analysts. They enjoy planning, strategy, and analytical tasks. They have great initiative. Rationals are strategists by nature and can help the team see the big picture: where the team is headed and why, and how things fit together. They know how to connect information.

Nontechnical, administrative, detailed work should never be assigned to a Rational, who will view it as mundane and contrary to their strategic mind-set. They excel in defining objectives, strategies, and goals and show great leadership in getting new ideas on the table and things off the ground. Rationals do not like to get into picky details. Thus, they are not always good in detailing work plans. It does not mean, however, that they are not detailed in their work. Rationals can be exhaustingly detailed when it comes to proving their case.

Independence is an emotional need for Rationals. They hate to be micromanaged. Sending them reminders or checking on their work is an insult to them. If you want to get under their skin, start looking over their shoulders and give them lots of constructive feedback. If they think their independence or competency is being undermined, they become defensive quickly.

Finally, many Rationals may be quiet and reserved in meetings and social gatherings. Small talk, which they find unproductive and meaningless, is not a strong suit for them.

How Best to Work with Rationals on Teams   Rationals are highly valued for their sharp thinking, natural planning skills, problem-solving abilities, strong initiative, and strategic vision. They help teams see the big picture and are committed to success. Rationals are highly creative, witty, and fast learners. They always rise to the challenge. Many are technically skilled, can build a work plan effortlessly, and turn out tremendous volumes of work. They are ultimate achievers, competing with themselves as much as with others. Their sheer mental strength enables them to conquer tough, complex problems. When pushed, though, their mental toughness can quickly shift into cold aggression.

Rationals appreciate others who are well focused, logical, and hard working to meet the team's objectives. They are motivated by the challenge of the subject. They are very goal driven, sometimes at the expense of others. Their internal drive and fast pace of thinking prevent them from waiting for others to catch on. They think fast but not often out loud, so a Rational may take great leaps forward in conversations or jump to the punch line without providing much train of thought. Rationals assume that people can make connections as fast as they do. Thus, patience and transparency are challenges for them. If you find yourself lost with a Rational, the best response is to acknowledge their good points and then ask them to share their thinking behind it: "I really like your thinking here. Please share with us how you got from point A to point B." You need to acknowledge first; otherwise, the Rational may feel you are questioning his or her thinking and be defensive. Another technique is to echo back the points and ask if you interpreted his or her thinking correctly. Echoing back is validating and respectful to a Rational. When all else fails, just say, "You're right." Sometimes that is all the Rational is looking for. As one Rational used to tell me, "I don't want to be right; I want to be perfect!"

In addition to speed and efficiency, Rationals like to do research, create options, analyze options, and arrive at a logical decision. They believe they can solve anything if they just think long and hard enough. Think along with them, and they will love you. There is nothing more accepting to a Rational than a respectful, thinking partner. Although it may not be apparent due to their aggressiveness, Rationals will change their positions if logic dictates.

Rationals need to be appreciated for their good thinking and recognized for their achievement. Although they are achievers and want things to be right, they feel most valued when their ideas are accepted by the team. This acceptance means their thinking was right. Rationals feel best when they feel right.

Success is the ultimate motivator for the Rational. Failure is not in their vocabulary. They abhor whiners and "can't do it" types. They think it is okay to be pessimistic, but only in a constructive, open-minded, and problem-solving manner. It works best to pose problems as challenges and not failures to Rationals. Rationals will not accept failures until they can rationalize them in their own minds. They have been known to rationalize mistakes incessantly. This overanalysis may not make others feel any better, but it is an emotional requirement for Rationals. It is almost like therapy. Rationals mourn mistakes and do not let things go very easily. So when you work with them on a team, make sure you allow time for this. For example, if something fails, Rationals will analyze the events that led to the failure. They are not looking for blame, just explanations. This retrospective analysis is a way of understanding why something did not work. In contrast, Guardians do not like to dwell on something that did not get done, and Artisans are focused on the here and now, not the past. Inside, Guardians and Artisans are screaming at Rationals to "let it go!" Artisans let things go very easily; they do not see the sense in mourning and cannot relate to this behavior at all. Nevertheless, Rationals need to mourn in order to move forward. For Rationals, hard work deserves a reward, and when that effort goes unrewarded, a Rational feels robbed.

Because Rationals like to think through problems and fear failure, they may be slow in making decisions. Not only do they want to analyze the situation, they also want to keep their options open in case something changes. Idealists are like Rationals in wanting time to think.

How do you turn a Rational around? Avoid treating Rationals emotionally by saying, for example, "You look pretty upset. Why don't you just try to calm down?" It is better to get on their analytical side than their emotional side. However, when Rationals get too much into their analytical mode to the detriment of the team, do not dismiss it. Help them think their way out of it. This will expedite the process and help the Rational.

Summary of How to Work with Rationals

- Be logical.
- Think along with them.

- Respect their ideas and initiative.

- Acknowledge them for their forward thinking and creativity.

- Give them independence.

- Do not micromanage their work.

- Never make them feel stupid or tell them they are wrong.

- Accept their need for analysis, planning, and challenging the status quo.

Idealists

Idealists value honesty, integrity, cooperation, harmony, and team cohesion. They are compassionate, caring, sensitive, and loyal.

Behaviors of Idealists on Teams   Idealists are natural team players and go to great lengths to please others in their interactions. They enjoy working with people and teams and are motivated by the behaviors of others. They are sensitive to people's feelings and disdain any personal attacks. They enjoy team cooperation and camaraderie and believe in team spirit and the ideals of achieving success together. Unlike Rationals, Idealists are not afraid to show their feelings. They may not always say it in words, but they will show it in their body language. They feel for others and want others to like them. They readily volunteer for assignments to demonstrate their willingness to give to others. In return, they hope to gain acceptance. The sooner an Idealist feels accepted, the better the Idealist feels about himself and will work productively. Being given an assignment on the team is a compliment to the Idealist: it shows respect, acceptance, and trust.

Idealists are good facilitators, observers, and listeners. They are keen to the feelings of others and will go along with the team as long as their values are not violated. Although they are very tolerant of others, frustrations can accumulate over time, and that energy can vent suddenly in the form of emotional anger. In other words, Idealists can carry a long fuse but eventually may explode emotionally.

Daniel, an engineer with a large cereal company in the Midwest, is a longtime friend and a classic Idealist. He is thoughtful, kind, sympathetic, knowledgeable, polite, honest, and humorous. He enjoys working on teams and gets along with everyone. But on occasion, Daniel can explode with anger over what appeared to be a mild event. For example, once he received an e-mail, sent to several people, that had a hint of criticism that he was being unresponsive to a customer. Immediately Daniel fired off a blistering reply. The e-mail itself was not the trigger. For Daniel, it was the last in a string of mounting pressures at home and work. Idealists like Daniel see themselves in this situation as victims, unfairly singled out and picked on. The injustice is hurtful to them, and they respond in kind. They may harbor bad feelings about people or emotional events for a long time. What is ironic is that everyone saw Daniel's response as uncharacteristic behavior, when in fact it was very characteristic of his makeup.

Idealists are often perceived as quiet, timid, and passive. Their behaviors are gentle, cooperative, and polite. Their nature is to let others go first, and they wait for permission to speak. This helps them avoid being out of step with the team and gives them an understanding of where their thoughts fit in or do not fit in. Being in step with the team is important to an Idealist. Presenting contrary views is difficult because of their inherent fear of conflict and not being viewed as a team player.

Their sensitivity to others is both a strength and weakness. Idealists feel a strong sense of trust and loyalty to the team. However, when that trust or loyalty is broken, Idealists take it painfully to heart. They believe that people are basically good and do not intentionally hurt others. Having that belief in people is wonderful, but it can result in many disappointments when those standards are not met. Emotions have a way of grabbing Idealists and not letting go. Idealists internalize, personalize, and mourn bad relationships. They are concerned about how other team members perceive them and want to repair any hints of a bad relationship. They want positive interactions and will even romanticize relationships.

How Best to Work with Idealists on Teams   Although Idealists may appear passive, they are listening, thinking, and processing information as much as anyone else on the team. Do not let their quietness fool you. They are mentally engaged, giving careful consideration to the content and dynamics of the discussion. Good teams learn to seek input from Idealists in a way that is caring and supportive. Idealists are less likely to contribute if they feel intimidated. Moreover, they avoid making decisions when pressured to take sides. An ultimatum is a nightmare for Idealists. The best course is to be patient and give them the time to think it through in their own way. Because Idealists want to avoid conflicts, decision making can be a struggle for them.

Idealists, in their drive to please others, are prone to overcommit to assignments and completion dates. Their "No, you go ahead first" attitude can slow a team's progress and may result in delays, missed deadlines, and procrastination. Where Rationals want to win, Idealists do not want any losers, including themselves. Not wanting any losers makes Idealists indecisive, preferring to avoid conflict over delivering bad news to someone. They want to be objective in their judgments yet not hurt anyone in the process. At times they hope for some outside force (an event or a higher authority) to help make the decision for them. Teams can help Idealists by guiding them through the decision and presenting options that are not win-lose propositions.

Idealists are motivated by the significance of a project. The team needs to show the importance of the cause, highlighting the potential benefits of the project. Idealists want to be appreciated for who they are and the ideas they contribute to the team. Being given team responsibilities means a lot to an Idealist, because it represents trust, respect, and honor. But carelessly dumping work on an Idealist is not motivating.

To Idealists, face-to-face team discussions may create potential conflicts, but they are also opportunities to strengthen relationships. Open and honest dialogue fulfills their need for team unity. In contrast, Rationals see team discussions as a forum to sharpen their thinking, and Artisans perceive team gatherings as a chance to make things happen. While Rationals fear saying something stupid, Idealists fear saying something false. This may lead to waffling behaviors or "I better check on it" type of remarks.

They appreciate praise, but public praise may embarrass them. They are concerned that such a display would appear selfish, self-centered, and arrogant. They do not want others to think that they are better than them. Idealists appreciate team achievements over individual successes.

Summary of How to Work with Idealists

- Be flexible.
- Be patient.
- Be collaborative.
- Be honest and open with them.
- Give them constructive, not hurtful, criticism.
- Be careful; they will take things personally very easily. They are prone to play the victim role.
- Be open-minded.
- Take time to listen and talk.

Guardians

Guardians value compliance, hard work, organization, respect, and punctuality. They have a natural drive to get the job done every time. Guardians are systematic, highly focused, cooperative, and loyal to others and their organization.

Behaviors of Guardians on Teams   If there is one word that best describes a Guardian, it is dependable. Guardians complete their action items, meet their goals, and follow all the rules and policies along the way. They play by the book and expect others to do the same.

Guardians are realists. They keep the team grounded in practical terms and views. They are optimists as long as the plan and pathway are clear. A team of Guardians will always get the job done but may lack the dynamism, creativity, and strategic thinking of Artisans, Rationals, or Idealists.

Guardians are consummate team players, first to volunteer for actions and always willing to give up their lunch hour to help their team succeed. In exchange, they want appreciation for their efforts. Guardians believe in everyone doing their fair share and contributing equally, especially in routine work. Their soul is in their work, whether at the office or at home. Guardians are dutiful to their work and less inclined to look too far ahead. Duty is clear and concrete, while planning is an exercise in wishful thinking. Guardians have high expectations of themselves and others. They believe there is a right way and a wrong way to do things. Taking short-cuts or letting things get disorganized is unacceptable.

Guardians can be insecure about their abilities and self-worth and require frequent validation through their work. Part of this trait is due to their strong desire to fit in, be accepted by others, feel secure, and have a sense of belonging to an effort. They have a need to be needed. They will work hard out of instinct, but they also like to be pampered and occasionally reward themselves for meeting goals. They work hard yet will gladly accept help from others as long as the work is done competently. Otherwise they will readily step in to make it right.

Change is a threat to Guardians. Rapid, unstructured change is disruptive because it creates instability, disorganization, and waste. Like Rationals, Guardians favor efficiency, brevity, and meeting deadlines. Guardians get easily frustrated by roadblocks, and they expect those in authority to remove those hindrances. Change impedes their progress. However, they accept change when it is well planned and well communicated. This trait makes Guardians more conservative and cautious than the other personality types. Their speech is less colorful than that of Artisans, less creative than that of Rationals, and more practical than that of Idealists. Most of all, they respect authority. Idealists and Guardians fear public criticism and potential diminution of their character, whereas Rationals and Artisans welcome new thinking, new ideas, new perspectives, and debate.

Guardians prefer task-oriented assignments over long-term, strategically based projects. They are motivated by praise, respect, and recognition of their work. They enjoy public acknowledgment, promotions, rewards, ceremony, and tangible awards. However, they may view trinkets as demeaning. It would be seen as a reflection of their value. Guardians are demotivated by inequalities, unproductive meetings, unstructured processes, disorganization, lack of tangible direction and results, and lack of success. Being unfairly criticized is highly offensive and hurtful to them. Similar to Idealists, Guardians dislike confrontation, personal conflicts, and disharmony among team members. They are concerned about others and want to help people but are less expressive than Idealists about it.

How Best to Work with Guardians on Teams   In unfamiliar surroundings, Guardians are reserved and cautious, especially when working with new people. They want the security of knowing whom they are dealing with and where they are headed. They feel more comfortable when they have clarity and certainty in their endeavors. To help them get comfortable, team members should make them feel welcome and spend time at the outset to thoroughly explain the project.

Guardians seek respect and appreciation for their work. They want to be kept apprised and participate in team decisions. They want to be respected and treated fairly at all times. It would be helpful to have clearly defined roles and responsibilities and ground rules for team meetings. They like meetings that are well organized and productive. Prework is definitely preferred over not being prepared. Guardians do not like ambiguity, preferring to see clear plans, rules, and pathways. It is difficult to follow and enforce rules if they are ambiguous. In a way, they are traditional in their work ethic and values.

Guardians hold themselves accountable and in turn want to work with others who take personal accountability for their work and responsibilities. They expect others to keep their promises and do what they agreed to do. Guardians like to see things completed with no sudden changes. If change is needed, they prefer having a compelling business case and a revised plan. Punctuality is important to them. They view someone who shows up late or unprepared as disrespectful and irresponsible. Unlike Idealists who may procrastinate, Guardians are appalled by procrastination.

Sources of frustration for Guardians are excessive analysis, slow decision making, lack of clear direction, and work delays. This can be mitigated by keeping them informed of any changes that can affect their work. Guardians suffer most when they feel left out and misinformed.

Summary of How to Work with Guardians

- Be trustworthy and honest.
- Be punctual and direct.
- Appreciate their hard work and dependability.
- Meet deadlines.
- Communicate, and tell them what is going on.
- Do your fair share of work.
- Be loyal to the team.
- Stay the course.

Artisans

Artisans value speed, creativity, and variety. They are energetic, enthusiastic, and creative.

Behaviors of Artisans on Teams   Artisans bring fun to a team. They seek stimulation and high impact. Artisans want to be thrilled, which means they love action. This does not necessarily mean physical action; mental activities work well too. Slow, methodical team processes will drive Artisans away. They see detailed work as boring and wasteful.

Artisans are at their best when strategizing new ideas, making presentations, and exploring new ways to operate. Like Rationals, they are broad, independent thinkers but in a faster tactical way. They have tremendous ingenuity and imagination, which enables them to see things in a different light. They can multitask and synthesize very quickly.

Compared to the other personality types, Artisans are the most transparent in their thinking. They readily express their opinions, feelings, and perceptions. At times, they may be too honest, judgmental, and open about how they feel and may appear insensitive to the feelings of others. Their transparency makes them fun to work with, and they establish relationships quickly. Their natural excitement is a source of great energy and spontaneity for the team. They are truly free spirits.

As with Rationals, their strength is in their independence. Rationals are great independent thinkers, but Artisans are great independent actors. They act and keep moving. Artisans work in real time since the past and future are not within their control. They move with great speed and efficiency. Unfortunately, not everyone can keep up with Artisans, who can switch gears from moment to moment. If you do not like their mood, just wait five minutes, and they will change. Sometimes they appear to be in constant motion, going from topic to topic and moving from activity to activity with little hesitation. They have tremendous energy and resolve. Artisans enjoy taking adventures and have an uncanny ability to persuade others to join them. Even Guardians, who are low risk takers, are likely to take risky adventures with Artisans and then go back for more. Artisans seem to fill a void in Guardians, but it is a double-edged sword. On project teams, Guardians have the most difficult time working with Artisans. Artisans do not share the same values as Guardians, who appreciate stability, punctuality, compliance, and organization. These traits are not as important to Artisans. Team rules and processes strangle Artisans. They believe these have a place but view them as artificial constraints. Artisans seek change in their world, and breaking down barriers is part of that. They wonder why a team would want to create more barriers, which seems foolish to them and a waste of time. Creating boundaries and rules are stifling. With such an attitude, Artisans are seen as rebels who want to disrupt order. Yet that is rarely their intent. What they want is change, which is inherently exciting and challenging to them, as well as their own space to express their creativity. Team rules and processes are acceptable when they yield immediate benefits.

One unique trait for Artisans is their bold, fearless mind-set. They seem impervious to worries, concerns, and criticisms and insensitive to the concerns of others. While Rationals appear insensitive because they show little emotion or expression, Artisans are insensitive for the opposite reasons: they are too expressive and emotional. They may talk over others, interrupt, argue, shift rapidly to new subjects, dominate discussions, and ignore what others are saying.

Artisans are risk takers and believe that you have to be willing to risk failure to succeed. To score big, you have to take big risks, and the Artisan is willing to take those risks. Artisans fear inaction and lost opportunities. Rationals are not risk takers because they fear failure and tend to agonize over their mistakes. Artisans do not mourn their mistakes. Failure gives them the opportunity to move to the next event. Life is one ride after another.

Rationals love independence; Artisans love freedom. Rationals and Artisans are change agents. Idealists and Guardians are change implementers. Rationals are idea initiators, whereas Artisans are more self-indulgent.

Artisans are colorful speakers, choosing descriptive words and resonant speech tones. They seem to use all their modalities of speech when they talk: mimicking sounds, gesturing with their hands, using facial expressions, and acting out events. They are prone to exaggerate their stories, not so much to sell an idea but to share their personal excitement with others. Sometimes they distort the truth. Nevertheless, their intent is not to lie or mislead others as much as to share the excitement of what they see and feel.

Artisans enjoy the thrill of the hunt more than the thrill of the kill. The bigger and the more challenging the hunt is, the greater the motivation is for them. That is because it requires greater demand on wit, creativity, cleverness, and finesse. Pulling it off is a great thrill for Artisans. While Idealists may procrastinate out of indecisiveness, Artisans naturally procrastinate for the thrill of just making the deadline. Therefore, they deliberately push the edge of the envelope to heighten reality to the richest level.

Rationals may appear arrogant because of their internal thinking processes. Artisans may seem arrogant because of their behaviors to live in the moment despite everything else that may be going on around them.

My grandmother was an Artisan and one of the most generous and fun-loving souls I have ever met. Her stories were poetic verses, filled with rhyme, fantasy, and magic. Her speech had a natural rhythm and melodic tone that drew others to her. She was the center of attention in the family. She enjoyed a good party and loved bringing gifts. Like many other Artisans, she was unforgettable. Her advice to me was to "always remember that a bad impression is better than no impression at all."

How Best to Work with Artisans on Teams   Artisans live to be the center of attention and seek immediate gratification. This does not mean they want the glory while others do all the work. When stimulated, Artisans are highly dedicated and tireless workers who thrive on challenge. They can apply tremendous focus and staying power. Similar to Idealists, Artisans need relevance. Where they differ is that Artisans want to act out their ideas and have a personal impact on others, while Idealists want other people to be affected by their ideas. Rationals and Artisans are excellent change agents, while Idealists and Guardians are change implementers and processors. As with Rationals, Artisans need independence and speed. Rationals need independent thinking, while Artisans need independent action. Artisans want to perform their own actions. They take pride in the action itself, while Rationals take pride in their thinking behind the action.

Artisans are great at multitasking, juggling priorities, and choosing among options. They are able to work quickly and make fast decisions. When you need something done right away or need spontaneity, look to an Artisan. Artisans are great tactical performers. They enjoy spur-of-the-moment things and need immediate gratification, so try to engage them when their interest level is high. Artisans want to see things play out. If you impede their progress, they will cleverly work around you. It is not so much working behind your back as much as their need to get what they want first. This great drive for instant gratification is a strength of Artisans and provides good energy for the team. The team's role may be to help the Artisan channel that energy productively. Idealists and Guardians give Artisans great comfort because they protect and look after them when they lose focus or move too rapidly.

Artisans may appear self-absorbed and indulgent. Their transparency makes them emotional and therefore destabilizing at times. An Artisan can become negative very quickly and very resentful and destructive if crossed by the team. Artisans do not work well on the sidelines. They need a stage to perform on, and denying them that opportunity would be a loss.

If you have the good fortune to have an Artisan on your team, do not see this personality as disruptive but as someone who is full of life and ideas. They are wonderfully opportunistic, providing a source of great spirit and creativity for the team.

Artisans are wizards in making presentations and persuading others. They are typically skilled in putting individual pieces together quickly and presenting an exciting and compelling story. Guardians can help ground the Artisan in proper procedures, and Rationals can make sure the information is accurate and logical. Idealists can help ensure that the presentation will connect with the audience and will be in line with the values of the organization.

Summary of How to Work with Artisans

- Respect their ideas and risk-taking behaviors.

- Speak quickly and directly.

- Recognize that they hate boredom and routine work.

- Help them stay focused and on task.
- Give them action and high-impact activities.
- Accept their tendencies to be disorganized and undisciplined in their approach.
- Let them do their thing. Do not try to do it for them.
- Have fun.

Overview of the Types

Figure 9.2 maps out the major differences and similarities of the four personality types when working in a team environment. Idealists and Guardians are more collaborative and passive than Rationals and Artisans. Guardians and Artisans demonstrate good tactical skills and are action driven in their behaviors. But because they are action oriented, they are prone to exhibit impatience. With Rationals and Artisans, independence is a strong need, and they exhibit aggressive behaviors when they are stressed. These two personality types are creative thinkers and think beyond the next step. High-level strategic thinking is a common trait for Rationals

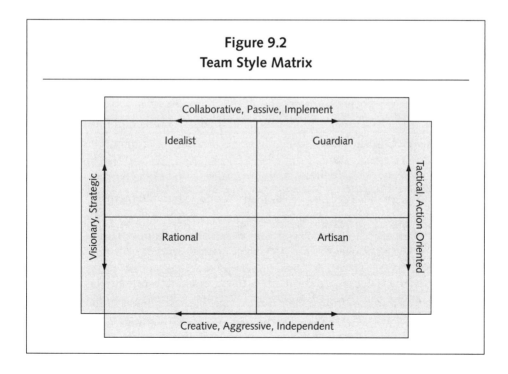

Figure 9.2
Team Style Matrix

and Idealists. What they lack in detail may be made up in their abilities to see the broader picture in terms of content for Rationals and relationships for Idealists.

PERSONAL VALUES VERSUS ORGANIZATIONAL VALUES

Our values are rooted in our personal culture, experiences, and personality type. Values are deeply hidden in personal space and represent individual diversity. In project teams, these human factors have a profound effect on the interactions among team members and team space. But how do individual values relate to organizational space?

From our values, we have personal expectations and desires. We are inspired when we feel our desires are attainable and supported by organizational and team space. For example, we may believe that hard work will lead to a promotion. For us to feel motivated and inspired, that belief needs to be reinforced by organizational space.

Our values are not isolated; they are subject to continued modifications and challenges from the environment. When our values are compatible with our surroundings, we are generally happy and stress free. We feel good when the behaviors of people around us are consistent with our beliefs. We tend to like people who say and do things that match what we believe in. Our values are tested by the values of our organization and project teams, however. In reality, our work environment represents the greatest challenge to our personal values. When we join a company, we are expected to accept the values of the organization. Company values are rooted in its history and institutional memory. Long-standing companies have deeply embedded values, which have been honed over many years of managing a business. There are three ways to identify your company's values:

- The company's vision, mission, objectives, and value statements
- The company's policies and key decisions
- The behaviors of managers and peers

The company's vision, mission, objectives, and value statements are usually clearly written and communicated in most companies. These statements offer a glimpse to the company's beliefs and values. But it is not always the case that the values are in fact demonstrated in the actions of the company.

In organizations, actions are manifested in two ways: the corporate policies and key decisions made over time and how well these values are practiced and reinforced in the behaviors of management, supervisor, and peers. Policies can be written to say all the right things, but behaviors are the true policies of an organization. The values stated may not be what is actually practiced. For example, an employee may feel pressured to give up family time to work weekends because of peer pressure from her team or company. When a boss sends out e-mails on weekends to the staff, what value message does that send? When a manager shades the truth to make a sale, what value statement is being made? When companies harm the environment to save on costs, how does that affect your values and motivation? Sometimes there may be a perception that employees are expected to compromise their values in return for employment. Some employees may experience a disparity between their values and the company's values. If a person's values are not in strong alignment with those of the company, then conflicts will occur. We have witnessed a number of these disconnects in many well-publicized companies that have crashed under their weight of deceit, greed, and dishonesty. A company is always at risk for a few unscrupulous employees, but the risk is also dependent on how well the management system rewards the right behaviors and disciplines employees who do not meet the values of the organization. For example, if a company's reward system is based on how many deals its employees can make, the company is valuing quantity over quality. A poor deal is considered as good as a great deal. Worse, a dishonest deal can count as much as an honest deal. Thus, having stated values alone does not create a values-based organization. These values must be demonstrated in actions; otherwise, they are just words on a page.

When it comes to organizational values, we may listen and understand, but we will not internalize them unless they meet our individual values and human factors. When there is good alignment between our own values and those of our organization, we feel at ease at work. Our behaviors at work would be similar to what they are at home. Do you show yourself at work, or do you hide? I am proud of my cultural heritage, and I would have difficulty working for an organization that did not make me feel comfortable showing my culture. I once had a manager who made fun of my Chinese lunches that I heated up in the microwave at work. He would say in the lunch room in front of others, "What's that awful smell?" or "What's that weird stuff you're eating?" I stopped bringing in Chinese food. His remark changed my behavior. It was not that the company supported that behavior, but it is what the company did not do: it did not select and train managers to be culturally aware and sensitive, and it did not communicate the values of respecting cultural differences in the workplace. The company may extol the values of diversity and even have a policy of respecting diversity, but the company's actions did not support it.

When company values do not match your values, you may be forced to change your behaviors. This modification of behavior may or may not be acceptable to you. Some people can readily adopt new behaviors. However, when behavioral modifications are made at the expense of your core values, those you believe in deeply, you will likely pay an emotional price. You may feel stressed at work, anger easily at work and at home, or work less diligently.

How real are your employer's values to you? How consistent are the company's policies, decisions, and daily actions? Do the behaviors match the content? Has the company translated its values into behaviors that you can see and describe? If the answer is yes, your company has done an effective job of living its values.

Other questions can be used to test the strength of your company's values:

- Is your company's commitment and actions to cultural diversity apparent to you?

- Are your company values explicitly stated when important company decisions are announced?

- Do you find yourself talking about the company's values to your spouse, family, and friends?

- Do you speak up in support of your company's values at work?

Inclusive organizations have a robust set of values, meaning that the values have a lasting connection with all employees. They value diversity, collaboration, teamwork, networking, development, and continuous learning. People feel valued, respected, challenged, and rewarded for their performance.

People who possess an inclusive attitude and behavior also have a broader set of values and are able to see beyond themselves. They have a talent for seeing different perspectives and are open to new and different ideas and people. They recognize that the best solutions are derived from deep pools of diverse thinking. Inclusive organizations breed inclusive behaviors, which broaden one's sphere of influence and opportunities for success. They provide training, consulting, counseling, and ombudsman resources that are intended to support their values.

It is helpful to periodically assess whether you feel your personal values are expanding or contracting. Cynicism, suspicion, and negativity can slowly creep into our view of the world. The lenses that we use to see the world can become clouded by mistrust, close-mindedness, and resistance to change. Most of these changes are derived from well-founded experiences and mistakes in our lives. Negative events in our lives have a lasting imprint on our personal values. We become risk averse and fear losing more than winning. It may be that as we grow older, the fear factor becomes greater and the benefits from taking risks diminish. As we become less tolerant of risk, perhaps we become less tolerant of change and other people as well. It is important to learn from our errors, but not to the point where it narrows our values. The years have a way of closing one's mind. Life already has its own limits. Why apply more? Cynicism narrows our ability to accept change. People's values may not change, but how they impose their values on others may change. People become more set in their ways and find it difficult to accept different views. Their circle of friends and colleagues become smaller over time. Their personal values may no longer overlap with those of their company or colleagues. Their values have contracted. This same concept applies to organizations whose values are behind the times. People leave these companies because their values no longer align to their organization.

Let us say you accept the gaps between your values and those of your organization. You may be partially satisfied and decide to stay. But your coping behaviors will affect your interactions with others. For example, some people avoid confrontation at all costs even if it means going against their personal values. This may occur when the boss makes a sarcastic sexual remark to you and you let it go because you fear losing your job or believe that group harmony is more important than a personal insult. Too often people trade off fear for pride. As a result, they repress their own values in preference of others. The better choice is to respect your values and develop your personal space. In later chapters, we discuss how to do this. (To learn more about how culture, experience, temperament types, and other human factors play out in real life, turn to the stories in Chapter Fifteen.)

SUMMARY

We need to understand people's expectations and give people hope and confidence that their expectations can be met or exceeded. After all, we all want the same things in life: to feel needed, valued, and fulfilled. Believing that those desires can come true is a powerful force that motivates and inspires all of us. Knowing what our desires are and how to fulfill those desires resides in our third space of human factors: personal space.

An important goal for all organizations is to value and promote diversity in the workplace. Achieving this goal requires not only a mutual understanding and acceptance of individual differences but a commitment to create an inclusive work environment. This is a daunting task given the multiple dimensions of diversity: ethnicity, age, gender, religious belief, education, personality type, skills, and other personal attributes. Creating a work environment where people feel valued and motivated is critical to the organization's success. Valuing individual diversity facilitates all the key elements of teamwork: communications, trust, transparency, accountability, decision making, learning, feedback, and recognition.

Individual diversity resides in personal space. This space contains our human factors, which consist of our core values and motivations, formed from the three basic sources of culture, life experience, and personality type.

First, we need to recognize that people come from different cultures in life, and each of those cultures has a unique language, customs, beliefs, foods, music, and other sociological factors. It is not unexpected to find that people of the same culture share similar behaviors and have a need to connect to each other. Second, people of specific generations demonstrate similar behaviors and beliefs that are derived from their shared life experiences. They may be geographically apart, but they are similarly affected by the events of their era, technological changes, and profound changes in their environment. Third, research has demonstrated that people are born with similar preferences or psychological typing.

David Keirsey identified four major temperament types: Rational, Idealist, Artisan, and Guardian. Each type shows a different behavioral pattern for learning, processing information, communicating, and interacting with their environment. No single type is better or worse for project management. Each type has special strengths and weaknesses. When these types are blended together on a team, the diversity of personalities generates greater creativity and higher-quality work than any one type can accomplish alone:

- Rationals provide competitive drive, logic, analytical skills, critical thinking, innovation, and initiative. They connect ideas, thoughts, and facts to form a strategic view and actions for a team.

- Idealists contribute patience, collaboration, thoughtfulness, sensitivity to people, intuition, and teamwork. They connect people and feelings to issues.
- Artisans generate energy, emotions, speed, actions, creativity, and fun. They help a team embrace change, see opportunities, take risks, and break paradigms.
- Guardians bring organization, processes, production, discipline, accuracy, and stability. They are able to successfully execute work plans and processes to meet team objectives.

Team Conflicts

Chapter Nine explored the key components of human factors and personal space. Human factors define who we are, what we believe in, and how we behave and interact with others. They determine how we act, perceive, and respond to our environment. Our individual set of human factors represents our diversity. We can tap this diversity to bring out the best in people or ignore them and lose this tremendous source of energy. Diversity can also create different points of views and conflicts which motivate a different set of human behaviors. As humans, we all want the same things from life: to feel needed, challenged, valued, and fulfilled. Yet because of our diversity, we seek those same things differently, and therein lies the potential for conflict.

Conflicts are unresolved disagreements between people or a threat of disruption to their lives. At one extreme, they can be physical conflicts between people, such as a fight, battle, or war. But in most cases, conflicts are mental disagreements with others. Conflicts cause people to behave differently. Both physical and mental conflicts have a strong emotional element attached to them. Conflict is a psychological state that takes people outside their behavioral norms, and it can be good or bad.

GOOD AND BAD CONFLICTS

Good conflicts are disagreements that are resolved in a positive manner and strengthen relationships, and bad conflicts are disagreements that produce negative behaviors and are destructive (Table 10.1). Constructive debate around different points of view is healthy. When team members question and challenge each other, these exchanges typically yield broader ideas, more creative options, and a better decision. For example, a team may disagree on their work strategies, but as long as people are open-minded, transparent, and willing to listen and compromise, a good team outcome is likely. Good conflicts do not generate negative behaviors among team members. The team reaches a mutually acceptable resolution with positive relationships and feelings. It is getting results and feeling good about them.

In contrast, bad conflicts are disagreements that are resolved in a negative way. Good team behaviors are not practiced. In fact, the interactions cause resentment and bad feelings among team members. Team members may talk over others, argue, stop participating, dominate others, speak negatively about each other, or walk away. Individually, conflicts may cause them to withdraw, lose sleep, or feel unappreciated. Win-lose confrontations are bad conflicts. When one party wins and the other party loses, the team suffers defeat rather than achievie agreement. Bad conflicts result in unsatisfactory outcomes, negative feelings, and weakened relationships among team members.

Table 10.1
Good and Bad Conflicts

Good Conflict	Bad Conflict
• Positive, constructive team behaviors are exhibited.	• Negative, destructive team behaviors are exhibited.
• Good team understanding.	• Poor team understanding.
• Team members are satisfied with the outcome.	• Not all team members are satisfied with the outcome.
• Relationships are strengthened among team members.	• Relationships are weakened among team members.

In good conflict, people take challenges constructively; in bad conflict, people take challenges personally and get defensive. Good conflicts are seen as opportunities to grow; bad conflicts are viewed as personal threats.

Two friends in a discussion over dinner can playfully disagree about who attended the better college, for example. They tease each other about the rivalry and poke fun at each other's alma mater. Both parties are having a good time, and they are both giving and taking. This playful banter is fun, congenial, and strengthens their friendship. They enjoy each other's company and behaviors. It is a good conflict—friendly behaviors with a positive outcome. But a bad conflict can occur between these same good friends if more personal negative behaviors are exhibited. Instead of talking about their colleges, they criticize each other's jobs or spouses, which creates negative tension. If this persists, tension can quickly become an emotional conflict. Anger, animosity, and retaliation may creep into the discussion.

The line between friendly disagreement and bad conflict is thin. What differentiates a good from a bad conflict is the shift to negative behaviors that harm their relationship. It may be that their friendship is resilient, and a bad encounter will be only a temporary setback. However, a team relationship may not be as strong, and a bad conflict can permanently diminish the relationship.

Figure 10.1 illustrates the continuum from friendly disagreement to tension and conflict and how bad conflicts are characterized by abnormal behaviors. Conflict

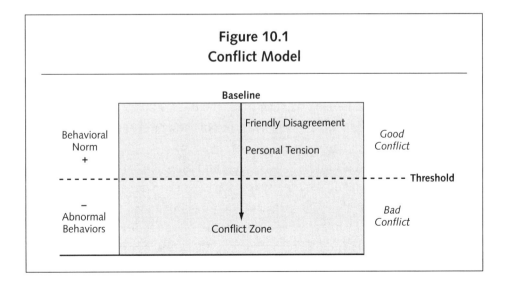

Figure 10.1
Conflict Model

Baseline

Behavioral Norm +

Friendly Disagreement

Personal Tension

Good Conflict

Threshold

– Abnormal Behaviors

Conflict Zone

Bad Conflict

drives people to a different behavioral state (lower box) and keeps them there until they find resolution or escape. It induces strong emotional feelings. They become self-centered, inflexible, stressed, impatient, insensitive, and close-minded. When people are in conflict, their behaviors can range from very aggressive to complete withdrawal in a fight-or-flight type of response.

Although there are good and bad conflicts, people prefer not to face conflict at all. They see it as a win-lose battle where the loser gets hurt and pays an emotional price. People can lose in many different ways: lose an argument, lose face, lose control, or lose a friend. The fear of losing is a powerful human factor. In fact, for most people, the fear of losing is a much greater force than the motivation for winning. Therefore, people hate conflicts. To cope with conflict, they fight or take flight. To better understand this human factor, we need to understand where conflicts come from.

Consider this story about a husband, Dan, and his wife, Abby, who lived in a quiet suburban neighborhood in New Jersey. Their neighbors, Rebecca and Chris, were pleasant people whom they had known for about three years. Their children went to school together, so it was natural that they visited once in a while. Dan noticed that his wife, Abby, had been visiting their neighbors quite often. She had been over there three times in the past two weeks, and when he asked her about it, she said she was just trading some recipes. This was a strange reply since Abby hated to cook.

The following week, Dan made a point of coming home early, and when he turned up the street, he noticed Abby and his neighbor, Chris, conversing by the side gate between their houses. When they spotted him approaching, they broke off abruptly, and Abby greeted Dan like nothing happened. When Dan asked Abby how Chris was doing, she answered, "Oh, nothing new, same old stuff." Dan noticed that she had a guilty look on her face, which fueled his concerns. His neighbor, Chris, was a good-looking younger man who did triathlons and kept in good shape. He also owned a company and had a certain smugness about him. Dan was not the jealous type, but he was suspicious that his wife was cheating on him. So instead of worrying about it, he took action and hired a work acquaintance to check out the situation and see if Abby was staying true to him.

The acquaintance followed his wife around for about a week. At the end of the week, he reported to Dan that he was not certain but he thought that Abby was seeing Chris on the sly and had seen them together at each other's houses while Dan and his neighbor's wife were both out.

Dan figured his suspicions were right. He thought, "How could I have let this happen?" and felt like a fool. He decided it was time to confront his wife. He was completely stressed out, angry, and afraid all at the same time. He promptly left for home after work and along the way rehearsed what he was going to say to his wife. When he arrived home, he found a note telling Dan to come over to the neighbor's house for some pizza. He was fuming now and thought, "Why doesn't she just move over there! That's enough!" Dan rushed over to his neighbor's house, and as he entered the side door, over thirty people burst into the room, shouting "Happy birthday, Dan!" It was the eve of Dan's thirtieth birthday, and Abby and her neighbor had plotted and prepared three weeks for a special surprise birthday for Dan. Dan was more surprised than anyone could imagine.

The moral of the story is to make sure you have a true conflict before you mistakenly create one in your mind. In fact, most conflicts are hidden, as this story illustrates. The stronger the perception is, the greater the reality of the conflict. It is unfortunate that so many conflicts arise from misunderstandings and misperceptions.

There were three sources of conflict in this story: a change conflict (losing his wife), values conflict (having an affair), and a behavioral conflict (animosity between Dan and his neighbor, Chris). These are the same conflicts that confront project teams as well.

CONFLICT OF CHANGE

Change conflicts tend to originate from organizational space. Changes may consist of policy changes, new requirements, reorganizations, new management, budget cuts, or a change in business plans. These changes may come suddenly, causing dramatic changes to a project, or they may consist of a series of small changes that cause a team to constantly adjust and adapt. Common changes in an organization are major work process changes, reorganization or restructuring, new ownership or management, technology changes, major events (such as mergers, acquisitions, new businesses, or competitive changes), or new projects and business opportunities. That these changes are usually outside the control of a team may add uncertainty and frustration to a team's work plans.

When people are confronted with the possibility of change, their responses may vary: they may see an opportunity for positive change, be curious to learn more, meet the possibility with skepticism and suspicion around the underlying reasons for the change, or be concerned over the potential personal impact.

People who are happy about change may be directly involved in the project and therefore have control. Also, they may not like their current state and welcome a change. For the latter, the pain of the current state is considered greater than the pain of change. They do not mind the risk of change.

Change is uncertain, and it is the fear of the unknown that frightens people. In the absence of information, people usually fill that void with worst-case scenarios and negative gossip. This behavior may be a defense mechanism of attempting to prepare themselves psychologically for possible disappointment. By assuming the worst case, they are actually giving themselves an upside and some headroom to hedge against a bad outcome. As long as these uncertainties of change exist, people will fall into fairly predictable patterns of behavior. To cope with change, they may initially deny the change, resist or avoid it, or assume the worst in the absence of information and respond with fear, worry, or anger. The severity of the response depends on the perceived impact of the change on the individual. The more personal and imminent the change is, the greater the individual will feel threatened. The greater the personal impact is, the greater the disruption will be on performance.

As Figure 10.2 illustrates, change challenges people's performance behaviors (for similar concepts, see Hiatt, 2006, and Kübler-Ross, 2005). An initial down cycle

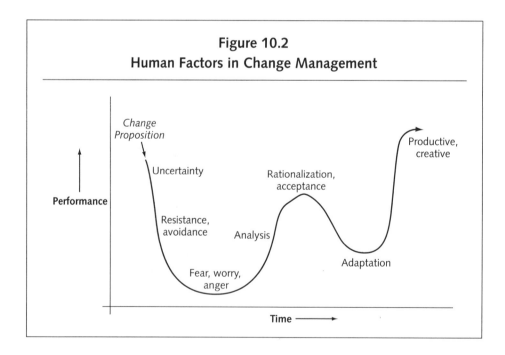

Figure 10.2
Human Factors in Change Management

is normal. Down cycles are characterized by negative behaviors. How deep and how long the down cycle persists depend on the intensity and extent of the negative behaviors. The job of the team leader is to recognize these human factors and work to minimize performance troughs in the change cycle. This is done by managing the human factors and behaviors that result in negative performance. Transparency and communications are keys. People want to know why the change is being initiated, why it is happening now, and whether they will have any control over the outcome. Understanding what is causing the change will help them gauge the seriousness of it. In other words, is the case for change real, perceived, weak, or strong? Can they control or influence this change? Often the need for change is precautionary or contingent on many other factors and future events. People may see some change propositions as red herrings.

The bad conflict from change is the threat of displacement from one's normal routine, future expectations, or function. In the status quo, people know what to expect and can plan for the future. In change conflict, people fear losing the status quo. Change represents a loss of control and creates a vacuum. One day everything is working well, and now the organization suddenly wants to change things. That is why people are resistant to change: it makes things unpredictable in a world that people struggle every day to control. People can no longer extrapolate into the future because they do not know what will happen. Their comfort zone is breached. A bad conflict results from a perception that the pain of change will exceed any personal gains. The mind-set is something like: "This is a bad deal, and I don't care to play." Adaptation is required, which usually means time and effort. People who are experienced and skilled in change management have a higher threshold for conflict than someone who is new at coping with change.

The fear of losing control affects change management. The organization can give people control by inviting their participation in the decision-making process, asking for input, and offering them choices in the change process. When people are left outside the process, they feel a loss of control and greater stress, which drives them to negative behaviors. That happens frequently in major change efforts. In those circumstances, the leader's role is to communicate and keep people well informed.

Team leaders can help manage change in these ways:

- Have a compelling business case for the change.
- Expect resistance, fear, and confusion during the change.

- Build trust by being honest and transparent.

- Involve all stakeholders in the process.

- Know who the opinion leaders are, and solicit their input.

- Communicate well, and engage those who will be affected.

- Capture concerns and issues, and promptly and honestly address them.

- Be available and visible.

- Identify and reinforce behaviors needed for successful change.

- Support and help people cope with change, and be empathetic.

- Share information broadly.

In times of change, here is what each temperament type would like to hear:

- Rationals: What are the drivers and strategies behind this change?

- Idealists: How will this change improve our future?

- Guardians: What are the specific plans, including roles and responsibilities, processes, and time line?

- Artisans: What is my part in this change? How will I be affected?

CONFLICT OF VALUES

Value conflicts occur when people have incompatible values or their personal values are challenged by others. The value conflict is tougher to manage than change conflict, because people cannot change their values as readily as they change jobs or projects. Value conflicts hit their personal space. It threatens the very things that they believe in and hold sacred.

Values are not compromised very easily, and when values are compromised, the reaction can be severe. A colleague had a conflict with his father over the California governor recall election of 2003. His father, a traditionalist, was a World War II veteran who had worked for a large U.S. chemical company for over thirty-five years. He believed in the American system, governmental and judicial institutions, and traditional democratic values. To him, having an actor like Arnold Schwarzenegger and more than two hundred other citizens running in an election to throw out a legitimately elected governor was a farce, an act of disloyalty and disrespect to the founding principles of democracy. It violated values that he believed in deeply. His son believed strongly that the incumbent governor had violated the trust of the California population, led the state into fiscal ruins, and lacked the ability to perform the job. This was an emergency situation that required extraordinary measures, and he believed that a recall was justified and moral. The two did not see eye to eye. Both had strong values around the issue but vigorously disagreed with one another. They had such a fallout that they ended up not speaking to each other for several months.

This was a bad conflict. They both lost. Both were simply being guided by their values, and both were right. It was not an ego conflict; it was a values conflict. This is why so many people get into bad conflicts when talking about politics or religion: they bring out differences in personal values.

In many cultures, open disagreements and conflicts are not honorable behaviors and may even be offensive and embarrassing to the family due to cultural values. Most cultures in the world believe group harmony takes priority over individual needs. They will protect their friendships and avoid conflicts at all costs. In the Asian culture, public confrontations and disagreements are considered rude and disgraceful behaviors that will shame the family and its standing in the community. Disagreements and conflicts are handled privately and among the right people.

We develop our value system as we grow up. More often than not, when these values are violated, they can set us off emotionally. These values affect how we work in teams too, because team members are likely to have different values, and therefore natural conflicts will emerge. Many conflicts among team members can be traced to differences or violations of core values. The need to be respected and trusted is a strong value in people. When these basic needs go unfulfilled, the result may be frustration, anger, and interpersonal conflict. Yet these things are hard to see since people's values are rarely explicit to others.

High-performing teams have processes in place to help see beneath the surface of behaviors. Processes such as fist of five, roundtable, and feedback (see Chapters Four and Eight) enable team members to share their thinking and feelings. As transparency increases, we reveal insights into how we think and what matters most to us. Some people see these feedback tools as team-building activities, but they are much more than that. They are processes that build consensus, inclusiveness, openness, and honesty among team members. By using these tools, you are sending a message that we value who you are and what you think.

In the absence of these tools and processes, there is less opportunity to learn people's motivations. Invisible conflicts can build among team members and if left unresolved may lead to negative feelings and behaviors. People are profoundly affected when their values are not respected by others. For example, someone who is passed over for a promotion by someone less skilled may feel betrayed by the organization. His values of trust and fairness are violated, and his behavior may turn to resentment toward the organization. Even if the decision to select someone else was done objectively, a person's values should be respected. To achieve this, management should ensure that the criteria and process for selecting people for promotions are transparent, well communicated, and followed to assure people that a fair process is in place.

Here are some examples of behaviors and remarks that can create value conflicts:

- Ethnic humor, for example, saying, "This exercise feels like a Chinese fire drill"
- Expressing little or no appreciation for someone's hard work and extra efforts
- Putting down others, for example, saying, "That's a silly idea," or "What you just said makes no sense at all"
- Excluding team members from discussions by, for example, talking over others, interrupting others, ignoring remarks of others, or dominating discussions
- Sarcasm
- Sexist remarks

CONFLICT OF BEHAVIORS

Behavioral conflicts are interpersonal conflicts among team members that reduce teamwork and performance. Commonly called personality conflicts, they occur when two or more people do not like to work with each other, which causes a disruption to team space. People have unique styles in how they communicate, express their feelings, process information, and interact with others. These differences in behaviors may be received differently by others. Conflicts occur when these behaviors negatively affect one another. It is not because of disagreements. Team members simply do not feel motivated when they work together. For example, one team member may come across as egotistical, intimidating, and arrogant, which the other members of the team dislike. Instead of wanting to work with this individual, they would rather see him fail or go away. Another team member may be extremely sarcastic and critical of other people. As a result, team members minimize their contact with this person.

These personality conflicts promote avoidance behaviors and discontent rather than teamwork, and the team's progress is impeded by these undesirable behaviors. It takes only one individual to destroy the motivation of a team. In fact, sometimes it takes only one bad conflict to ruin a team relationship. That is why behavioral conflicts are such threats to a team. The six key team behaviors (trust, transparency, accountability, valuing individual differences, interdependency, and learning and recognition) are essential for good teamwork. Also, good team processes (team meetings, roles and responsibilities, communications, decision making, measuring performance, and feedback) will drive desired behaviors and help a team avoid team-wrecking behaviors. When team processes work well, good team behaviors follow and bad behaviors are eliminated or reduced. (More discussion on managing team conflicts is contained in Chapters Eleven and Twelve.)

TEAM SYNERGY AND ANTAGONISM

Figure 10.3 illustrates that positive and negative conflicts will always exist within a team. It is rare to find a team without conflicts. In most cases, mild positive and negative disagreements occur but are inconsequential in nature. This fluctuation

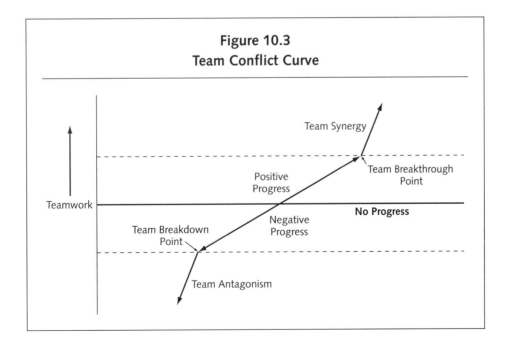

Figure 10.3
Team Conflict Curve

is shown as an upper (positive) and lower (negative) band (between the two dotted lines) on the chart. The team experiences periods of positive and negative teamwork, and the team moves up and down the continuum. This is normal. When positive conflicts are well managed by the team, the level of teamwork will rise as a result of greater team understanding, open communications, transparency, and acceptance of different opinions. When positive team behaviors predominate over time, the team may reach a breakthrough and achieve synergy, a step change in teamwork: the team is more productive working together than working individually. The whole is greater than the sum of the parts. Notice that the level of teamwork takes on a greater slope when synergy is achieved. The team experiences high performance, and team members feel highly committed to the success of the team.

Conversely, when negative conflicts occur, teamwork is reduced. Its effects can be mitigated (stay above the dotted line in Figure 10.3) if the conflict is not allowed to escalate. Negative behaviors can reduce teamwork when conflicts persist among team members. When the scale of negative team behaviors is excessive, the team can fall into a steeper slope of decline. At that point, the team experiences low morale, poor collaboration, and negative team performance. Team members may feel lost or unengaged or, worse, have antagonistic feelings toward the project and each other. When the team drops into an antagonistic state, it takes considerable energy and effort to return to an acceptable operating range (to return above the lower dotted line). Synergy creates team energy; antagonism consumes team energy.

Team Synergy

Team synergy can be observed and felt by all team members:

What You See

- High positive energy and enthusiasm
- Lots of communications, with people talking to each other and asking questions
- A willingness among team members to give their time, attention, and support to others
- High output, high quality, and ahead of schedule
- Smooth decision making and balanced participation from everyone
- A sense of having fun, good humor, and expressed feelings

What You Feel

- You have strong "want to" versus "have to" feelings.

- You want to share your opinions and information.

- You want to share what you feel and think.

- You want to do more and do it better, and you are never satisfied.

- You want to share the credit and praise and recognize each other.

- You feel the team solves problems and makes decisions much better than you can alone.

- You feel empowered and secure in taking risks.

- You feel tremendous pride and confidence in your team.

Synergy is a state that a team reaches when relationships are strong, team members are highly motivated and interdependent, and mutual trust is established. Building trust is a catalyst for accelerating work output, building positive relationships, and creating high-quality work and decisions. Synergy is a feeling that one has for the team and the work. A person who experiences synergy on a project team feels that the team can do almost anything and that a member would be willing to help in any way. Team confidence is high.

One of the best opportunities for synergy is in self-managed teams, which are self-directed, permanent work teams. The team is responsible for defining their day-to-day work activities, work assignments, and structure. The team has authority over how the work will be allocated and performed. Mutual trust and accountability are cornerstones of self-managed teams. Team members are equals and accountable to each other rather than to a supervisor. It is a high-risk venture (they will be scrutinized by management, must prove they can operate without a boss, and must work together well) but a high pay-off proposition (high employee morale, cost savings, high output). To be successful, self-managed teams must achieve team synergy. They require a high level of interdependency, trust, and a must-win attitude. Self-managed teams are motivated to prove themselves and by definition do both their work and the work that their boss would have done. Synergy is the underlying reason to create a self-managed team.

Synergy is not fixed; it is a fleeting, almost elusive state. Any team can experience it, but it is difficult to sustain throughout a project. Synergy can come and go in a team when team members turn over, roles and responsibilities change, or leadership changes. But when synergy does happen, it feels special, and people always remember it, not so much in terms of the project achievements, although that is very satisfying, but more so for the relationships that are built. Synergy is not a sudden phenomenon. It is a cumulative state: the team's investments in content, process, and team behaviors are compounded over time to yield extraordinary benefits.

Team Antagonism

When negative feelings and relationships build within a team, work suffers, and the team may be vulnerable to a breakdown. When this occurs, team antagonism is created, and people operate at a much lower level. Antagonism drags the team downward. It is not a good place to be.

You will know when you have team antagonism by what you see and sense:

What You See

- High negative energy or low energy
- Poor communication; people are talking at each other and advocating their individual positions
- More takers than givers
- A struggle to get work done, variable quality at best, and behind schedule
- No consensus, low participation, and high absenteeism
- High "presenteeism" (people are present but not productive or engaged)

What You Feel

- Strong "have to" versus "want to" feelings.
- You refrain from sharing what you feel and think.
- You want to do just the minimum and get it over with.
- You compete for credit.
- Praise is scarce.
- You feel the team cannot solve problems or make decisions on its own.
- You feel tremendous stress, resentment, or hostility in the team.
- You feel risk averse.

Team antagonism is cumulative. It is created when project teams grow apart and mutual trust is low. Behaviors that create the greatest team antagonism include poor communications, put-downs, aggression, condescension, selfishness, disrespect, finger pointing, personal sarcasm, exclusion, harassment, and distrust. Antagonism not only wears a team down; over time, it becomes more and more difficult to reverse. Repairing relationships is one of the toughest things that a team can do.

The one behavior that contributes most to team antagonism is poor listening, which occurs when people are talking but no one feels understood. When teams are confronted with problems, people's preferred style of communication is usually advocacy rather than listening. It is good to share views, but it should be done with an open mind and open ears. People speak to the issue and advocate what they think is the right course. They have opinions, ideas, and assumptions that they feel add substance to the issue, and they want others to acknowledge their thoughts. Rather than listening, people are busy processing and formulating their own opinions and are waiting for their turn to speak. They are all trying to give voice to the issue, but no real listening is occurring. When people do not feel heard, they feel unappreciated and devalued. That is when antagonism sets in.

SUMMARY

Team conflicts are unresolved, interpersonal disagreements that can lead to increased or decreased team performance. In good conflicts, the team is able to resolve problems and differences using positive behaviors. The end result is a satisfactory outcome for all, with strengthened relationships. A bad conflict is a team disagreement that leads to poor team behaviors, an unsatisfactory resolution for some, and weakened relationships. Bad conflicts generate negative emotional energy and can drag a team down. In bad conflicts, people shift to a defensive state, and they can become self-centered, impatient, frustrated, angry, and destructive.

Misunderstandings can lead to misperceptions and bad conflicts. Positive team-building behaviors such as open communications, transparency, and team feedback reduce bad conflicts. The most common types of conflict are change, value, and behavior.

Change conflicts stem from a fear of change and uncertainty. Change represents a loss of control and a disruption to the team. To embrace change, the team must be convinced of the benefits of change and move forward together. Not everyone will be convinced, and this leads to conflict. In addition, we need to recognize that people adapt to change at different rates.

Value conflicts occur when people's personal values are challenged. The type of values tested may include honesty, integrity, ethics, or cultural differences. People do not compromise their values readily. Value conflicts are the things that people believe in and are the most difficult to reconcile when challenged.

Behavioral conflicts are personality conflicts, which reduce teamwork and performance. People have unique styles in how they communicate, express their feelings, process information, and interact with others. These differences in behaviors may be received differently by others. Aggressive behaviors may not be welcomed by passive personalities and vice versa. These personality conflicts may promote avoidance behaviors and discontent rather than teamwork.

Most of the time, teams experience periods of both positive and negative levels of teamwork. When negative team behaviors dominate, work suffers and the team is vulnerable to breakdown. Breakdown occurs when team antagonism is created. The desired state is team synergy, where breakthrough performance is achieved. When positive team behaviors predominate, the team achieves breakthrough performance and synergy. Synergy creates team energy; antagonism consumes team energy.

How Conflicts Affect
Personal Space

Personal space is tested when external changes occur in strategies, budgets, personnel, management, competitors, markets, and other factors. Change conflicts commonly originate from organizational space, while behavioral conflicts occur from team space. Value conflicts may arise between individuals and the organization, and they may also occur between team members. Value conflicts are the most difficult to resolve and have the most profound effect on work interactions. Each person's space is unique, and therein lays the potential for intra-team conflicts, especially if team members do not value individual diversity.

Not all conflicts are bad. Most conflicts are more positive than negative and increase our understanding, transparency, and acceptance of others. Bad conflicts push people into abnormal behaviors and cause them to shut down or confront. Over the course of the team development cycle, good and bad behaviors occur in everyone. How individuals choose to respond to these conflicts depends on their own values. Those who are in conflict can become self-centered, insensitive, frustrated, and angry.

PASSIVE-AGGRESSIVE THRESHOLD MODEL

Conflicts have a profound effect on personal space, and people respond to external challenges differently (Figure 11.1). My passive-aggressive threshold model illustrates that each person has a certain threshold for taking personal action. A threshold is the lowest point at which a response occurs. It is the point at which people freely express their thoughts and feelings: the lower the threshold is, the greater the likelihood of action, and the higher the threshold is, the lower the likelihood of action. What causes a person to take action depends on the urgency and level of importance of the situation: the higher the importance is, the greater and faster the response. If the house is on fire, for example, people move fast.

When it comes to team interactions, people may not speak out and take action on an issue unless it has personal meaning. They will not participate in team discussions unless they have sufficient interest and motivation to engage. Motivation can come internally, especially if it supports their values and interests, and it can come externally from organizational space or team space. Input is fed from both internal and external sources. This is especially true in team conflicts. Internally, everyone has a natural threshold for taking action during disagreements. Action thresholds vary from individual to individual, circumstances to circumstances, and even day to day. What drives someone to voice disagreement is highly dependent

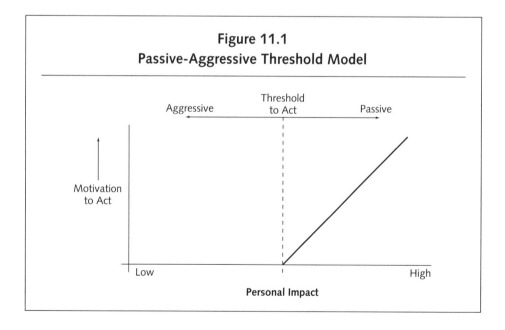

Figure 11.1
Passive-Aggressive Threshold Model

on his or her experiences, consequences, and personality type. It also depends on the behaviors of the team. If the team is prone to have bad conflicts, then people are less inclined to speak up because their threshold to speak up is high.

A person who continues to adopt a higher and higher threshold (the threshold shifts to the right) will become less assertive and more passive. This shift to the right may result from past failures, bad outcomes, and negative experiences. For example, when people feel their ideas are not being valued, they may decide to shut down and not offer ideas anymore. They become more self-effacing and discouraged, and their internal dialogue is poor and self-defeating. If a boss puts an employee down for taking a risk, that employee will be less likely to take another risk without the boss's permission. Moving to the right is subordinate, nonassertive, exclusionary, and fearful. Fear erodes self-confidence. In extreme cases, the employee withdraws completely and seeks satisfaction elsewhere.

In contrast, people who shift their threshold too far to the left adopt a low threshold, which means they are highly reactive, demanding, and controlling. They may dominate others, intimidate people, and lose their tempers quickly. Road rage is an example of assuming a low threshold. They demand a lot from themselves and other people and never appear satisfied. Moving to the left is also an exclusionary and fearful behavior. When people move too far to the left, they exclude others; when they move too far to the right, they exclude themselves. Fear of failure or a fear of being wrong can create a low threshold. A low threshold is just as bad as having too high a threshold.

Moving to the right is not a negative or cowardly behavior. For the most part, avoiding conflict is a way of respecting others and letting others go first. It shows a high degree of care and concern for others. The nonassertive person may be highly motivated to please others and takes great satisfaction in seeing others assert themselves. This is a positive trait. However, taken to an extreme, where we continually relinquish our rights to others, it is not a good long-term behavior. If the motivation is due to fear and not kindness, we are giving up a part of ourselves to others. No one wants that.

One risk of being too passive or aggressive is that these behaviors can quickly become a habit. Your threshold is stuck in one gear. Over time, remaining silent and letting things go can slowly take you to the right, and before you know it, your threshold has become permanently high. Worse, when the time comes that you need to be assertive, you will not be able to find it in yourself. You will simply be out of practice. That is the danger of having too high or too low of a threshold: it can get away from you quickly if you do not use your mental muscles once in awhile. You get into a comfort zone and are content to stay there.

This behavioral creep can happen to anyone. They claim a lack of energy or lack of sufficient motivation to act. Yet as they creep further to the right, it takes more and more personal energy to get themselves back to the center. It becomes a downward spiral that they may not even see but others will. People who are afraid to make decisions often say they are not good at it, but no one can be a good decision maker by avoiding decision making. To be a good decision maker requires making a lot of decisions and feeling secure in accepting bad outcomes. Sometimes good decisions result in bad outcomes. Some people will not speak up because others do not seem to listen to them. Like many other things in life, speaking up is a learning process, and it takes practice and feedback to become good at it.

Some people carry a high threshold when they are unfamiliar with people but warm up quickly as they become more comfortable (that is, less fearful). Some people simply require more time to process information, but the train of the conversation is running too fast for them to jump on. We need to remember that people have different reaction times. When important team decisions have to be made, a good technique is to give people time to collect their thoughts and then go around the table asking for each person's opinion.

A team has the power to develop a low or high threshold for itself. It can encourage disagreement and build a safe environment to disagree, or it can suppress disagreement, driving the team's threshold to a high level. That, however, usually results in mediocre to poor performance. When people are not speaking out, good ideas are lost.

Although this human factor is well recognized, teams seldom discuss this behavior because it is a soft issue, an intangible, and something too emotional to discuss. So teams try to cope with it by staying focused on deadlines and the content of the work.

It is not uncommon for project teams to shift to the right and become passive in decision making. One form of this behavior is groupthink, where a team is more motivated to agree than disagree and starts to narrow its diversity of thinking. Some groupthink is good in terms of agreeing to work objectives, strategies, processes, and actions. Where it falls apart is when teams start getting complacent, do not encourage other ideas, challenge each other less, or give in more quickly. They start lowering their standards.

FEAR FACTORS AND PERSONAL SPACE

Here are four examples of how fears and inner conflicts affect our behaviors.

The Road to Abilene

Fear of conflict can lead a team to take passive team behaviors. The Abilene paradox (Harvey, 1974) is a phenomenon in which a team is so accommodating and fearful of conflict that the members will agree to do things that no one really wants to do. But instead of voicing their disagreement, they support what they perceive are the wishes of the team and go along with it. They take the path of least resistance (the road to Abilene) rather than face possible team disagreement. All personality types are prone to take this path.

Figure 11.2 illustrates how groupthink or passivity can drive a team to a position that no one wants. Consider this example. A division manager holds a leadership team meeting and introduces the concept of strategic staffing. The division has never had a long-range plan for developing succession plans, competency needs, and hiring goals. After some discussion of what strategic staffing represents, the team shows curiosity and initial interest. Taking this as a positive sign, the manager brainstorms an idea of forming a cross-sectional team to study the issue, do some benchmarking, identify best practices, and develop a work plan. To each team member, this sounded like way too much and too soon. Also, team members instinctively were not sold on the idea yet. Some wondered if they really needed another study team, and others thought that it sounded like a big commitment that merited more discussion. Despite these doubts, no one dismissed the idea right away. Instead, one member expressed some positive aspects about the idea: "Yes, engaging our staff is always good." Others nodded, and another team member said, "It wouldn't hurt to get more thinking and data around this."

Although the manager was merely testing the concept, no one dared to be the first one to voice opposition. Hearing no opposition, the manager asked, "Does anyone not want to do this?" The room was silent. The manager then said, "Good. I think the next step would be to get people from each of your work groups to form this study team." It was captured as an action item, and the leadership team moved to the next agenda item. Although the manager was only testing the idea on the team, this intent was not transparent to the team. Based on the enthusiasm and body language of the manager, the team assumed the manager was pushing for the

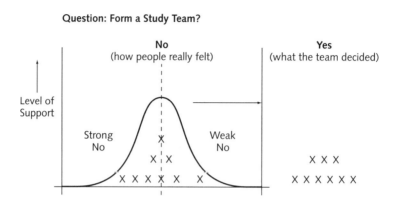

Figure 11.2
The Road to Abilene: Moving to a Place
Where No One Wants to Go

Question: Form a Study Team?

| No (how people really felt) | Yes (what the team decided) |

Level of Support

Strong No   Weak No

Note: Each X represents a team member.

formation of this study team, and no one was willing to speak up against the idea. They were essentially fearful, unwilling to take a personal risk, and they all moved to the right together as a team.

Several underlying fear factors drive this behavior, each of them associated with the personality types of Rationals, Idealists, Guardians, and Artisans:

• Fear of failure and criticism. The goal is to avoid being blamed for a bad decision. (Rationals)

• Fear of conflict. There is a desire to avoid confrontation. (Idealists)

• Fear of rejection. There is a desire to be accepted and not to be ostracized. (Guardians)

- Fear of embarrassment and ridicule. The worry is that one's opinion will not be respected or valued, leading to a feeling of being minimized. (Artisans)
- Fear of accountability. There is a desire not to be responsible for a wrong team decision. (All personality types)

At times, these same fears can paralyze us in situations where actions are required. We avoid facing certain responsibilities in the fear of conflict or fear of rejection from our teams. The most common response is inaction—for example

- Not confronting unacceptable performance and retaining low performers.
- Not stopping a worker who makes culturally insensitive remarks, letting it go, and rationalizing it as good humor.
- Not addressing the elephant in the room—that is, people are afraid to talk about a major issue that is looming in front of everyone and impossible to miss, yet no one knows what to do with it. It may be too big to discuss or too embarrassing, sensitive, or taboo (sacred cows, for example). We are afraid to raise it so we remain silent and suffer the result.
- Not taking personal accountability for a bad decision, hoping no one will notice.
- Not explaining your decision to the team you manage, thereby avoiding any challenges.
- Not praising others, fearing it may appear insincere or patronizing.
- Not making a decision, wanting more and more analysis in order to be 100 percent sure when only an 80 percent decision is needed.

Fear of Weakness

A variation to the Abilene paradox is the fear of weakness. We are sometimes paralyzed by our own egos and pride when we are overwhelmed by too much work or difficulty. Instead of asking for help, we suffer in silence rather than admit defeat or weakness. We all seem to believe that only the strongest survive and those who show weakness are eliminated. Also, no one wants to be seen as the weakest link on the team. We see this play out in other ways, such as not stopping to ask for directions when we are lost or not wanting to recognize others for fear of appearing soft. Weakness is a fear of all personality types.

I recall being involved in a large team project where everyone wanted to do their best. We set aggressive goals and time lines. The work was enormous, but we wanted to complete the team project on time. Into the fourth week of the project, we all were working long hours to deal with the growing workload. We were aspiring managers, so none of us complained. Finally, during a conference call, one team member admitted to feeling overwhelmed and stressed and wondered how others felt. In no time, others chimed in and confessed that they felt exactly the same way but did not want to say anything negative for fear of hurting team morale. Ironically, our inability to face the truth to each other was actually bringing down the project. The fear of appearing weak or losing ego should never be a barrier to good project management. It was total relief to the team when our colleague spoke up honestly. After that, we were more realistic about the project. His confession actually reenergized the team and built greater trust, and we went on to complete the project on time.

Fear of Taking Risks

One prominent human factor in team decision making is risk taking. Risk taking does not come naturally to all people, and we all have different risk tolerances. Teams and individuals express risk tolerances in different ways: we avoid risks (defer making decisions), transfer risks (giving problems to someone else), and hedge our risks (inflating budgets, extending time lines, adding extra review steps, and overanalyzing data). The risk tolerance of a team is not necessarily the composite of the individual team members. Having one or two high- or low-risk takers on the team can create conflict and drive a team to make the wrong decision.

Risk has two dimensions: what is at stake and what is the probability of success or failure. As we discussed in Chapter Three, when people have a lot at stake, they exhibit greater commitment and involvement. Team members will have uneven stakes in the outcome of the project and therefore have high or low fears of taking risks in the project. When the stakes are high and the probability of success uncertain, teams have difficulty making decisions. High stakes and the lack of reliable information or precedence will motivate a team to delay, defer, or avoid making a decision; transfer its risks to others; or hedge risks by doing more research and data collection. The fear of making the wrong decision is high in projects with high uncertainty. Risk aversion is a major issue in team decision making and a source of conflict. Teams can take two measures to manage risks in projects:

- Establish a management or decision review committee for the project. This oversight committee can help support and give protection to the team by sharing or even shouldering primary accountability for the outcome. More important, the committee helps determine the level of acceptable risk.

- Be explicit with the uncertainty or risk. Use decision and risk analysis methodologies to assess and integrate risk into the project. This may entail more data gathering and research, but decision and risk analysis helps to characterize and quantify project risks.

Teams should not fear risks but manage them using organizational space and good decision-making tools and processes.

Road to Mediocrity

Another team phenomenon is the risk of overcompromising in team decision making (Figure 11.3). Because of our desire to achieve team harmony and cooperation, we are afraid to upset others. Organizations seek diversity in teams and recognize the creative power of diversity in solving problems and improving processes. We accept that diversity is good on team projects, and therefore the more diversity there is, the better. The team gains more perspectives, more alternatives, and more opinions. However, the risk is that diversity can force teams to the middle rather than to best solutions. In our effort to please everyone and honor the opinions of everyone, we can fall into the trap of overcompromising and settling

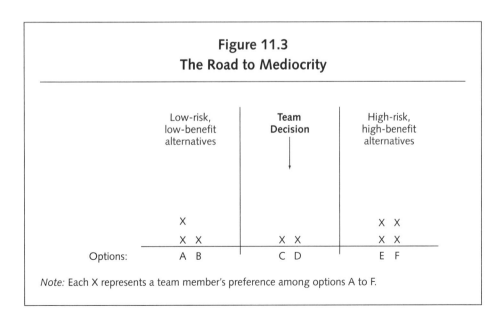

Figure 11.3
The Road to Mediocrity

| Low-risk, low-benefit alternatives | Team Decision | High-risk, high-benefit alternatives |

Note: Each X represents a team member's preference among options A to F.

for a no-conflict solution rather than the most effective one. Certainly, the best solution sometimes may well be a compromise. However, success requires superior solutions, not mediocrity. Those who spend too much time in the middle of the road will get run over. We do not want to settle for mediocrity. Diversity should add, not dilute, value.

No one is free of fear factors. Each temperament type carries a unique set of fearful behaviors (Table 11.1). This does not mean we run around frightened all the time; it just means we have some fears that are stronger than others, and they are related to our values. Teams need to be sensitive to these intrinsic fears in people and try not to play into them.

Those who fear rejection or conflict are allowing others to control their behaviors and are thereby reducing their personal space. Letting others control behaviors is a symptom of low confidence and self-defeating internal dialogue. Both organizational space and team space can limit personal space if we let them. We get squeezed (Figure 11.4), and our self-confidence and self-esteem suffer. Also, apathy can take over as we think, "What I say won't make any difference" or "What I say will drag things out or make things worse, so I won't say anything." This is a self-centered, small space behavior. What squeezes our personal spaces? Fear, conflict, and stress are the biggest culprits. They operate silently in our minds and become self-replicating as we let them control our personal space. It is like a virus

Table 11.1 Fear Factors by Temperament Types			
Idealist	Guardian	Rational	Artisan
• Fear of causing conflict or disharmony	• Fear of rejection	• Fear of being wrong	• Fear of being ridiculed
• Fear of embarrassment	• Fear of being criticized unfairly	• Fear of failure	• Fear of being controlled by others
• Fear of disappointing others	• Fear of insecurity, lack of money	• Fear of looking stupid	• Fear of inaction

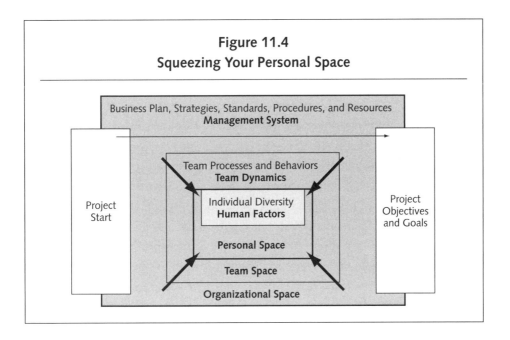

Figure 11.4
Squeezing Your Personal Space

Business Plan, Strategies, Standards, Procedures, and Resources
Management System

Project
Start

Team Processes and Behaviors
Team Dynamics

Individual Diversity
Human Factors

Personal Space

Team Space

Organizational Space

Project
Objectives
and Goals

that has crept into our brain. It disturbs our internal dialogue and makes us look inward, where we care more about ourselves than others.

Idealists and Guardians are prone to avoid conflict and give up their personal space. When we are assertive, we are maintaining our space. When personal space shrinks, it lowers our self-confidence and self-esteem in a vicious cycle. Speaking out and challenging the team to take different perspectives require confidence, energy, and unselfishness. Giving up a small amount of personal space may not be significant in the moment, but these moments can sometimes turn into years. We should be more fearful of losing space than fearing conflict. When we are in conflict, under stress, or afraid, we are at risk of losing personal space. When we allow organizational space or team space to dictate our behaviors, we are shrinking our space. We let the company run our lives, let our friends define who we are and how we are to act, and let fear determine our behaviors. A bit of fear can be healthy, motivating, and keeps us alert, and many personality types use fear productively. However, we need balance in our lives where we can respect ourselves and respect the right things in both organizational and team spaces. The right things are those that are consistent with our values, culture, and experiences. Aggressives take personal space, while passives give up space. Give and take or compromise is important in teamwork, but a person who constantly gives or takes space is not true to self or the team.

As illustrated in Figure 11.5, when positive and negative stimuli are received from our environment, we respond accordingly to the importance of the stimuli and the state of our personal space. Personal space is our inner self, a place where internal interactive thinking occurs and human factors are formed. An internal dialogue or thinking process takes place as we process new information, interpret its meaning against our human factors, and express those perceptions in our behaviors. I call it an internal dialogue because we tend to silently weigh and debate things in our minds. This can be an intellectual or emotional dialogue, depending on our predominant personality type. Each person has a unique set of human factors and therefore may respond differently to the same stimuli.

Stress and conflict are the most challenging stimuli to our human factors because they have a powerful effect. How we choose to respond to stress or conflict is up to each of us. Each of us is in full control of our personal space, and we there-

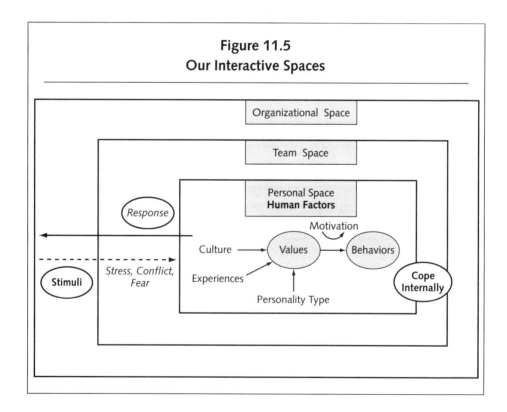

Figure 11.5
Our Interactive Spaces

fore have a choice in how to respond. Many people are good at managing stress and conflict; some are not.

Every behavior has a consequence. The consequence can be something good, like finding a solution to a problem, or something negative, as when people respond angrily. The consequences of our behaviors are captured internally in our culture or experiences within our space. Culture and experiences are environmental factors that we learn over time. We build a consequent history with situations and people, especially when our interactions produce profound effects. We do not easily forget our high and low experiences. Regardless of our responses, we have to live with the consequences of our actions. Living with the good and bad consequences requires coping skills and inner strength.

Managing conflict can therefore be viewed as a three-part model: stimuli, coping, and response (Figure 11.5). Stress, conflict, and fear stimuli can come from all three spaces: organizational space, team space, and personal space. How we choose to manage our behaviors is based on our human factors. When we initiate a behavior, we are hoping to get a positive consequence or avoid a negative one. Either way, we hope to get what we want or get a consequence that we can live or cope with. Just as our ideal goal in project management is to get results and feel good about it, our personal goal is also the same: to get results (a desirable consequence of our behavior) and feel good about it (coping with the consequence internally).

CONFLICTS AND PERSONALITY TYPES

Behaviors are determined by genetic and environmental factors, and each personality type behaves differently under conflict. Everyone has a different threshold level for conflict, and it changes depending on the circumstances and people involved. One person may feel conflict when criticized by someone at work, while another person may feel no conflict under the same circumstance. Some people confront conflict, while others avoid it. The ability to cope with conflict is defined in large part by genetic code. This section examines how each personality type deals with conflict.

Rationals

When it comes to conflict, Rationals are eager to face new challenges. Rationals are initiators, problem solvers, and drivers who want to attack and conquer trouble right away. They enjoy a good mental tussle and are likely to take the lead on resolving a conflict. As one Rational used to tell me, "I like to meet conflict head-on."

To a Rational, the best conflicts are ones that require hard thinking, research, and analysis to solve. They like to solve conflicts through logic and reasoning, which works well for content conflicts but not for people conflicts. In fact, Rationals do not like relationship conflicts and distance themselves whenever possible. Their patience and listening skills are not at their best when confronted by personal conflict. Rationals are uncomfortable in emotional situations, especially when people break down and cry or yell. When this happens, Idealists console, while Rationals escape. Often Rationals escape physically to get quiet thinking time. They need time to warm up to emotional issues.

In conflict, Rationals prefer to analyze. People conflicts are drawn internally for evaluation and resolution. Rationals weigh their options and choose the right path. Non–people type conflicts represent a challenge to Rationals, and if they have to, they will work unceasingly on it. Unresolved conflicts frustrate them. If they feel responsible, they may agonize over it for a long time and have trouble letting go. In all, Rationals provide high energy, logical thinking, and creative ideas during conflict situations.

Idealists

Idealists do not like conflict and avoid not only conflict but situations that may lead to potential conflict. Having to make hard decisions is a challenge for Idealists, and they strategically avoid getting themselves into this situation. When conflict arises, Idealists have a strong need to isolate themselves or escape from the problem, for example, by taking a nap or going to a movie to let their emotions recover. Idealists require time to make a decision. They prefer to look introspectively for an answer. They want to think things through thoroughly, making sure their decision is not emotional but objective. They may solicit opinions from others or just hope that the problem will resolve itself. Idealists may believe that somehow it will work out on its own, a belief that fate will make the ultimate decision. In more practical terms, they tend to carry a belief that something will occur that will make the decision clearer for them. One strength of Idealists is that their intentions are pure: to do good and not cause harm.

Guardians

Like Idealists, Guardians do not like conflict and avoid it as their first instinct. They view conflict as a disruption, an impedance, and a barrier in getting things done. What makes Guardians highly effective in dealing with conflicts is their wonderful ability to compromise. They are unselfish team players, willing to make sacrifices for the good of the team. They are tactful, diplomatic, and cooperative in their interactions with others during conflicts. But they do not sacrifice to the point of being unfair to themselves or others. They will seek counsel and trust authoritative opinions. Guardians make their positions known and can be stubborn, but are willing to let go and support the majority view in order to move forward. Their loyalty to the team and organization is admirable, and their cooperative attitude helps catalyze consensus. In contrast to Idealists, Guardians seek external validation from a rule, policy, or precedence before making a decision.

Artisans

Artisans handle conflicts well. They are gifted in their abilities to think in the here and now and not be overly concerned with making the wrong decision or stepping on toes. They are bold risk takers who are happy to be in the middle of the action and will apply themselves as much as Rationals do. Their effectiveness under fire can be attributed to their creativity, directness, and energetic engagement in conflicts. Sometimes they may move too quickly to the answer, and they commonly lose interest if the conflict becomes long and drawn out. Also, whatever is the most convenient may not always be the best answer. Artisans like quick, cut-to-the-chase solutions. Artisans care about personal relationships and show great kindness and generosity to others in need, although these qualities are not always apparent. They can be sensitive and perceptive about people. They may seem cool sometimes, but only because they have found something else of greater interest.

Summing Up the Types

Guardians and Rationals, when stressed, want to be in control. Guardians like to control the process. Rationals like to control the thinking. In comparison, Artisans and Rationals go after speed and efficiency—the faster, the better. Artisans see conflict as a risk-taking opportunity and a chance to be a standout. Idealists see conflict as an opportunity to heal people. In conflict, Idealists and Guardians tend to wait for permission to act. Idealists wait to avoid conflict; Guardians wait for the conflict process to be framed and defined. In contrast, Rationals and Artisans jump on conflicts and problems. Both want to act fast on issues—and sometimes too fast for Idealists and Guardians to get on board. Rationals see a mental challenge, and solving a problem is an intellectual game. Artisans are notably the best in urgent conflict situations, and Guardians are the best in cooperatively reaching a compromise.

Each personality type brings a special set of skills and emotions to both good and bad conflicts. Their strengths and weaknesses are complementary and depend on the type and urgency of the conflict.

SUMMARY

The passive-aggressive threshold model illustrates that our motivation to take action varies from individual to individual, circumstances to circumstances, and even day to day. A person who continues to adopt a higher and higher threshold will become less assertive and more passive in behavior. And those who shift to a lower threshold become more reactive and aggressive. Ideally, we should be centered in our passive-aggressive behaviors and respond to conflicts in a positive, constructive manner.

Behaviors are often driven by fear. Fear can even drive people to behave contrary to their own beliefs. Groupthink, such as the Abilene paradox, is an example of a passive, accommodating behavior that can lead teams to bad decisions. Fear is a human factor that creates bad team behaviors and squeezes space. Furthermore, when people let outside factors drive their behaviors, they lose personal space and self-confidence. Each personality type displays a different set of fearful behaviors, and recognizing these characteristics enables us to reduce team conflicts.

How we choose to respond to stress or conflict is up to each of us. Managing conflict can be viewed as a three-part model: stimuli, coping, and response. Stimuli such as stress, conflict, and fear can come from all three spaces: organizational, team, and personal. Our internal and external responses to conflicts are dependent on our human factors and consequent history. Every behavioral response has a consequence, and we internally cope with each consequence. Just as our ideal goal in project management is to get results and feel good about it, our personal goal is also to get results (a desirable consequence of our behavior) and feel good about it (coping with the consequence internally).

Personality types deal with conflict differently. Idealists and Guardians tend to avoid conflicts, while Rationals and Artisans like to confront it. Each type has strengths and weaknesses: Idealists seek what is right but may procrastinate and avoid decisions which create conflicts; Guardians are strong implementers of change but require clear guidance; Rationals initiate change but may overanalyze it; and Artisans are bold and decisive but may take unreasonable risks.

Expanding Your Space

Wwe devote tremendous time and energy coping with stress, adapting to change, and managing conflicts. Hardly a day goes by that we are not confronted with some new challenge, problem, or demand on our time. Conflicts are regular events in our lives, yet how well we manage stressful stimuli affects our behaviors and relationships with others. Our response to conflicts is individualistic and situational and is dependent on the degree of importance to us, our knowledge of whom or what we are dealing with, our consequent history with that person or type of conflict, and our underlying human factors. Ideally, we want to face conflicts confidently, respond skillfully, and, most important, feel good about the situation when it is over. People should be good responders, not good reactors. Reactions are spontaneous, instinctive, self-centered acts, while responses are thoughtful, caring actions. We want to make good, intelligent responses toward resolving conflicts and avoid having to cope and carry conflicts forward in our lives and thereby become stressed, overwhelmed, and mentally worn.

Our goal is to get results and to feel good about it. Unfortunately, all too often, we either do not get the results we want and feel badly about it, or we get the results we want but end up causing others to feel badly about it. Just like in project management, we want productive interactions and positive outcomes. We want to be good at preventing and resolving conflicts as opposed to always absorbing and coping with conflicts. As Figure 12.1 illustrates, the goal is to reduce incoming conflicts, respond skillfully in resolving conflicts, and decrease the need to cope with unsatisfactory results. It is our human factors that control how well we process and cope with conflicts.

Our ability to address and resolve conflicts lies in our inner space. If you find your personal space getting tighter under conflict, meaning that you get fearful, defensive, and selfish, then you are not operating at your best. Getting tighter in personal space never resolves conflicts; it only exasperates them. We do not want to reduce our space when in conflict. Losing personal space means we are losing control of our own behaviors. This occurs when our personal space is being controlled by the behaviors of other people or being overdriven by the factors from organizational space, such as accepting an authoritative decision that is in conflict with our personal values. In conflict, we tend to strike out and control what is outside us, when in reality the loss is occurring inside us. We somehow feel that controlling process and content will restore emotional control in ourselves. Guardians show this behavior more than the other three personality types, but all personality types exhibit this behavior. In conflict situations and stress, behaviors are motivated more by fear than anything else. When threatened, we protect ourselves and seek to satisfy our own needs first. For all personality types, we selfishly seek safety when we are frightened. Fear has a way of squeezing personal space and reducing personal control. Reducing personal space to strike out or satisfy others and thereby

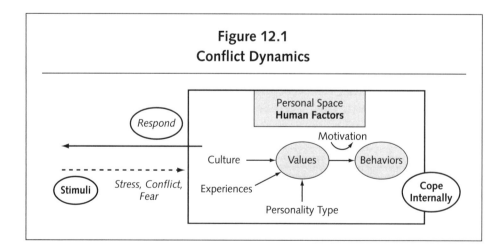

Figure 12.1
Conflict Dynamics

avoiding conflict is not a good strategy. The best strategy is to expand your personal space.

How do we expand our spaces to improve our abilities to manage conflicts? It is common to find that passive personalities want to be more assertive, emotional personalities want to be calmer, and analytical personalities want to be more sensitive, which seems to make sense. However, it is unrealistic to suddenly transform personal space into something that it is not. Rationals do not suddenly become Idealists, and Guardians do not suddenly become Artisans regardless of how hard they try. We cannot fight our own biology, especially under conflict situations.

The way to manage conflicts and develop interpersonal effectiveness is to expand personal space. That means to reach beyond ourselves with positive influence into team space and organizational space (Figure 12.2). Our behaviors have a positive impact on the behaviors of the team and organization. This is in contrast to a contracting space, where our behaviors are increasingly controlled by other people and the organization.

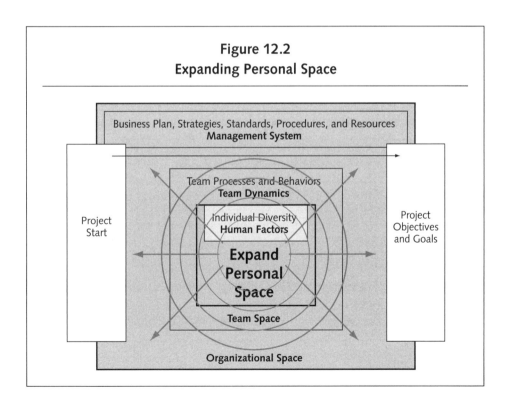

Figure 12.2
Expanding Personal Space

Business Plan, Strategies, Standards, Procedures, and Resources
Management System

Team Processes and Behaviors
Team Dynamics

Individual Diversity
Human Factors

Expand Personal Space

Project Start

Project Objectives and Goals

Team Space

Organizational Space

When we give up space, we give up control of it and lose influence. This can result from being overly passive or overly aggressive. For example, when we refrain from voicing disagreements to avoid conflict with others, we are giving up space. When we recognize poor performers and let them have control over our feelings and work, we are giving up space. When we allow others to dominate a meeting and push people into a wrong decision, we are giving up space, and when we permit people to talk over others and disrespect others, we diminish our personal influence and effectiveness.

TANGIBLE BENEFITS OF EXPANDING PERSONAL SPACE

Expansion gives us strength in four key areas. First, an expanded space creates informal power and increases our sphere of influence. Informal power refers to the level and extent of our influence on other people's behaviors. In other words, how well do our behaviors motivate others to listen to us, help us, be open with us, and work for us? In project teams, we are expected to lead and direct people who do not work for us. In most cases, we have little or no supervisory authority over the work of others. This is one of the most frustrating challenges facing project managers today. How do they get people to do what they want? The goal is not to manipulate people but to motivate them to work collaboratively. Why are we inclined to readily help some people and not others? What motivates us to give our time and effort to someone else? The answer lies in our informal power. Expanding personal space increases informal power. Informal power is neither granted nor bestowed; it is earned through positive interactions and sustained through leadership.

Second, expanding personal space helps prevent and reduce incoming conflicts. When people are willing to give us the benefit of the doubt or are willing to compromise or accommodate our position, they have faith and trust in our behaviors created by our past interactions with them. They have retained a positive consequent history about us, and until that established history is broken, they are willing to give us more than they would otherwise. This giving behavior results in fewer confrontations and conflicts for us. Also, our reputation is a form of informal power that helps us to fend off and resolve conflicts. If we have a reputation of honesty and integrity, people will trust us more readily. Therefore, by increasing our personal space, we are building a strong buffer against conflicts.

Third, expanding our space brings out the best in people and increases our scope and capacity. When we are perceived as someone who gets the job done and makes others feel good about it, then we have a formula for team success. People like to work with those whom they trust and are motivated by their behaviors. By expanding personal space, people feel safe to express themselves and to go the extra mile to please. When we have positive influence, people gravitate to us and want to work with us over others. A "want to" attitude (versus a "have to" attitude) is what generates discretionary performance in people: "I want to do more, and I want to do it better." When people are willing to do more, we greatly increase the scope and capacity of our team to grow and improve.

Finally, expanding personal space gives us inner strength. People who are assertive are less fearful. When we expand our space to reach others with our feelings and opinions, we are less fearful of what others may think or do. We are less unafraid because we possess a stronger belief in ourselves that we can handle whatever is thrown at us. We have the inner space not only to absorb the results but also respond.

HOW TO EXPAND PERSONAL SPACE

Here are seven good strategies for expanding personal space. The intent is to look beyond yourself, reach out to others, and extend outside your personal space in a positive and constructive manner.

- Value diversity.
- Build a positive account balance with others.
- Be visible.
- Practice inclusive behaviors.
- Send the right signals.
- Be assertive.
- Know your response options to conflict, and use them skillfully.

Value Diversity

Understanding the human factors and diversity of people is key to expanding our personal space. First, it increases our acceptance of the behaviors of others. Instead of judging other people's behaviors through our personal values, we demonstrate a greater respect and acceptance of the diversity in others. Their values are just as valid as ours. We listen to understand first, before jumping to judgment. We recognize that our way is not always the best way to do things. Honor the differences in others, and they will honor you.

Second, we become sensitive to diverse human needs and understand what motivates and demotivates other people. By understanding another person's personality type and diversity, we can appreciate why people may do things differently from us. The things that motivate or demotivate us are not likely to be the same for someone else, and we need to recognize that and not get frustrated. We become more effective when we give the right incentives to people. We all have a fire in our gut; what fuels our fire varies from person to person.

Third, we modify our personal behaviors to be more compatible with others. By understanding cultural, generational, and personality differences, we can take a more diverse and personalized approach in working on teams and with others individually. If we model the desired behaviors of others, others will be drawn to support us.

The bottom line is that our space expands when we are able to reach others at a personal level.

Build a Positive Account Balance with Other People

We expand personal space by supporting others. Each encounter or interaction with another person is an intellectual and emotional transaction. It is human nature for people to do good things for each other. It makes people feel good and fulfills a human intellectual or emotional need. We see it as quid pro quo: if I go out of my way to help you, I will expect you to do the same for me. Good deeds are often rewarded by appreciation, recognition, gifts, loyalty, trust, friendship, and endearments. Like many other good things in life, positive relationships do not occur without time and effort. We must believe and invest in each other if we are to be a successful team or organization. Building a positive account balance with team members is a proactive behavior and helps to prevent disharmony and conflict in relationships. We must invest in others in order to build positive relationships. It is a two-way street.

Doing things for others with the expectation of gaining a favorable relationship with the other party is often referred to as social capital, political capital, or goodwill. In the context of teamwork, I like to call it personal capital: an investment of time and effort to help other people for the purpose of establishing a positive, collaborative relationship.

Here are some examples of how to build personal capital with others:

- Volunteer to help others with their workload.
- Support their ideas in front of others.
- Listen to their problems, and give constructive feedback.
- Ask for their opinions.
- Give praise and recognition for their achievements.
- Include them in your communications and business events.
- Share new tools and methods.
- Share information.
- Meet their deadlines on tasks.
- Promptly respond to their e-mails, voice mails, and requests.
- Show up to their meetings on time.
- Volunteer to do things for the team.
- Initiate process improvements for the team.
- Share your achievements and credit.
- Mentor and coach others.
- Give others opportunities to grow and develop.

The value of personal capital is in the eye of the beholder; that is why it is important to understand human factors and diversity. Challenging an Idealist to a debate is not building personal capital, but asking about their feelings or relationships is. Interactions are transactions with the potential for both give and take. Givers are net investors; takers are net withdrawers. In relationships, it is very difficult to make withdrawals (requesting help from another person, for example) when you have no personal capital invested (or have not even opened an account with the other person). In fact, if your history has been negative with this person, you are likely barred from his or her "bank."

Not all transactions and investments are the same. What you give and what is given in return may not be immediate but may take time to grow. Some investments are good, and some are bad. There are no guaranteed returns.

The bottom line is that our space expands when we build personal capital with others.

Be Visible

It is difficult to make a positive impact if you are not visible to others. Be an active contributor, communicator, and leader. This requires a willingness to take risks and stretch beyond your personal space.

To expand personal space, you must mentally and physically get involved with team and organizational activities. You must actively engage in all three spaces and ensure that you have ongoing projects in both team space and organizational space. Make time to meet people at all levels in the organization, participate in organizational and team events, establish and maintain a network of contacts, speak up on issues and problems, volunteer for assignments, and visibly support others. Visible team players are action oriented: they get involved in determining new strategies, goals, standards, policies, and processes.

You can increase personal space by being a change agent. Contributing to organizational and team successes requires a proactive mind-set in identifying new opportunities, developing creative alternatives, and proposing exciting improvements. This may entail creating and marketing new ideas, facilitating discussions, being willing to take risks, and being forthright with your views.

Let people see you as a catalyst for change. The process and behavior of creating new ideas can be more important than the content. Visibility is created when people see you as a positive generator of ideas.

When you do good work, others believe in you. When you work hard, follow through on your commitments, and solve problems, you gain the trust and belief of others, which makes you more visible. People will see you as positive, reliable, and competent. Do not be afraid to show your personal successes, and be proud of your accomplishments. High team performance always makes you more visible to others.

Great character builds greater visibility. Let people see your best side. People of high honesty, respect, and integrity stand tall in the minds of others. When you demonstrate your highest character, others take notice. You may hear remarks like, "That was big of you to do that," "You have a big heart," or "You are a stand-up person."

The bottom line is that our space grows when we get involved, offer new ideas, work hard, and show character.

Practice Inclusive Behaviors

Allow others into your personal space. When people feel welcomed to approach you, ask you questions, and solicit your help, you have a space that they want to come to. They feel safe to talk to you and know that you have their best interest at heart. When you are willing to receive others, they will be eager to work for you and enter your personal space. In contrast, when people feel intimidated by or even fear your behaviors, they do not feel compelled to come to you. Our behaviors can bring people in or leave them out. Being inclusive starts by not excluding yourself. As we learned from the Abilene paradox, being overly passive raises your threshold to act, squeezes your personal space, and results in excluding yourself from the action. The same principles of inclusion apply to you: get engaged, practice being involved, and recognize and reward yourself for good performance.

Work with people who will stretch you. We learn a tremendous amount from other people, especially those who are leaders, mentors, managers, experts, teachers, and thought leaders. It is important to include these people in our lives. You may find it intimidating at times to interact with people who are smarter or more experienced than you, but this adventure will stretch and develop you. Not only are these people willing to share their knowledge, but you learn much just from watching and listening to them. It pays to seize the opportunities to work with these people on projects and in meetings. As they say, you are the company you keep.

Acknowledging and inviting other people's opinions are ways to demonstrate inclusive behaviors. When people feel welcomed to join a conversation or contribute to a team effort, they are motivated to give more of their time, skills, and knowledge to the effort.

The bottom line is that our space expands when we invite people in.

Send the Right Signals

Send positive signals from your personal space. Signals are nonverbal and behavioral cues that we send to others. They are the impressions that we give people when we interact with them on an ongoing basis. What is your daily behavior with people? Are you cheerful, serious, or indifferent most of the time? Do you regularly praise or recognize others? Do you take the time to sincerely ask how they are doing? Do you gladly participate in team events or only when you must? Do you take time to encourage and voluntarily help others? Do you promptly return telephone calls and e-mails?

Signals are the little things that people pick up and remember about you. They are a combination of what we do or say directly or indirectly to people. Nonverbal communications are powerful transmitters of our feelings: a simple smile or a handshake can quickly change how people feel about us. Positive signaling takes effort. People who give positive signals are good team leaders.

The first signal sets the tone for what follows, so the most important time to give a positive signal is when we first meet people or when people first approach us. First impressions are indeed lasting impressions, and a smile or a positive reception quickly puts people at ease and motivates others to do the same for us.

Transmit desired messages clearly and frequently. If we wish to communicate an important message to others, then we need to transmit both our intellectual and emotional beliefs. For example, if we think safety is an important value that needs to be continuously expressed, we must transmit our feelings about it through our behaviors. People can sense whether we are truly a believer or a pretender.

The bottom line is that our space enlarges when we send positive signals to others.

Be Assertive

Speak from your personal space. Assertiveness is about expressing what we feel clearly and confidently without violating other people's space. It is about respecting our mutual space: we should neither give up space nor let others take away our space. When we let someone else speak for us, we are giving up our inner self. When we fear conflict, we are allowing others to control our behaviors and giving up personal space. To protect our space and become more assertive in conflict situations, we begin by trusting what we feel and verbalizing it. No one can ever deny or refute what we feel. It is personal space; no one can ever feel what we feel, which means we have absolute legitimacy in this space. This legitimacy enables us to speak directly and with great confidence. The key is to stay in our personal space and not cross over in attempts to control or judge others.

Here are some examples of staying in personal space:

- Make I statements. *Correct:* "I don't feel supported by you" (speaking from personal space). *Incorrect:* "You don't support me" (speaking in the other party's space, a violation). *Correct:* "I really depend on you, and when your work is not done on time, my work also suffers" (speaking from personal space). *Incorrect:*

"Your lack of follow-through is irresponsible and indicates that you are not a good team player" (speaking in the other party's space, a violation).

- Always judge the observation, not the person. *Correct:* "These statements do not sound accurate to me" (judging from personal space). *Incorrect:* "You are so stupid for saying these things" (judging another person's space). When we judge the person, we are making assumptions about the other person's space. This is a space violation.

- When we dominate and repress others, we are violating another person's space. We need to stay in personal space when giving negative feedback or constructive criticism to another person. *Correct:* "When I read the project charter, my understanding of the project's objective is to reduce the number of defects in the product. Am I wrong?" (speaking from personal space). *Incorrect:* "You're wrong! Didn't you read the project charter? It clearly states that the project's objective is to reduce the number of defects in the product" (invading the other person's space).

Using these correct ways to express ourselves prevent conflicts and miscommunications. People are likely to judge others who appear to judge them. Being assertive does not mean being dominant, aggressive, and vocal. Assertiveness comes from trusting our inner voice, being confident with ourselves, and not being fearful of what others may think. When we have a broad, expanded space, we are less fearful and less vulnerable to attacks from others; when our space is small, our vulnerability is high. Assertiveness builds personal space.

When we possess either a highly passive or aggressive style, we are losing space. In using aggressive behaviors, we lose space by excluding people. Our space expands when people fill our lives, and aggressive behaviors, such as when we dominate or intimidate people, scares others off. It is no doubt that people do not want to work with us if we choose to disrespect or belittle them. As a result, our space becomes smaller. In using passive behaviors, we tend to assess our value through the eyes of others and allow them to drive our behaviors. To be assertive, we need to find our sweet spot: the ability to become aggressive or passive when we need to without excluding ourselves or others. Being assertive increases personal space in two major ways: giving us the ability to move easily between aggressive and passive behaviors for a given situation and building self-confidence. As shown in Figure 12.3, assertive people have the ability to flex their threshold to the right or left to fit the situation.

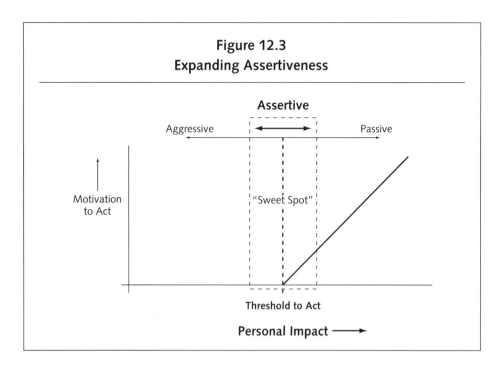

Figure 12.3
Expanding Assertiveness

Assertive

Aggressive ← → Passive

Motivation to Act

"Sweet Spot"

Threshold to Act

Personal Impact ⟶

Passives can expand their space and improve their assertiveness by following these guidelines:

- It is okay to say no.
- You are not responsible for how other people feel. You can neither control nor be responsible for someone else's personal space.
- Your fear of conflict or confrontation is likely far worse than the actual consequences of your actions.
- Waiting for permission to act is a lost opportunity.
- You have more emotional strength than you think. Let them challenge you.

Aggressives can expand their space and improve their assertiveness by following these guidelines:

- Honor other people's space. Intrusions are usually not welcomed.
- Those who want to be independent and alone will end up in life being independent and alone in their space. Accept other views and alternatives.

- Let it go. There is no need to occupy other people's spaces. Giving space to other people is far more important than being right.

- Slow down, and let other people catch up. Better yet, let others "drive" for awhile.

The bottom line is that assertiveness strengthens personal space.

Build Conflict Response Options, and Use Them Skillfully

Nothing grips a team more than conflict. Very few of us are good at resolving conflicts, so we try to avoid them, ignore them, defer them, work around them, and even try to give them to others if we can—anything but having to face them. As a team, it does not get much easier. We apply more brains to the problem, but we also have to reach team consensus too. It just seems to require so much time, emotional energy, and pain to resolve. Avoiding them is not always the best option. When team disagreements linger, the team is at risk for potential bad conflicts. A better solution is to expand our abilities to manage conflicts by using the right response options for the situation. Conflicts come up suddenly, and we need to be equipped to handle the challenge. There are a number of tools and techniques to respond to conflict, and two basic models are offered here. One is my adaptation of the classic Thomas-Kilmann model (1974) (see also Blake and Mouton, 1964; Kerzner, 2001), and the other is based on my three-space model of project management.

Classic Model   How we respond to conflict varies from individual to individual. Figure 12.4 illustrates the spectrum of choices in responding to conflict that we will call the *classic model* (it is a modified Thomas-Kilmann model). This spectrum resides in our personal space. When we face conflict, we basically have a natural preference for reacting assertively or unassertively. Rationals and Artisans tend to react quickly and assertively, while Guardians and Idealists likely behave unassertively. In extreme situations, Rationals and Artisans may be aggressive and dominating. They seek to win over others. For Guardians and Idealists, extreme situations may induce a more withdrawing behavior. They may literally shut down and refuse to participate at all. However, we should not rely on only our behavioral tendencies for managing conflicts. We are all capable of responding aggressively and passively given the right set of circumstances. We all have internal thresholds for being assertive or passive.

In conflict, people can seek four tracks from the classic model: aggressive, passive, avoidance, or cooperative (Figure 12.4).

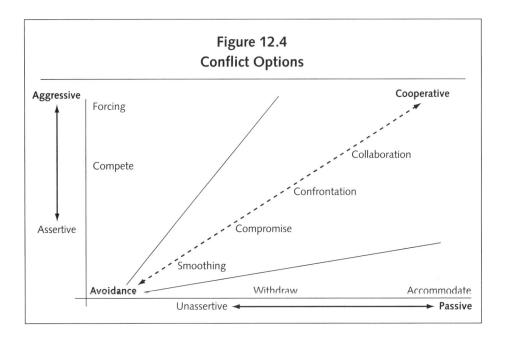

Figure 12.4
Conflict Options

Aggressive

Cooperative

Forcing

Collaboration

Compete

Confrontation

Compromise

Assertive

Smoothing

Avoidance

Withdraw

Accommodate

Unassertive

Passive

Basically, the aggressive track is an "I win, you lose" response: I want my position to prevail over yours. The opposite response, "you win, I lose," is the passive track: I accept your position over mine. Avoidance occurs when you purposely evade the issue and do not want to address the issue at this time. Finally, when parties seek a win-win outcome, they are using the cooperative track. Each track represents a different set of response options.

Aggressive Track This set of behaviors ranges from assertiveness, where we try to bend others to accept our position, to using our authority or power to "force" people to a given view. This conflict response is effective when competing, controlling, or compliance behaviors are required, such as legal and enforcement actions, emergency response, mandatory work requirements, health and safety rules, and stopping unethical practices. Typically these conflict options are valuable when situations call for decisive actions or immediate corrections. When these options are used to hurt or intimidate others, they create more conflict than they resolve. Rationals and Artisans are prone to show these behaviors.

Two common types of aggressive behaviors are forcing and compete. Forcing is directing others to behave in a manner that they may or may not agree with. It is an ultimate aggressive behavior where a person uses his position of power and authority to force others to his view. He may force things on others for their own good. People who use forcing often assume that the other party will submit to their demands, thereby achieving a quick victory. Of course, any victory may be met later by defiance or retaliation by opponents. Forcing may be necessary to achieve immediate compliance to prescribed processes or behaviors.

Compete is an aggressive "I win, you lose" behavior. One party is highly satisfied, while the other party is highly dissatisfied. This conflict style favors strong personality types who can dominate or overpower others. Also, people with organizational authority, such as politicians, public officials, management, and teachers, practice this behavior. Competing is a high-stakes game that results in a winner and a loser. For a team, it poses a risk of alienating others.

Advantages of using aggressive options are that they are fast, a quick win, effective, authoritative, proactive, and powerful. Disadvantages are that there is no buy-in, the behavior is exclusionary, and the other party is resentful.

Passive Track   At the opposite end of the spectrum are passive or unassertive behaviors where people give up their positions to the other party: they allow the other party to win. Like aggressive behaviors, passive behaviors are also exclusionary in nature, but instead of excluding others, they are excluding themselves. These are effective options for someone who feels the benefits of moving forward outweigh the detriments of continuing the conflict between parties. It might be better to cut losses now than risk a greater loss later to the team. For example, a willingness to accept an opposing view may be effective in preserving the peace, setting a cooperative tone across the team for future discussions, and demonstrating flexibility in resolving issues.

Accommodate means accepting the other party's position regardless of whether the conceding party agrees with it. You are willing to "lose" to let the other side "win." This could be a gesture to save time, an easy way to avoid conflict, an act of subordination, or a lack of confidence in your position. Withdraw means taking your position off the table. This does not necessarily mean giving in to the other side but, rather, choosing to retract your position. Withdrawal does not mean that you have adopted other options. You are open to hearing and debating other positions.

The advantages of a passive track are that it avoids further disagreement and bad feelings and allows the team to move forward. The disadvantages are losing personal confidence and influence and being perceived as weak or subordinate to others.

Avoidance Track   Avoidance behavior is a no-interest behavior. We choose to neither compete nor accommodate the other party. This is different from passive behaviors in that we are not withdrawing or giving up our position to the other party. Our position still stands, but we do not want to discuss it at this time. We agree to disagree and retain our position and agree to go forward without further discussion. I can either physically leave or declare my disinterest in working on the issue further. I will revisit it if I feel like it.

Neither party feels satisfied in avoidance mode. Avoidance behavior may be appropriate in certain circumstances. In an emotional issue, a person may elect to avoid further conflict until he has regained his composure. Avoidance is less of a track than the other areas, but avoidance can also have a progression of behaviors too, such as physically hiding from the other party, ignoring the other party, and being in communications but agreeing to disagree.

An advantage here is that conflict does not escalate into something worse and buys time to gather more information, cool off, or seek advice. Additional time may heal the problem, or it may not be the right time to address the problem, and waiting may be the best solution. The disadvantage is that there is no conflict resolution. You must internalize and cope with the problem and may develop feelings of frustration and guilt.

Cooperative Track   Cooperative behaviors are exhibited when both parties receive satisfaction from the outcome. These behavioral options are not separate alternatives but a continuum of choices with increasing partnership as one goes higher:

- A smoothing response is to play down the conflict, emphasize common interests, and avoid discussing any hurtful or divisive issues in order to gain cooperation from the other party. Statements like these are common: "It's not a big deal. We can always come back to it later," or "If it doesn't work, we can always change it back." This is a coaxing strategy.

- Compromise is a give-and-take or split-the-difference proposition. No one wins entirely, but no one loses entirely either. Each side gives up something in return for agreement. Neither side is fully satisfied but is sufficiently satisfied to move forward. It is a common bargaining technique.

- Confrontation is a joint problem-solving approach: each side is willing to work out an optimal solution for both parties. The process entails gathering facts and information, understanding each other's position, and seeking a solution. It is more of a deliberation than a compromise, and each party walks away satisfied.

- Collaboration is the highest cooperative state. Each party is fully satisfied with the conclusion and agrees. It is a win-win for both parties. Each party gets results and feels good about the outcome.

The advantages are that both parties walk away with a mutual win and feel good about it, although it scales up from a weak win-win with smoothing to a very strong win-win in the case of collaboration. This track seeks satisfaction of both parties. The disadvantages are that it requires more time, patience, creativity, and interpersonal skills.

Ideally, we want to be assertive and collaborative: to openly and honestly state our thoughts and feelings in a constructive manner that reduces neither our space nor the personal space of others. When personal space is small, we are more prone to take an aggressive or passive track. In an expanded space, we have more confidence, energy, and motivation to take the cooperative track. In Figure 12.4, the spreading solid lines around the cooperative track symbolize the fact that collaboration results in greater space as people successfully work together. Collaboration has a multiplier effect when team synergy is achieved.

To strengthen your collaborative skills

- Expand your personal space to see the other sides of the issues. Be willing to compromise and seek mutual understanding.

- Explore options. There are always alternatives.

- Look for creative win-win solutions.

- Be able to recognize and respect the temperament types of others.

- Flex your personality style to be more compatible with other types.

- Be inclusive with your verbal and nonverbal communications.

- Demonstrate good listening skills and patience.

- Show care and concern for others.

- Respect the opinions of others.

- Avoid personalizing issues.

- Be positive.

Three-Space Model   When interpersonal conflicts occur, people tend to focus on their space. After all, conflicts are emotional disagreements that take us out of our behavioral norms. We are motivated to find an answer so that we can return to our normal behavioral state. The classic model offers behavioral choices for resolving conflicts: aggressive, passive, avoidance, and cooperative. These coping behaviors are generated from personal space. However, we should not feel that all conflict responses must come from personal space. In fact, if we tried to manage all of our conflicts alone, we would be literally overloaded. Overloading can lead to severe anxiety, stress, and frustration. No one can do it alone.

The three-space model (Figure 12.5) is about learning how to use the three spaces to give us more options, relieve our conflict load, and lessen our cope-and-carry baggage. Many people do not realize that they can readily recruit help from organizational and team spaces to resolve their interpersonal conflicts. They are lifelines to use when we need help. The three-space model offers numerous advantages for resolving interpersonal conflicts.

Organizational Space   Organizational space offers innumerable ways to resolve conflicts. It has rules, policies, regulations, values, procedures, standards, strategies, and authority. If the conflict is around resources or getting cooperation from other

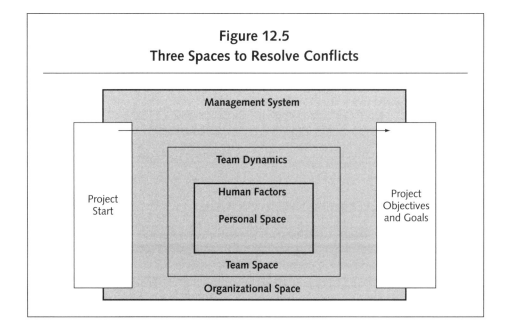

Figure 12.5
Three Spaces to Resolve Conflicts

departments, it often helps to seek a solution through management rather than line personnel. Department managers are responsible for resource allocation. If the resource is not made available, it may become a choice of priorities, which again may involve a management decision. Guardians are the best in using organizational space to help resolve conflicts. They have a deep respect for authority, rules, policies, and procedures and refer to authoritative sources to build their positions on issues.

Here are some examples of using organizational space to help resolve conflicts:

- You have a disagreement with a colleague over the priority of work assignments. Instead of debating the issue, you go to your manager for immediate clarification.

- You and a colleague are debating the interpretation of a regulation. Instead of engaging in argument, you contact the authoritative governmental agency for its interpretation.

- You wish to suspend an employee for unacceptable job performance and are worried about facing the employee. Instead of confronting the employee alone, you call on human resources to review the case and help you administer the process fairly and legally with the employee.

- People in your business function are complaining to you that they feel grossly underpaid compared to those in other companies. Instead of avoiding the issue, you request that your company provide competitive salary and benefits data for people working in the same region and in the same discipline.

Team Space   Using team space to resolve conflicts involves forming a project team, a partnership, an alliance, or recruiting others to help. By bringing people together to address a problem, you are asking them to share a common space. More and more people and organizations are relying on teamwork to help solve problems and improve processes. We can also use this same concept to help address personal problems and conflicts.

Following are some examples of using team space to help resolve conflicts:

- You and another manager have a tough decision to make on a capital project. You each have different views and personal stakes in the project. You form a project team of experts to thoroughly evaluate the alternatives and make an objective recommendation to both of you.

- You are leaving your office facility when a person you do not recognize approaches you to ask if she could use your security badge to get back into the building. She claims to have left her badge on her desk. You do not want to violate security rules. Instead of saying no and fearing a conflict, you offer to help her contact a colleague of hers inside.

- You have a large team working on a complex project. The team is enthusiastic but inexperienced. Their progress is slow, and conflicts are emerging. You bring in a facilitator to help the team with team processes and conflicts.

- You and your colleague disagree over the validity of a conclusion in your report. Instead of continuing debate, you have the report reviewed by a senior team member and agree to accept her opinion.

Using Organizational and Team Spaces to Resolve a Personal Conflict   I had just concluded a long business trip in Houston and was eager to return home. When I arrived at the airport, I found that weather problems had canceled many flights, including mine. Passengers were advised that the flight was being rescheduled for the next day. Many passengers were quite frustrated by this change and were told that the airline had no other solutions for them. The airline employee at the gate was inundated with complaining passengers. Instead of joining the crowd, I headed to the airline customer service desk where people were trained to handle situations like this, a move up to organizational space.

I waited in line behind a young couple where the woman appeared very flustered and the man was angry. They had some heated words with the employee and then huffed off, swearing at the employee. How was I going to follow that act? I thought that the last thing this airline employee needed was another angry customer. Instead I looked for a leverage point to create some team space. I walked up politely to the counter and gave the employee a smile and said, "I don't think they pay you enough for this job! How do you do this every day?" He mentioned that he had done it for seven years and that this was not half as bad as some of the cases he has faced. I said, "Boy, I give you a lot of credit." At that point, he replied, "Thanks, what can I do for you?"

I told him that I apologized for having to lay more work on him, but I was a frequent flyer of his airline and really needed to get home: "I know things are a mess and we're stuck here, but I need your help in getting home to San Francisco. What would you do if you were me? Can you think of any creative solutions?"

He paused and offered, "I haven't any solutions, but let me try a couple of possibilities for you." After about five minutes, he said, "I'm not supposed to do this, but I can get you on another airline, and I have to convert you to business class."

I asked if that meant an extra charge, and he said, "Just go catch your flight at gate 56. And hurry if you want to make it!"

What a great guy! Why did he make a special arrangement for me? He certainly did not have to do it. What motivated him to help me were several things:

- By greeting him with a quick smile, I sent a signal that I was not going to be angry with him.

- I respected his space by sympathizing with his position, which his response indicated he appreciated it.

- I told him that I was a frequent flyer of his airline and needed to get home tonight in hopes that he would sympathize and respect my space in return (personal capital), even though it may have been a bit superficial.

- I then created team space by asking for his help: "What would you do if you were me?" I was inviting him into my space, and he took the invitation. Now we were sharing space, and we felt like partners, not adversaries.

- By creating team space, we were working collaboratively to get a win-win. My win was going home, and his win was feeling good about doing something extra for a deserving person.

In conflict situations, being a partner emotionally is just as important as engaging in the intellectual or logical component of the conflict. Soft skills are critical. In this case, I used humor, flattery, empathy, and a smile to try to create an emotionally positive, problem-solving tone. Also, emotional engagement should be done first, especially if the person is an Idealist or Artisan and thinks emotionally first. Positive feelings always lead to intellectual solutions.

Change thinking, and it will change behaviors. Everything I did helped me change the employee's thinking about me. If I had behaved angrily toward him, he would have resisted helping me. I had to try changing his thinking in order to change his behavior toward me.

DETERMINING YOUR CONFLICT MANAGEMENT STYLE

The three-space model offers additional options for resolving conflicts. There are no hard-and-fast rules on which space is best for resolving a particular conflict. It is individual and situation dependent. Just as with the classic model, the best conflict option depends on (1) the degree of importance to you and your threshold to act, (2) your knowledge of whom or what you are dealing with, (3) your consequent history with that person or type of conflict, and (4) your underlying human factors. What is your threshold to act, and which space do you favor when you are confronted by a given conflict? What is your predominant style: passive, aggressive, avoidance, or collaborative?

To assess your conflict style, Exhibit 12.1 provides three conflict scenarios and five possible response options. Read each scenario, and then for each response option (A, B, C, D, and E), identify (1) which of the three spaces are involved (organizational, team, or personal); (2) which of the four classical conflict tracks they illustrate (aggressive, passive, avoidance, or cooperative); and (3) which of the four options (A, B, C, D, and E) you would pick. The answer key is listed on the last page of this chapter.

Discussion on your choices. Was it easy for you to identify the three spaces for each choice? If you took personal action to address the problem, then you were operating in personal space to try to resolve the problem. If you were depending on others to address the problem, you were either using team or organizational space. Organizational space would involve using company policy or rules, referring the matter to an authority, or relying on management to do something.

Did you find that you favored one type of response option over others? Do you feel you have a high or low threshold for taking action? Did choice E, the cooperative team space (win-win), feel the best for you? Given that we have three spaces and four response tracks with different options within those tracks, a broad range of options is available to help resolve these problems.

The key point is that there are many viable options to manage problems and conflicts. Some things are better done aggressively in personal space, and others are probably better handled by avoidance in organizational space. Choosing an option that you are comfortable with may not be the best option. To be an effective manager, you need to expand your space and learn to use all options. It takes much practice and experience.

Personal space expands when you effectively use organizational space and team space in conjunction with classical response options to manage conflicts.

Exhibit 12.1
Conflict Scenarios

Case 1: You arrive at the lobby of your office building and a coworker (whom you have seen around the office on occasions) is smoking. Your company facility is a smoke-free zone. You know secondhand smoke is a health hazard. What do you do?

A. You promptly say: "Excuse me, this is a smoke-free facility. You can't smoke here."
B. You move away to the other side of the lobby to avoid the smoke.
C. You take your complaint to the lobby security officer.
D. You hope someone else arrives in the lobby to say something to the coworker.
E. You say: "Excuse me, this is a smoke-free area, but you can smoke outside. Would you like me to show you where the nearest smoking area is outside?"

Case 2: Your manager is hosting a presentation by the human resource manager, and about thirty people are in attendance. The presentation is about the new company salary program. She appears to be a very nice person, but she is a soft speaker. You are sitting in the back row and can barely hear her. What is your response?

A. You say: "I can't hear you. You need to speak up."
B. You sit and try to hear as much as you can and will pick up what you missed later from your colleagues.
C. You write a note and pass it up to the host (your manager) in hopes that he will say something to her.
D. You make a side comment, "Can you hear her?" hoping someone else feels the same way and will speak up.
E. You try to catch the attention of the speaker with a polite hand sign that she needs to speak up.

Case 3: You are standing in line waiting for lunch with your friend at the company cafeteria. The line is rather loosely organized. There are four stations, but only two are open. You have been waiting for ten minutes, and you are both very hungry and concerned about making an after-lunch staff meeting on time. You make your way up front when suddenly another cashier opens up a station to your right and a person behind you immediately runs up to the station. What is your response?

A. You shout: "Hey! you jumped ahead of me. I'm next."
B. You wait for the next available station.
C. You don't say anything, but you complain to the cashier that they need to control the line better.
D. You are annoyed but wait for your friend's reaction first to see what she wants to do.
E. You step to the counter and say: "Sorry, we were next, but we can order together if you like."

SUMMARY

Expanding personal space means to reach beyond ourselves with positive influence into team and organizational space. Our behaviors have a positive impact on the behaviors of the team and organization. This is in contrast to a reduced space, where our behaviors are increasingly controlled by other people and the organization.

Expanding personal space builds informal power, reduces incoming conflicts, motivates others to want to work with you, and gives you inner strength. Just as in project management, our goal is to achieve results and feel good about it. We want to be good at preventing and resolving conflicts as opposed to always absorbing and coping with conflicts.

There are seven key strategies for expanding personal space:

- Value diversity. Our space expands when we reach others at a personal level.

- Build a positive account balance. Our space expands when we build personal capital with others.

- Be visible. Our space grows when we get involved, offer new ideas, work hard, and show character in our behaviors.

- Practice inclusive behaviors. Our space expands when we invite people in.

- Send the right signals. Our space enlarges when we send positive signals to others.

- Be assertive. Assertiveness strengthens personal space.

- Know your response options to conflict, and use them skillfully. We want to be good responders, not reactors, to conflict. Personal space expands when we effectively use organizational and team space in conjunction with classical response options to manage conflicts.

Answer Key to Exhibit 12.1

A: Personal space, aggressive track (satisfy my needs first)

B: Personal space, avoidance track (avoid conflict)

C: Organizational space, passive track (exclude myself, defer to authority)

D: Team space, passive track (exclude myself, defer to others)

E: Team space, cooperative track (satisfy both my needs and theirs)

Managing Good and Bad Behaviors

We all have strengths and weaknesses and good sides and bad sides to our personalities. Although our good and bad behaviors appear as opposites, they are actually complementary and mutually dependent. Optimism and pessimism, for example, are opposites, but we can readily switch from one to the other or blend the two. We move easily from one behavior to another. Just as in life, we are a mixture of good and bad, strong and weak, and high and low. We can have a high moment and then suddenly experience a low moment. One is fed by the other. Great sadness can lead to great happiness. The feelings that we get from one are accentuated by the other. We appreciate health when we are sick and wealth when we have been poor. A new-found love is so fleeting, yet a love that is lost is never forgotten. One is the seed of the other. Out of adversity comes great triumph. We see these forces play out often in our lives.

Our bad side dominates in times of stress and conflict; our good side dominates when we are praised and appreciated. We have an upper-level force and a lower-level force, and we tend to cycle between those two states. When we are friendly and open with others, we are up. When we get harsh, impatient, or defensive, we are down. Unfortunately, no one lives in perfect balance, and we occasionally encounter people who are lower-level dominated or upper-level dominated. The most obvious lower-level-dominated people are bullies, whiners, intimidators, and those who seek to control others. Those who are transparent, caring, and receptive to others are upper-level dominated and tend to be a positive force on a team. Thus, we have both upper-level and lower-level behaviors. Lower-level behaviors and upper-level behaviors are different for the four personality types (Table 13.1).

Extreme conditions can reveal both good and bad behaviors in our personalities. My dad once said that if I really wanted to know someone, I should take that person out to the golf course. Golf is a great sport for revealing your true behaviors: you can experience great joy or great frustration on every shot. Golf has a way of bringing out a person's true temperament. A person may behave well for about nine holes but never for eighteen holes. It is inevitable that our innate personality will emerge in a round of golf. That test has never failed me yet.

It does not take a round of golf to reveal anyone's undesirable side. Lower-level behaviors are inside all of us. If we choose to, we can easily move into our lower state: we get selfish, impatient, insensitive, or short-tempered. There are plenty of motivators and pathways to this bad side. For example, when we have high expectations of ourselves and fail to perform to our standards, we tend to be hard on ourselves. We are disappointed in our own behaviors and push harder to improve, be valued, and accepted. However, our self-disappointments can be a strong force in shifting us to our lower-level state, where we suddenly shut people out, isolate ourselves, or even get mad at ourselves. We do not have to accept these lower-level behaviors. In our personal space, we can choose where we want to be. We can take a better course: learn from our mistakes, forgive ourselves, and move on. We do not have to beat up ourselves. Forgiveness lightens the mind and frees the body from the burdens of inferiority. It may be natural to languish temporarily in personal disappointments, but those who do not get over these disappointments tend to carry them forward in a negative way. Too many people hang on to their regrets and self-disappointments, which can lead to a perpetual, self-defeating internal dialogue. Artisans and Guardians are best in letting go; Rationals and Idealists have the toughest time. Letting go and moving forward is an upper-level behavior. Moving to our upper level gives other people a better view of who we are and what we are capable of doing. We cannot shine from our lower level. Upper-level behaviors illuminate who we are, while the darkness of the lower level represses our spirit and talents.

Strong team players consistently exhibit upper-level behaviors. They have a positive internal dialogue that resists lower-level thinking. Upper-level players pro-

Table 13.1
Upper- and Lower-Level Behaviors

Upper-Level Behaviors	Lower-Level Behaviors
Idealist	
• Creative	• Procrastinates
• Problem solver	• Worried, emotional, upset
• Caring, builds relationships	• Overly sensitive to criticism and threats
• Helps ensure people are connected	• Paralyzed, no output, withdraws
• Patient	• Becomes a noncontributor
	• Complainer, lets things erode
Guardian	
• Outstanding implementer	• Resistant to change, stubborn
• Hard worker	• Controlling, bossy
• Conscientious, loyal to team	• Focuses too much on process
• Driven to get the job done on time, on spec, within budget	• Becomes very rigid, picky, narrow
	• Internalizes problems
Rational	
• Self-starter, initiator	• Dominates: calls all the shots, poor listener, talks at people, constantly challenges others
• Technical and analytical thinker	• Argumentative
• Great planner, strategic-minded	• Defensive, arrogant, always right and never wrong
• Sees the big picture	• Impatient; moves forward without consensus
• Idea generator	
Artisan	
• Fast thinker, fast doer	• Unreliable, unpredictable
• Wonderful risk taker	• Hates excessive processes and structure
• Enthusiastic, high energy	• Gets distracted and ignores others
• Performer	• Immature, insensitive
• Persuasive	• Judgmental
	• Will not follow norms

mote cooperation and move the team forward by demonstrating the following attributes:

- Positive attitude about people
- Problem-solving mind-set
- Future orientation
- Transparency and openness with others

In contrast, lower-level players have the following traits:

- Defensive
- Self-centered
- Insecure
- Fearful
- Negative outlook

DEALING WITH DIFFICULT PEOPLE

People who spend their time in their lower levels are often difficult to work with. One of the great sources of stress on a team is putting up with difficult people: those who impede the actions and progress of others. Their behaviors reduce productivity and teamwork. Dealing with difficult people can be almost painful; they seem to inflict an emotional pain on others, possessing a negative power and control over the team's interactions.

Difficult people show predominantly lower-level behaviors and consume team energy by taking away time, resources, and attention, and making everything an effort. The team feels diluted, tired, discounted, and frustrated when dealing with the persistently difficult person. People feel devalued because the team accepts negative behaviors and makes concessions to placate them. A persistently difficult person will pull the team down to a lower level. If the team settles into a lower dynamic state, performance suffers. Operating at a lower level makes the team susceptible to conflicts and lowers the team's set point (Figure 13.1), which is the average behavioral level of the team. With a lower set point, the team is more prone to bad behaviors (such as resistance, impatience, fear, and defensiveness) than good behaviors (such as listening, giving to others, and transparency). Instead of striving for the best, they are content just to finish the work.

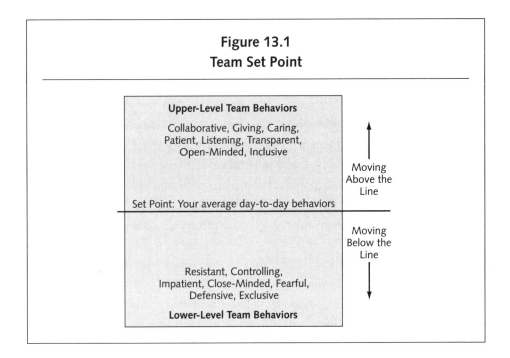

Figure 13.1
Team Set Point

Upper-Level Team Behaviors

Collaborative, Giving, Caring,
Patient, Listening, Transparent,
Open-Minded, Inclusive

Moving
Above the
Line

Set Point: Your average day-to-day behaviors

Moving
Below the
Line

Resistant, Controlling,
Impatient, Close-Minded, Fearful,
Defensive, Exclusive

Lower-Level Team Behaviors

A team has a high set point when

- Debate is encouraged, and conflicts are quickly resolved.
- Everyone is transparent in their views and feelings.
- The team wants to work together rather than apart.
- People care about each other.
- Bad behaviors are not tolerated.
- The team regularly seeks behavioral feedback.
- Reinforcement and recognitions are behavioral norms.

Who Are These Difficult People?

We are all difficult people at times. We all have our moments where we impede the actions of others. We get short at times and dip into our lower level when we are stressed or in distress. When we are in our lower level, we are less likely to behave normally or rationally. We all know what to do and say when we are calm and relaxed, but we cannot seem to recall those things when we are under stress. That is why we do not like to work under pressure. Pressure brings out our bad behaviors such as impatience, anger, and defensiveness. They occur when we get stuck in traffic jams, wait in long lines, are embroiled in interpersonal conflicts, and face other stressors, such as bad bosses or money problems.

A difficult person is quite different from people who have difficult moments. Difficult people are personality types who have gone bad. Difficult Guardians are controlling, stubborn, highly resistant, and negative to change. Difficult idealists disengage from the team, become pessimistic and victimized, refuse to contribute to what they call a "lost cause," and may take pleasure in watching others fail. Difficult Rationals roll over people, become condescending and insensitive to others, are defensive and critical, do not listen well, and withhold information from the team. Difficult Artisans are selfish, unfocused, unreliable, moody, and judgmental.

Difficult people spend most of their time in their lower level, while others spend most of their time in the upper level (Figure 13.2). Difficult people prefer to operate from their lower level and develop a lower set point. Commonly they are not transparent, do not collaborate with others, seek their own views, control the team

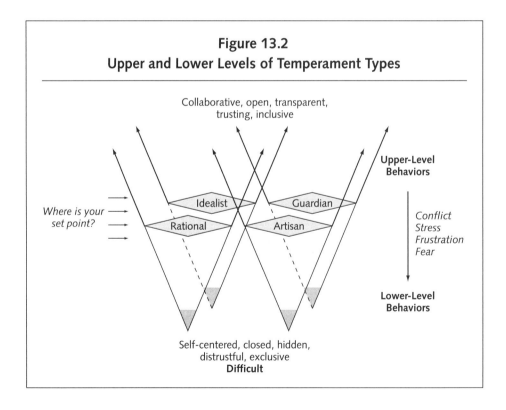

Figure 13.2
Upper and Lower Levels of Temperament Types

Collaborative, open, transparent, trusting, inclusive

Where is your set point?

Idealist   Guardian

Rational   Artisan

Upper-Level Behaviors

Conflict
Stress
Frustration
Fear

Lower-Level Behaviors

Self-centered, closed, hidden, distrustful, exclusive
Difficult

with their behaviors, and consume energy from the team. They can be very successful and accomplished people and are often very bright, enthusiastic, and hard working. However, they do not work well with others, prefer not to work on teams, and do not seem to care. They believe they can work faster alone and with greater resolve than working on a team. Being unencumbered by team rules frees the independent individual to move forward. It is true that one can work faster alone, encounter less resistance, and may be preferred for certain types of work, but it is unlikely that an individual can outperform a skilled team.

The most common problem with difficult people is that we do not know how to work with them. The way to cope with and manage them is to be aware of what they are doing and how you are responding.

Behaviors of Difficult People

Difficult people operate from a lower dynamic state in their personality style. The more difficult that person behaves, the lower he or she is.

There is a misconception that difficult people are always aggressive, abusive loudmouths. True, these behaviors are difficult to cope with, but they are not the only difficult behavioral set. Passives also consume energy by avoiding conflict, withholding information, deferring decisions, avoiding responsibility, and seeking sympathy. Passivity does not mean inactivity. Those who display passive-aggressive behavior can resort to sabotage or back-stabbing behaviors to exert influence. The lower level is filled with both "bad" aggressives and passives.

What Is It Like to Be in the Lower Level?

The lower level is dark and hidden, a mosaic of secret rooms, blind corners, twists and turns, and nooks and crannies. I have seen people drop to their lower level and never find their way out. Sadly, they have lost their way in life. The deeper they go, the more alone and self-centered they become. They are insecure, fearful, deceiving, and so suspicious that they hardly trust anyone except for those who they know well.

Why Would Anyone Want to Go There?

Their intent is not transparent. They prefer not to reveal themselves, because it is protective and defensive in nature. When things get tough, they dive for cover. When people are stressed or threatened, they naturally seek refuge. They want to escape. At times of conflict, they lash out and insult or yell at other people in order to escape the situation. The lower level can be a very powerful place. It has great influence on others and consumes energy from *others.*

A profoundly negative event in life can drive people to their lower level, isolating themselves from the pain. In some cases, difficult people evolved into a lower dynamic state through years of complacency, and their bad behaviors became a habit. No one helped them and over time, they normalize their bad behaviors. The National Aeronautics and Space Administration called this gradual tolerance of an unacceptable condition "normalization of deviance." We slowly accept a deviation of our normal behaviors, and it becomes our second nature. Our internal dialogue accepts it. We learn to accept a bad behavior internally; it becomes a comfort zone.

Hiding is a common trait for difficult people. Rationals may hide behind logic, hoard information, and withhold opinions. Their knowledge is power. Guardians may hide behind the process and justify their actions based on agreed-to actions and precedence. Difficult people prefer to work from their lower level despite their impact on others. Their behaviors give them a sense of safety and independence that they naturally seek.

Dipping into your lower level can also be productive and motivating to yourself and others: it is like the famous saying, "I'm mad as hell, and I won't take it anymore." Being able to dig deep for some inspiration and confidence can be very resourceful. But dip too often, and the strength becomes a weakness. You may know people who use their lower-level behaviors too often, and it develops into a weakness for them. Unfortunately, they do not see it and they develop a blind spot in their personality.

Lower-level behaviors can be managed, and we can also cope with people who demonstrate these behaviors. People who persist in their lower levels erode teamwork and success and steal energy and enthusiasm from the team. They are takers.

What Are Difficult People Trying to Accomplish?

Difficult people are takers: they want to take others down to their emotional level. They are extremely self-centered and want others to support their behaviors. They want others to feel their anger if they are angry. If they are whining, they want others to sympathize with them and whine with them. To support their behaviors, they want others to help them justify their anger. They want to hear things like, "You have every right to feel angry." When they get defensive over an issue, they want to hear things such as, "You are right" or "I'm with you." Basically they are fearful and are taking cover in their lower level.

What Can You Do When You Encounter a Difficult Person in Conflict?

There are a number of ways to resist them:

- Do not join them in their lower level, do not feed it, do not empower it, and do not reinforce it.
- Elevate your thinking and behaviors, and practice positive upper-level behaviors.
- Switch your thinking. If the person is content driven, go to a process mode; if the conflict is around process, go to content.
- Understand that the common underlying element of difficult people is fear. By addressing their fear, you can resist the negative effects on you.
- Do not get upset; it is not your problem. People with low self-esteem need to put others down, control the situation, draw attention, or seek sympathetic approval to feed their insecurity.
- Do not hate them; feel for them. Difficult people do not know any better, and lack the knowledge, skills, and self-assurance to elevate themselves.

What Are the Most Common Lower-Level Behaviors in People?

All personality types have lower-level traits; some are found in all four types, and others are more associated with one personality type. The most common lower-level behaviors are complaining or whining, highly aggressive or dominating, controlling, impatient, and poor listening.

The Whine Cellar   Some people seem to enjoy being the office cynic, the complainer, or the poor victim. Cynicism and pessimism are lower-level behaviors that serve to attract attention and extract sympathy from others. Some types of Idealists are prone to operate in this mode. They like to go into the "whine cellar" and complain about almost anything. This is really a power play on their part, and some are quite skilled at it. People who are cynical and whine about the work are not good team players and consume energy from the team.

The key to avoiding the whine cellar trap is not to go there in the first place. In fact, make sure you do not support them for being there. Second, acknowledge the problem, and do not encourage any more whining. Sometimes it works best to write down the complaints. In that way, you demonstrate to the whiner that you have heard him and he does not need to repeat his story over and over again. Once the problem is acknowledged, help him find his way out of the cellar. You can do this by getting him to take constructive action to address it. Asking him to solve it right off is probably too big of a leap. It is far easier to ask him to gather more data and facts about the problem. It helps to work with facts as opposed to perceptions. By doing this, you help the person start on a positive, upper-level direction. You can lead him upstairs, but he needs to break through himself. It does not help to call a person a whiner since that judgment would not be well received. Instead, take the conversation forward to a future perspective, move the discussion to a problem-solving mode, and pinpoint actions that can be taken to address it.

The Dominant Domain Dominant behaviors are common on teams. Those who exhibit this lower-level behavior become authoritative, insensitive, critical, and controlling. Dominant behaviors fulfill a strong emotional need to control the situation and focus inwardly on their ego and intellectual need to be right. This is a common trap for Rationals. They have a need to prove they are right about everything, and they have difficulty letting go. Reversing a dominant behavior is tough because when dominance prevails, their listening stops. This results in decisions being made without team buy-in, people looking for retribution, and division and exclusion within the team. Dominant behaviors can be managed with strength in team processes, facilitation, and leadership. If dominant personalities exist, it is best to employ an assertive facilitator or install a strong team leader. Dominance requires equal or greater strength.

Difficult dominant people want other people to join in their lower state and feed their dominant behaviors of being exclusive, arrogant, aggressive, and insensitive. Instead, focus on the content, the logic, and the facts. Invite other opinions and honor team processes. If a person is in a dominant lower level, help her move to a higher level. First, acknowledge what she has said. Respect her thinking. Then ask her opinion on other ideas; shift to a new process to get others to participate and break the dominant cycle; call for a process check and reset the discussion on another topic (content); or address a behavioral topic (which Rationals have less energy for).

Controlling Behaviors Exerting excessive control is another common lower-level behavior. It is a place where people go when they are frustrated, have a low level of trust, or are not getting their way. Controlling behaviors are self-centered behaviors exhibited by all personality types but in different ways. In lower-level states, Artisans exert their controlling influence by ignoring team agreements and disengaging from team processes. Rationals are aggressive and dominating. Idealists get highly emotional and impatient, and Guardians control the work, tasks, and processes.

Guardians favor control. They like rules, laws, and processes because they offer control and semblance of order. When rules are not in place, the environment becomes disruptive, unfair, and disorderly to them. So in response, Guardians seek control and order through actions. They step in and stubbornly do the work and expect compliance from others. Idealists use emotional control behaviors when they feel hurt or see conflict. Typically their behavior is an emotional pleading or fighting type of response.

The best approach to reducing control behaviors is communications. Most often, the control behavior is in response to something that has gone wrong in the eyes of the person. Many times, it is simply a misunderstanding. The person does not like where things are headed and wants to rein in the team. Process checks and team assessments are excellent preventive measures to avoid controlling behaviors. If someone does not like where the team is headed, make it safe for people to speak up. As a team, try to talk your way upward. This requires mutual listening and understanding. To help the downward Guardian, recognize the need for change, agree on specific actions, and move on and get to work. For frustrated Guardians, action speaks louder than words.

Impatience   Impatience is a common lower-level behavior. We get impatient with our colleagues, bosses, children, spouses, and friends. When we lose our patience, we show it by getting frustrated or angry. We lose a sense of personal control and do not have the emotional energy and willpower to stay patient. On teams, when we are not satisfied with the progress, our patience starts to erode. We are ready to move on, but no one else is. We feel impeded.

Rationals and Artisans are fast movers and tend to lose patience when things slow down. They want to take action but have to wait for the team. They feel that they can go only as fast as the slowest person on the team. Guardians get impatient when no work, actions, and decisions are being made. Idealists get impatient when they feel people are being uncooperative and disrespectful.

Fundamentally, patience is about the value of time. We have great patience to wait and listen if we feel the time is well spent. We have a time clock inside us. We maintain a high level of patience when our interest level is high and are willing to spend the time to make it work. Impatience readily translates into lower-level behaviors when we feel our time is not being well spent and someone else has control of it (as in team meetings). That is why impatience often results in an emotional outburst and feelings of great frustration. Our time clock simply goes off. Impatient people can be difficult to handle. They walk ahead of us, run to the front of the line, make negative remarks, and have annoying impatient behaviors: they tap their feet, drum their fingers, groan, and roll their eyes. Sometimes we wish we could hit their snooze button.

Our patience is tested when progress is stalled and processes are not working well. Open-ended discussions with no time limits, slow decision-making processes, or lack of effective facilitation are common patience busters. Frustration sets in when our expectations are higher than the actual performance level, and one major source of frustration is when we feel our time is being wasted. Impatience is self-imposed; no one makes us impatient. We do it to ourselves. We are most prone to impatience when we are tired, stressed, and constrained by outside forces.

There are some ways to build greater patience in team meetings:

- Impatience is a self-centered behavior. Look outside yourself and put yourself in another person's perspective. What may be unimportant to you may be essential for someone else.
- Have a realistic agenda and time allocations.
- Address the most important issues first.
- Have a facilitator and timekeeper for team meetings.
- Minimize competing priorities by improving your time management.
- Avoid doing multiple things at one time. Focus on one process at a time. Park any off-topic issues.
- Agree on how much time to spend on an agenda item, and stick with it unless the team agrees to continue.

Poor Listening   We are poor listeners when we drop to our lower levels. When two people are talking from their lower levels, they are too deep into their own space to hear each other. In fact, they are too deep in their own holes to hear anything. They are out only to satisfy their own needs. In order to communicate, both parties need to be listening, and that requires both parties to be in their upper levels.

TECHNIQUES TO HELP THE TEAM STAY IN THE UPPER LEVEL

Where we choose to reside in our upper-lower states depends on our human factors and team environment. In project teams, our behaviors are motivated by team dynamics and processes, and in order to succeed as a team, everyone must count and contribute their best to the project. This type of motivational power is not all self-driven; it also relies on the psychological support of others. Maintaining an upper-level behavioral state for the team requires a dual effort in both personal space and team space. This section reveals key behaviors and techniques for motivating upper-level performance.

Personal Space: Recognition, Respect and Trust, and Relevance

To help others stay in their upper level, we need to extend our positive feelings to them. Most people are not persistently difficult; they just have difficult moments and require an occasional lift. We can influence others and keep them in their upper levels by practicing three simple behaviors: giving recognition, showing respect and trust, and making others feel relevant—the three R's.

Recognition　Recognition is the simplest, most underused team-building behavior. People are reluctant to recognize each other, and we often forget to acknowledge people for their extra efforts. Most people are uncomfortable praising others, perhaps fearing they may embarrass the person or appear superficial. In a competitive culture, we may fear that by praising others, we may be lowering our own stature. But this is an illusion of our insecurities. Praising others is a sign of leadership and maturity. The best leaders catch team members doing something right and recognize them on the spot. Giving someone sincere praise is one of the most powerful things that we can do. It may be nothing more than a kind pat on the back, a short e-mail note, a positive remark on the phone, or even a smile. It may seem small in terms of time and words, but it can have lasting impact on others. Praise is a relationship builder and a motivating behavior for a team. The key is to be timely, honest, personal, and specific with praise. If someone gave an excellent presentation, a remark such as "nice job" is not as effective as, "Mary, I thought your presentation was great. You spoke well, hit all the right points, and were poised during the group discussion."

Artisans enjoy public praise and recognition. A party in their honor is a great choice, especially when many people are present. Rationals appreciate praise when the recognition is based on their achievement and creativity. Idealists shy away from large public ceremonies around their personal achievements. They are concerned that others may see this public praise as being selfish, arrogant, and pretentious on their part. They prefer personal appreciations, a nice gift, a handshake, or a thoughtful card. Personal sincerity has a positive effect on Idealists. Guardians want to be valued for their work and efforts, and a team recognition award can have good impact. They do not put much value in trinket awards. Equating their worth to a trinket is an insult to them. They view their work as an unselfish and meaningful contribution to the team. Guardians accept money, which to them represents worth and security.

Respect and Trust   The second set of team behaviors is respect and trust. Respect and trust are feelings that you give someone. They are far more than just words and are different for each personality type.

Artisans want to be respected and trusted for their boldness, creative thinking, and problem solving. They feel trusted when given freedom to create new ideas and take unbridled actions. Idealists want to be respected for who they are, their honesty, and their collaborative spirit. They feel respect and trust when people respond to their feelings, intuition, and concerns. Rationals feel the greatest respect and trust when they are given independence and recognition for their ideas and are allowed to create that larger picture for the team. They respond especially well when the team expresses how the person's vision has helped guide the team to success. Guardians want to be respected and trusted for their hard work, discipline, and contributions. They want to feel that the rest of the team appreciates and accepts their work.

Relevance   Everyone wants to work on something that has real meaning and value to the organization; otherwise, the commitment will be low. All team members should feel significant, that their skills and talents are appreciated and valuable to the team's objectives. The key is to ensure that the content is highly relevant to the people who are working on the team. Once the value of the work is clear, then the people can be linked to it.

We can make the work highly relevant in these ways:

- Convey the importance of the project and the challenges.
- Explain the qualitative and quantitative benefits of the work.
- Get management to reinforce the importance of the work.
- Praise and recognize the content of the person's work.
- Pinpoint how the person's work is contributing to the success of the project.

- Make sure everyone has a contributing role to the team's key decisions and outputs, including presentations.

The three R's instill trust and confidence in others. When people feel confident, trusted, recognized, respected, and important, they also feel truly inspired to do more for the team. Inspired people are self-motivated, upper-level players. Motivation induces us to act, while inspiration moves us to perform at a higher level.

Team Space: Involvement, Behavioral Expectations, Transparency

The top three actions that we can take to produce higher-level performance are to create strong team involvement, set high standards and expectations, and be transparent with others.

Create Strong Team Involvement   Involvement builds energy, spirit, teamwork, and commitment, thereby keeping people in their upper levels. Involvement keeps people engaged and connected with the team (no one should lose sight of the team). It is like adrenaline. When everyone is involved, every team member stays emotionally and intellectually charged about the team project. People must feel challenged intellectually and have an emotional stake in the outcome. Neglect will cause people to retract, withdraw, or even sabotage the team's progress. High-performing teams are inclusive and maintain team involvement in these ways:

- Rotating team roles and responsibilities
- Including everyone on the team meeting agendas
- Giving everyone a lead responsibility for a piece of the project
- Assigning work that fits well with each person's strengths and interests
- Using team processes that encourage involvement (see Chapter Four)

Set Behavioral Expectations   People want to be clear on team expectations. Guardians want to know what work needs to be done and by when. Idealists want good teamwork and a shared purpose. Artisans want to know what is at stake and what roles everyone will be playing, and Rationals want to see the big picture and know what the goals are and why.

Typically expectations are around content and process and rarely about behaviors. Maybe they are too soft and sensitive to discuss openly. Nevertheless, they have a profound effect on the team. When the expectations for behaviors are not defined up front, people are left to operate from their own individual set points. Skipping this step is truly a lost opportunity. Like having a shared vision and values, the team should take the time to define the team's set of desired behaviors. When a high standard is set, people will rise to the occasion. It pays to be open and explicit about behavioral expectations.

A team can establish a higher set point by agreeing on some key behaviors:

- We stand by our decisions as a team. It is okay to disagree and challenge each other in team meetings, but once we make a team decision, we stand by it together when we leave the room.

- All ideas, issues, and decisions belong to the team. There is no such thing as my idea versus your idea.

- Listen to understand first. We strive to see other points of view and keep our minds open. We seek to generate alternatives and diversity in our thinking.

- Do not talk over others. We respect all opinions. We allow people to finish their thoughts before others speak, and only one person speaks at a time.

- No one dominates. We give everyone equal time to speak. Everyone speaks freely, but no one monopolizes the time. We are concise with our points and invite others to speak.

Be Transparent   Transparency is a catalyst for teams to go higher. It is about showing yourself, conveying the honest thinking and feelings behind your words. One of the key causes of conflicts is lack of transparency on teams. Rationals may refrain from disclosing their thinking and feelings in fear of being second-guessed or being wrong. Guardians and Idealists may prefer to stay quiet to avoid creating discontent. People will not open up unless they know and trust the other party well. Artisans are the exceptions: they say what is on their minds and have no personal barriers in sharing how they feel. Artisans are not afraid to quickly judge and react. Unfortunately, too many people prefer not to be transparent and offer these common excuses:

"Expressing my feelings is a sign of weakness."

"My personal feelings are not appropriate to share with the team."

"No one wants to hear that kind of stuff."

"Explaining myself takes too much time."

"I may come across as being negative."

"It's a waste of time to explain all that."

"I want to stay objective."

Here is an example of using transparency when dealing with difficult people. A friend wrote to me, "I had been through a lot today with someone who is extremely difficult to work with. After trying everything I could, I decided to be very transparent with him, and he was just shocked that it came from me. I pinpointed details on how he manipulates certain situations and how he disrupts my performance and that of other coworkers. Basically he was taking everyone to their lower level, and I couldn't handle it any longer. After this talk, his disposition changed from being defensive to a realization that he was in fact being disruptive. I was shocked when he admitted to his manipulations, apologized to me, and actually thanked me. He said that was courageous of me to approach him. He didn't know the negative impact he had on others because no one had ever confronted him and that he respected me for what I did. Amazing!"

Transparency is an upper-level behavior that can help defuse discussions. Whenever you ever find yourself facing a potentially volatile person and are fearful that this person may react negatively to your comments, be transparent, and say what you honestly feel right off the bat to defuse the situation. For example, say something like, "I feel nervous about raising this problem with you because I don't want to upset you and make you mad." The other person will usually respond by saying, "Don't be silly. I won't get upset. Now what's on your mind?" Stating your honest feelings is a powerful technique in dealing with conflict situations.

SUMMARY

People have two psychological states: upper and lower. People in their lower state are poor listeners, impatient, self-centered, defensive, and fearful. People in their upper level state are open-minded, tolerant, giving, and collaborative. They seek refuge in their lower state when they are stressed and insecure. Ironically, people are less stressed and more secure when they are in their upper state. To avoid the lower level, we either have the internal strength to take the upper path or receive help from others to raise our behaviors.

People in their lower state are difficult to work with. Those who persist in their lower level are considered difficult people who inhibit and impede others. The best strategy for dealing with difficult people is to resist going down to their level by staying in the upper level. Difficult people want to take you down with them. Do not take the invitation. Rise above it.

The most common lower-level behaviors are

- Whining—playing the victim game, a common trap for Idealists
- Dominance—the need to be right, a common trap for Rationals
- Control state—the need for compliance, a common trap for Guardians
- Impatience—a time trap for all personality types
- Poor listening—a lower-level trap for all personality types

The keys for staying in the team's upper level are

- The three R's: recognition, respect and trust, and relevance
- Creating strong team involvement
- Setting behavioral expectations
- Being transparent

When people feel confident, trusted, recognized, respected, and important, they also feel truly inspired to do more for the team. Inspired people are self-motivated, upper-level players.

Raising Your Game

Being in the upper or lower level is a personal choice, not something imposed by others. Where you want to operate at any given moment is up to you. There are no reasons to wait for permission or to compete for a top spot. The upper level has unlimited capacity and power.

Some people think that they have to win over others in order to gain stature and higher esteem. Others see their self-worth in their jobs and careers. Esteem is in your own mind. You make your own level and stay there because you want to be there. The motivation comes from within, not outside yourself. You can raise your game if you want to.

Raising your game means raising your set point. To do that, you need to stretch yourself beyond where you are today. This will require taking some risks, continuously setting your sights on something higher than today, and being willing to accept failure. People who are afraid of doing something different or taking on something beyond their comfort zone will not grow and extend themselves above their current set point. To change your set point means that you have to develop your self-confidence and abilities to do more, learn more, and challenge your resolve and inner strength.

Strategies and techniques for raising your game depend on your set point. If your set point is already high in the upper level, your strategy will be to help other people raise their level of performance—to inspire others. You will find that by giving to others, you will get a certain lift in return. This is the personal reward and satisfaction that you will receive from your acts of generosity and support of others. In fact, the lift you get will be much higher than what you give and much higher than what you may expect. Some examples of actions to take are teaching, coaching, tutoring, counseling, mentoring, volunteering, and facilitating. These actions are things that you can do in your current job and life in general. It may be as simple as giving positive reinforcement, appreciation, and encouragement to another person each month, each week, or even each day. Participating in charitable events, public service, and community activities elevates your sense of self and others. These activities involve giving of yourself to others without expecting any direct returns. To get to a new set point, you must think outside yourself and extend yourself to others on a sustained basis. This may take weeks, months, or even years in some cases. You cannot raise your game or expand personal space if you do not look beyond yourself.

Mentoring has gained a great deal of momentum in recent years because of the changes in the workplace and demographics. As the boomer generation nears retirement age, organizations will struggle to replace their skills, knowledge, and experience. In anticipation of this loss, more and more companies and organizations are encouraging mentoring by senior employees and offering part-time work to early retirees in order to retain and transfer precious knowledge and skills. This is called "silver mining." Mentoring should not be instituted just for mining old knowledge; it should be an activity that people of all ages practice. We have seen this successfully practiced in schools where fifth and sixth graders mentor first and second graders. This behavior needs to be developed early in life and sustained to support lifetime learning. It is easier to learn behaviors when we are young. It is important for young people to know how to think outside of themselves, care for others, and establish a high set point in life.

People who are above the line (possess a high set point) have a tendency to do more of the same—that is, raise their personal expectations and standards. If hard work has brought personal success, then more hard work should yield greater success. If personal achievement and initiative gave success, then more initiative and achievement will bring even more success. Despite these good intentions, this upward movement is rarely sustainable. As one moves up, getting to a higher level does not mean raising personal expectations. What happens instead is that people find greater frustration rather than raising their game. This is somewhat of a paradox. Setting higher and higher expectations is a risky game because people are likely to burn out. They do not enjoy work anymore. Worse yet, they may not enjoy life as much.

Rationals are prone to get into this mode. They set high goals for themselves and find that they are failing; failure is not acceptable to Rationals. They either solve it or rationalize it. This is an inner strength and inner weakness for Rationals. Idealists and Guardians are also prone to this effect; for example, people are deeply hurt when their faith, trust, and loyalty to their company fail. The loyal employees and shareholders of Enron, WorldCom, and others had great trust in their companies and values but ultimately were hurt when these organizations violated their values. As employees put in their years, their belief and commitment to their companies grow, along with their 401(k) and company stock holdings. The great reluctance of employees to reduce their overweighting of company stock is a clear reflection of their loyalty and belief in the company. As a good friend said to me, "When I decided to diversify and sell most of my company stock, I felt I lost a strong attachment to the company right after that." Believing in your company's values is important, although sometimes it carries a high personal risk. Idealists and Guardians may assign a level of belief that is not commensurate with the practices, actions, and reality of the organization. Passive belief causes complacency, which leads you falsely higher.

If you are spending more time below the line, meaning that your net behavior is still in the lower level, your best opportunity is to increase your understanding and perception of yourself. You can successfully rise above the line in these ways:

- Seeking feedback from friends, family, counselors, colleagues, and supervisors

- Identifying the drivers that are pushing you into the lower level

- Understanding what benefits you are deriving from these lower-level behaviors, for example, some form of self-reinforcement

- Thinking more positively and maintaining a positive internal dialogue

- Identifying what is holding you down, which may entail exploring and seeking help in understanding your current state

- Improving your health, which may include exercising more, improving your diet, getting more sleep, and reducing stress

The key is to get lighter by shedding the psychological weight that is keeping you in the lower level. Also, you may try to contribute more to your team and relationships and hold yourself fearlessly accountable for your actions. When you raise your set point, you increase your personal capacity to do more, see more, and expand your influence.

SHAPING YOUR UPPER-LEVEL BEHAVIORS

Whether you are above or below the line, moving your set point higher will take commitment, time, and effort. To get there, an action plan will be required. Some of these suggestions might work for you:

- When you face a difficult situation, think "upper level." Ask yourself, "What would an upper-level person do in this situation?" This will help catch yourself before you fall.

- Have a daily cue to remind yourself to stay in your upper level. For example, place a sticky note or dot on your: bathroom mirror (so you can see it first thing in the morning), rearview mirror of your car (if you are inclined to get frustrated when driving), computer monitor at work, or notepad to help you during meetings.

- Pinpoint specific lower-level behaviors that you wish to avoid.

- Establish personal goals, and reward yourself when you achieve them.

- When you drop into your lower-level behavior, ask yourself how you could have avoided it or recovered faster in the future.

There are common barriers that each personality type shares. Being able to transcend and conquer these limitations will reap personal rewards. Here are some examples of improvement opportunities for each personality type that will lead to a higher set point.

Rationals

- Accept and admit failure.
- Show yourself to others; be more transparent.
- Be a good listener, and make others feel that you are listening.

Idealists

- Try not to take things personally.
- Be transparent with your struggles so others can help you.
- Manage your time to avoid procrastination.

Guardians

- Be open, and embrace change as an opportunity to grow and develop.
- Let go, and be selective on what you must control.
- Be patient; it will get done.

Artisans

- Manage your time to be more punctual.
- Show others you care and are sensitive to their needs.
- Show more patience for process and rules.

RISE ABOVE TO GET BEYOND

The best strategy to cope with lower-level behaviors is to try first to raise your own personal level and then try to raise the level of others. To achieve good listening behaviors, both parties need to be in a listening mode. This means that neither party can reside in the lower level. Using lower-level argumentative behaviors to win over others is a losing strategy. When two parties are arguing from their respective lower state, no effective listening and understanding are being achieved. Winning over another person is not an uplifting experience for the loser. Defeating another opinion does not give rise to mutual understanding. That is why a win-win strategy is so important between parties. Instead of winning a debate, we should aim to raise the other person's view and seek a win-win outcome, which comes about when you are able to simultaneously raise your own level and the level of the other person. This takes considerable patience, selflessness, and seeing the other person's point of view.

This section discusses the tools and techniques for raising your level and the level of others (Figure 14.1).

How to Help Others Rise to a Higher Level

If you are trying to raise someone out of a lower level, giving praise and positive recognition will not suffice. In fact, you are likely to raise more ire than cooperation. Also, it does not help to try to manipulate the uncooperative person. The key is to give the person a simple lift in the upward direction.

An upward lift means to motivate the person to listen, broaden his or her thinking, and accept other possibilities and options. There is a continuum in the art of managing agreement with an uncooperative party that I call the ladder of collaboration

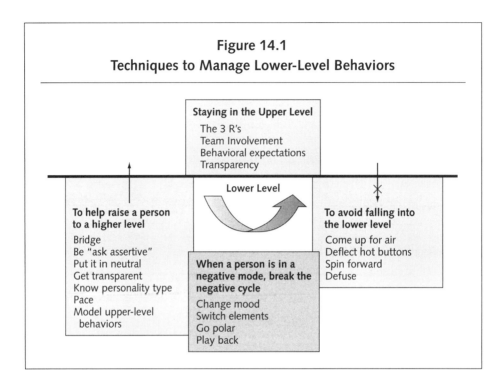

**Figure 14.1
Techniques to Manage Lower-Level Behaviors**

Staying in the Upper Level

The 3 R's
Team Involvement
Behavioral expectations
Transparency

Lower Level

To help raise a person
to a higher level

Bridge
Be "ask assertive"
Put it in neutral
Get transparent
Know personality type
Pace
Model upper-level
  behaviors

When a person is in a
negative mode, break the
negative cycle

Change mood
Switch elements
Go polar
Play back

To avoid falling into
the lower level

Come up for air
Deflect hot buttons
Spin forward
Defuse

(Figure 14.2). The idea is to position the other party to listen. Listening will lead to understanding, which in turn positions the conversation for compromise. Continued cooperation can even lead to collaboration in the longer term. It is difficult to move someone from the lower level to a position of compromise and collaboration in one stroke. People deep in their type are not in any state to be cooperative. They are inwardly focused, seeking an emotional or intellectual need. For example, the deeply seated Rational wants to be right in his thinking; until that need is fulfilled, that person will stay in his lower level. Once the need is fulfilled in some way, the person will begin to emerge and be willing to listen to and accept other alternatives. At that point, the content can be further debated and negotiated. Mentally positioning a person to compromise is just as important as communicating the content of your issue.

Techniques for Helping Others Reach a Higher Level

There are several good techniques to use in conversations, meetings, conflicts, negotiations, and e-mails to help others rise to a higher behavioral state and move up the ladder of collaboration.

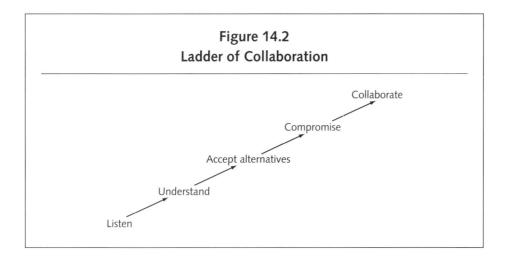

Figure 14.2
Ladder of Collaboration

Listen → Understand → Accept alternatives → Compromise → Collaborate

Bridging Bridging is a conversational technique of acknowledging what other people say and do, a highly effective technique for helping other people rise to a higher level. Many meetings become disorganized discussions because everyone in the room is speaking about their own ideas, busily processing what they are hearing, or mentally composing what they want to say next. At times this may become a debate of ideas and a competition of whose thoughts will win over the team. It is common for discussions to be nothing more than going from person to person, thought to thought, and finally closing down. Meeting participants are highly focused on themselves and their issues.

Bridging is about looking beyond yourself, acknowledging others, showing respect, being transparent, and trying to connect thoughts before making your own comments. For example, say we are having a team discussion about planning a special team meeting. One team member, Janet, suggests, "Why don't we have a slate of management speakers? I know a couple of division vice presidents who would be excited to do it. What do you think?" and then John says, "I have a great idea! How about a team-building event, and we can have it off site?" Another person says, "We could have it at the company lodge," and yet another adds, "And the lodge can provide a caterer for the food." Although their intent was to brainstorm ideas, Janet, after hearing these responses, may feel a bit ignored, devalued, or rejected and think, "I guess nobody liked my idea. I shouldn't have said anything." These are not good feelings to have.

When people make a sincere effort to contribute a thoughtful remark, they deserve sincere acknowledgment. When no acknowledgment is made, their disappointment is clearly visible in their body language. As a consequence, depending on the dynamics, Janet may back off or come back with another remark to test her idea. Also, if she does not have a trusting relationship with the group, she may feel put down and has to cope with the rejection she feels.

The better technique is to bridge by first saying, "That's a good idea, Janet. What topics would they cover?" or "I like your thinking, Janet. What do you think about having a team-building activity too? What do others think about these ideas?" No doubt Janet would appreciate these responses, which are personalized and accepting. People always have a choice: they can create a subtle conflict with Janet, draw energy away from her, or make the outcome for the team positive and synergistic. The best choice is to be inclusive of Janet's suggestion and create a shared space rather than compete for space. No one has to take space away from others to win. Taking a moment to bridge a colleague can make a big difference in team dynamics.

Of all conversational techniques, bridging is by far one of the easiest to do and has the greatest impact. It gives people intellectual and emotional support, which you see immediately in their body language. It is a highly effective technique for creating a more inclusive and positive discussion. The key to having positive conversations is to demonstrate that you are listening and understanding the points of others and that you appreciate and respect their contributions. Whether this technique is used at work or at home, you will likely avoid many conflicts and be pleasantly surprised by the reaction of others.

Here are some examples of bridging remarks:

"Thanks for mentioning that."

"I like what you just said."

"Your point is well taken."

"I like the way you said that."

"Thanks for asking."

"Good observation."

"You make an excellent point."

"I'd like to build on your good comment."

"I'm glad you said that."

"You raise an important question."

"That's a great catch."

"I'm going to capture the point you just made."

Be "Ask Assertive"   Instead of always stating your position, you have the option of asking instead of telling. This is a powerful technique for problem solving, negotiating, and resolving conflicts. Asking questions demonstrates openness and interest in hearing what others think, as in the example with Janet and John: "I like your thinking, Janet. What do you think about having a team-building activity too? What do others think about these ideas?" By asking questions, you are opening up the individual's thinking to other possibilities and casting light on the field of play instead of narrowing the views of others.

Here are some examples of "ask assertive" questions:

"I'd like to better understand your point. Can you please give me an example?"

"I hear your concerns. What is it about this issue that you oppose?"

"I would like your support. What would it take to get your endorsement?"

"I hear your arguments against it. What things have you heard that you like?"

"What steps can we take to solve this?"

"What is holding us back from making a decision?"

When you ask a question, people tend to listen more intently than when you are telling. One of the simplest yet most effective techniques to invoke listening is to say, "May I ask you a question?" The response is usually yes. This immediately puts the person in an automatic listening mode. When a difficult person goes into the lower level, asking questions will help raise his thinking, but you must get the person into a listening mode first. Here are other good questions to invoke listening:

"May I throw out an idea?"

"May I share an observation?"

"May I make a suggestion?"

The purpose for being ask assertive is to increase understanding, broaden thinking, and generate constructive dialogue. Unfortunately, sometimes this technique is used for opposite purposes. This occurs when a person springs a rhetorical question to chide or make a personal statement, such as, "Why did you choose to push ahead without first checking with me?" or "Why did you fail to follow my instructions?" Another misuse occurs when a person uses this technique to show up another (with the message that he knows more than the other person)—for example, "Are you sure you have uncovered all options?" when this person knows there are other options. So instead of honestly seeking more information, the person is asking a question to advance his own cause—a Trojan horse approach. This type of questioning is deceptive and manipulative. When you are confronted with these situations, guide the discussion forward by asking a question back, such as, "What options do you have in mind?"

Put It in Neutral   This is a technique to motivate better listening. When two people are engaged in a stubborn debate and neither party shows any active listening, it becomes nearly impossible to reach mutual understanding and agreement. To reach common ground, efforts must be made to strike a balance between advocating and listening. Instead of arguing one side or another, good collaborators know how to regain active listening when the debate gets too deep. I call this "putting it in neutral before you drive." When a person is telling you something, it is analogous to driving a car. There can be only one driver at a time. When two or more people are trying to tell their side of the issue at the same time, the conversation usually goes nowhere. And a conversation with three or four drivers at the same time becomes chaotic. "Putting it into neutral" means shifting the dialogue from telling to mutual listening. You put the car in neutral and listen: no one is driving, and both parties are listening. This is done by asking a question, acknowledging a point, playing back what you heard, or even changing your physical position. The technique is to stop driving, and by acknowledging and asking the other person a question, the other person stops driving too.

For example, when Rationals get deep in their advocacy, they are poor listeners. When you are dealing with Rationals in this situation, first play back what you have heard. It is important that you show Rationals that you fully understand their position and arguments. You honor their thinking by acknowledging their points. Once they feel understood and respected, they will be ready to hear your point of view, especially if you phrase it in this way: "I like your thinking about moving our IT services overseas and find your market assumptions to be valid. May I build on your thought?" or "May I get your opinion on another idea that I have?" A Rational will be listening and ready to help.

Help Others Get Transparent   In discussions, an effective way to improve transparency is to use an inquiry technique by asking the person for more information, the reasoning behind her opinions, or where she sees the benefits. These probes are extremely useful in gaining a better understanding of the person's rationale. Examples of questions that you can use are, "What is driving you to feel that way?" "Please help me understand your thinking behind this," and "Please help me understand the benefits of your position." By helping the person become more transparent, you are raising the understanding level among participants. You can also try asking, "What is holding you back from supporting these other proposals?" or "What do you see are the differences in opinions?" All of these work well. When this is done right, the person is usually pleased that you were interested in her thinking because it shows recognition, respect, and relevance—the three R's.

Verbal and nonverbal cues are important in this technique. How you say something is as important as what you say. Probing for understanding can backfire if the person perceives your inquiries to be an interrogation or put-down.

Understand Personality Types to Improve Interactions   Learning the traits and behaviors of the four personality types is invaluable in understanding how others would like to be treated. Treating others as you would like to be treated is still the golden rule, but it is not always reliable. We are born with natural tendencies, and we process and communicate information differently. Our motivations are linked to our intellectual and emotional needs. What may be motivating to you may be demotivating to others. We have seen this in different cultures and generations of people. Recognizing another person's personality type takes training and experience. However, being able to recognize the four basic types will improve your interpersonal skills, not necessarily because you will treat people any better but because you will be more tolerant and accepting of others. By interacting and talking with others, you will broaden your understanding of them and learn to accept those who are different from you. Learning the basic personality styles is the secret to strengthening your interpersonal and managerial skills. It is the best investment that anyone can make in appreciating diversity and coaching for greater team performance.

Pace   When you are trying to get agreement from another person, try to match or pace the body language, speech pattern, and tone of the other person. By doing this, you are sending positive nonverbal cues, and he will feel more comfortable and receptive to your presence. For example, when a person is speaking slowly and softly, it would be intimidating for you to speak in an aggressive, loud, and fast-paced manner. If the person is standing and talking down to you, physically stand up to be on the same plane with him or ask him to sit and chat. By pacing, you are subconsciously getting in sync with the other person, who will appreciate your cooperative demeanor. Paying more attention to nonverbal communications will enhance teamwork skills.

Role-Model Upper-Level Behaviors   If you see and treat others as having good upper-level intentions, they may shift to a higher view. Just because the other person may not have the advantage that you have in operating from a higher level does not mean you should talk down or shut the person out. Upper-level behaviors have positive effects on others, and role-modeling them can have a positive influence on others. The challenge is to bring out the goodness in all people.

Some people may feel that these techniques can be perceived as manipulative. But manipulation occurs when the intent is to disrespect, hurt, or devalue other people for personal gain. The techniques here are not for manipulation. They are intended for positive purposes: to improve teamwork, acknowledge and recognize others, and help others rise to their higher level of performance.

Another concern is being patronizing. As long as you are in your upper level and the other party is in a lower state, you are by definition in a position to be condescending. You can mitigate that by using a technique that fits your style, calibrating the tone and strength of what you are saying, being patient, and trying to raise your interpersonal level slowly. The technique of putting it in neutral before you drive is a good example of being patient when trying to lift someone else.

RAISE YOUR GAME

Table 14.1 presents techniques to maintain upper-level behaviors. The keys are to acknowledge and praise others, respect others, broaden thinking, increase listening, and build mutual understanding.

Techniques to Break a Negative Cycle

A negative cycle occurs when a person is not satisfied with a situation and will not let it go. He or she is stuck in a lower level, like a wheel spinning in place, and needs help to break out of it. The solution is to change this person's thinking, which will also change his or her behaviors.

Table 14.1
Techniques to Raise Your Game

Bridge by acknowledging the other party first
1. "I really like what [name] just said about . . ."
2. "I have feelings similar to [name] and [name]."
3. "I would like to build on [name's] point and [name's] point."
4. "I believe [name's] thinking and my thinking are on the same track."
5. "I'd like to hear from [name]."
6. "Thanks, [name], for raising that important issue, I had a similar thought. How about if . . . ?"
7. "Let's not lose [name's] good point that . . ."

Bridge by praising the other party first on content, process, or behavior

Content
1. "Thanks for mentioning that."
2. "I like what you just said."
3. "Your point is well taken."
4. "Good observation."
5. "You make a good point."
6. "I'm glad you said that."
7. "That's a great catch."
8. "You helped me realize an important question."

Process
1. "I like the way you said that."
2. "I'm glad we made time for this."

Behavior
1. "Thanks for asking."
2. "Thanks for sharing that thought of . . ."
3. "I appreciate your openness and honesty."
4. "I appreciate your transparency."

Bridge by using playback to respect others
1. "I hear you say that . . ."
2. "Just to follow up . . ."
3. "So your point is . . ."
4. "I want to make sure I heard you correctly. Your point is . . ."
5. "If I may summarize, you said . . ."
6. "I share your view that . . ."

Table 14.1
Techniques to Raise Your Game, continued

7. "You really struck a chord in me when you said . . ."
8. "I hear your concerns that . . ."
9. "I think I understand your position of . . ."
10. "I can see where you drew your conclusion that . . ."
11. "Please correct me if I'm wrong, but did I hear that . . . ?"

Invite advocacy to respect others: You may precede (the better choice) or follow your thoughts with, "I would like to:
1. "hear your feedback on . . ."
2. "invite your thoughts about . . ."
3. "get your opinion regarding . . ."
4. "bounce this off you about . . ."
5. "get your wisdom regarding   "
6. "see how this strikes you about . . ."
7. "hear your take on this."

Be "ask assertive" to broaden thinking
1. "Please tell me what your thinking is behind . . ."
2. "Can you share your thinking on . . . ?"
3. "Can you please expand on your thought that . . . ?"
4. "What is motivating you to say . . . ?"
5. "Please help me understand your feelings or thinking about . . ."
6. "I would like to better understand your point. Can you be more specific or give me an example?"
7. "What are your feelings about . . . ?"
8. "How were you able to connect [point X] to [point Y] so well?"
9. "Your point is right on. Please walk me through your thinking again."
10. "What would it take to get your support?"
11. "I noticed, [name], that you look a bit concerned. Do you have a different thought?"

"Put it in neutral" to increase listening
1. "May I ask you a question?"
2. "May I build on your comment?"
3. "May I throw out a related idea?"
4. "May I share a related observation?"
5. "May I make a suggestion?"
6. "May I share a quick thought?"

Table 14.1
Techniques to Raise Your Game, continued

7. "You just triggered a thought that further supports your point [or "builds on your point" or "may be related to what you just said"]."
8. "I have a question for you."
9. "Can you help me?"

Be transparent to build mutual understanding, and speak from your personal space
1. "Would you mind if I played devil's advocate for a minute?"
2. "This feels right to me. Does anyone else feel the same way?"
3. "I'm sorry, but I feel a bit lost. Can someone help me get back on track?"
4. "Am I too negative about this?"
5. "I feel the energy level has fallen. Would you like to move on?"
6. "What was going through my mind as you were speaking was . . ."
7. "Here's how I feel about . . ."
8. "My feelings tell me that . . ."
9. "One thing that appeals to my thinking is . . ."
10. "I felt good when . . ."

Change the Mood A negative cycle persists because people are feeding it with lower-level behaviors. You can break the cycle by changing the person's mood. Think positive, and your body language and demeanor will naturally follow, and you will be communicating much more constructively. Another way to change the mood is to inject some good humor. Nothing breaks a bad negative cycle faster than a bit of good humor. Good humor means that you say something amusing but at no one's expense unless it is your own. This means no sarcasm or put-downs. A good technique is to poke fun at yourself or something neutral, such as a process. Humor, when used properly, is a sign of trust and openness. It means that people are able to have fun.

Switch Elements (Content, Process, and Behaviors) to Restart a Discussion If a team is in conflict over content, switch elements by asking a process question or discuss a behavior. Conversely, when a team struggles with process, they should move to a discussion on content. When the team is struggling with both content and process, they should discuss behaviors. Switching the perspective of the problem by way of process or behavior can help restart the team and find new grounds for agreement.

Go Polar   "Go polar" means taking the opposite view and using reverse psychology. When you find yourself in a discussion where all your suggestions are going nowhere and you would like others to make suggestions, take an exact opposite position. Say something such as: "Well, it doesn't sound like it's worth suggesting any ideas" or "Maybe we should just quit." The response is usually a change in behavior. People start helping instead of rejecting or criticizing.

One time ten of us were crammed in a tiny meeting room. Everyone was feeling tight and uncomfortable. I suggested that we try to find another room on the floor. This was met by great cynicism: "It would be a waste of time" and "The other rooms are probably just as bad." I then suggested that we contact building services for some help, which was met with, "Forget it. That person will take all day to do the search." At this point, I decided to switch my polarity and said, "I guess it sounds like everyone wants to stay here!" I had tried to make positive suggestions and when that did not work, I switched 180 degrees. And the team responded, "Oh, no! We don't want to stay here! Let's try to look online for an open room." Just like that, they switched from a negative mode to a problem-solving mode.

You can also apply this technique to situations where you have made a mistake and wish to elicit a positive rather than a negative response. If you make a mistake, instead of getting defensive, just use some humor and polarize it: "Boy, I must be the dumbest person in the world!" People will likely smile and respond in support of you. This is better than the traditional behavior where people try to explain their way out of it, hoping that others will understand your mistake. Rationals have a tendency to behave this way. Polarizing is a better choice.

Playback   A negative cycle can persist until either the energy runs out or you leave the scene. A better technique is to simply play back what you heard, which stops the person from continuing in a negative mode. For example, when a person gets negative on something, just replay what you heard, and ask if you got it right: "Let's make sure I heard you right. You're upset that the team did . . . and you feel left out." The point is not to agree or disagree. Here is another example: if a person is upset about a change in a work process, you echo back, "You're upset about the work process change?"

Acknowledgment does not mean you are agreeing with the person. You are verifying what you just heard. The key is not to get dragged down with the person. You should try to stay neutral. What works best is to state what you felt and heard, get confirmation, and then move into a positive problem-solving mode by asking, "What would you like to see happen?" Once you have captured the content and feelings of the person, there is no reason for the person to recycle the complaint. If she does, simply say, "I think we already covered that. What would you like to see happen?" One important question to avoid is, "What can I do to help you?" By saying that, you are supporting the negative cycle, risk going down to the other person's level of discontent, and taking on her problem. It is not uncommon to fall into this trap.

Playback is consistent with moving to neutral before you drive. This technique protects you from going down and helps open the other person's mind to more productive alternatives.

Techniques to Avoid Dropping into the Lower Level

Sometimes you may find yourself falling into the lower level and wish you could catch yourself before that happens. Here are some techniques to prevent you from falling too far.

If You Dig in Deep, Know When to Come Up for Air   Have you ever gotten into a disagreement with another party, and you both just kept trying harder and harder to convince each other, to no avail? Each party is convinced he or she is right, and neither will back off. After a period of no progress, both parties end up in a black hole, wondering how they got there, and then frustration sets in. When you find yourself in a hole, the first thing to do is stop digging.

As we struggle in conflict, a natural reaction is to want to resolve it or escape. In fact, in our well-intended attempts to dig out, we are actually digging deeper and making things worse. Also, when we are in our lower level, our behaviors send negative signals regardless of our words. Therefore, in any verbal conflict, we should avoid arguing the same position more than two or three times. In conflict, it is best to stop and come up for air by switching to an ask assertive mode and thereby seeking to understand first, then be understood, seek a point of mutual agreement (seeking common ground), summarize each other's points, or take it off the table. Otherwise, continuing the dialogue will likely dump people into their lower level, invite others to take sides, or result in a bad conflict. Any time you decide to go in deep with someone, have an exit strategy.

Deflect Hot Buttons   We all have our hot buttons: things that upset us and dump us into our lower level quickly. Hot buttons are hardwired to your values. The connection generates great energy and strong emotions and usually provokes a regretful response. The behavior that pushes your button threatens what you believe in and who you are. It can be a sensitive topic, an offensive word, a fear, or a threat. I know people who get upset when others are critical of their work. When a hot button attack arises, you need to have the wherewithal to recognize it. To cope with this threat, try to deflect the attack. Here are some ways to manage this attack:

- Buy time to calm down by echoing back what you just heard: "Let me make sure I got it right. You said . . ."

- Ask a clarifying question: "That's interesting. Can you give me an example?" or "What is compelling you to say that?"

- Ask how others feel about it. For example, if someone makes a challenging statement that is sensitive to you, do not react emotionally. Simply ask, "How do others feel about that remark?"

- Go into an "I" response and state how that remark made you feel and ask if that is what the other person intended: "I feel hurt by your statement. Is that what you intended?"

- When dealing with hot button issues with friends and family members, it is best to avoid them or gently set them aside. Close friends and family members know your hot buttons better than anyone else and use them when they feel threatened by you. In that situation, it is better to try to deflect or defer them rather than engage in a hot-button-pushing contest and regret it later.

Spin Forward If you catch yourself falling into your lower level, just spin forward: "to go forward" means to say something in the context of the future (forward looking) and "spin" means to say something positive. For example, your colleague approaches you for help, but you are tied up on a rush assignment and say, "Oh, gee, can't you see I'm busy?" If you catch yourself, just continue, "But you know, I think I can break free in about twenty minutes, and we can tackle your problem then." When your boss dumps another assignment on your desk and wants to know when you can get it done, you may instinctively say something such as, "Wow, I'm so overloaded." If you catch yourself, just continue, "How about if I look over this and get back to you later today?" With this method, recovery is fast and sweet. A short statement can make a big difference in how you come across to others. People tend to remember your closing remark more than anything else, so always spin forward.

Being transparent means to show yourself and speak up when you feel differently about things, but it is just as important to try to finish on a forward-looking and productive path. If you cannot find a forward spin, ask someone else for theirs: "Can anyone offer me a solution?" "What can we do to help solve this issue?" "What ideas do you have to help address this problem?" "Can anyone help me here?"

I recall a time when I had to notify an employee of her termination. I told her that her performance was poor and that I had decided to let her go. After some discussion on the termination process, the employee started making some negative remarks about the work environment and the people around her. She got emotional and began blaming others. She claimed that the process was unfair and the work unreasonable. I did not want to get into an emotional, lower-level discussion with her. Instead, I chose to spin forward: "May I ask you a question? How would you like to see this conversation end?" It was a forward-thinking question. She immediately stopped her negative train of thought and answered thoughtfully that she would like to end on good terms and would like time to think about her circumstances and choices. I told her that I appreciated hearing that and offered my support in helping her close her employment. We concluded in a respectful manner. By spinning forward, you can quickly change a negative situation to a positive one.

Defuse Emotional Situations   In highly emotional conflicts, the person with the higher emotional state will pull you down. When people are angry, it is difficult to reach collaboration or compromise. To get there, emotions need to subside. When encountering emotional anger, it is better to let the person vent and dissipate the emotional energy. Try to listen to the concerns, and avoid entering the person's space by saying things such as, "You're acting like a jerk," "Please calm down," or "How dare you raise your voice to me!" Trying to counterbalance the emotional state will only escalate the behavior and make you the personal target for the anger. A better strategy is to try to put the discussion in neutral by asking clarifying questions or agree to continue the discussion at a later time. This allows people to regain their composure and avoids escalating the conflict.

SUMMARY

"Raising your game" means to establish a higher set point in your team behaviors. To change your set point means that you have to develop your self-confidence and abilities to do more, learn more, and challenge your resolve and inner strength.

This chapter covered numerous concepts and techniques for raising your game. How you proceed depends on your set point and your fluency in using these techniques. People who slip easily into their upper or lower state have a higher or lower set point. The set point is a point within your upper and lower levels, and it is where you choose to operate from on a daily basis. Each person has a set point and controls it. The more you operate outside yourself, the higher your set point is. If your set point is "above the line" already, your strategy will be to help other people succeed and raise their level of performance. Some examples of actions that one can take are teaching, coaching, tutoring, counseling, mentoring, volunteering, and facilitating. If you are spending more time in your lower level, your strategy is to increase understanding of your behaviors through feedback and self-assessment.

Several techniques were presented on how to rise to a higher level, help others reach a higher state, avoid falling into one's lower levels, and break negative cycles. The key themes are

- Each personality type has different opportunities to improve their behaviors.
- Higher-level behaviors consist of using techniques to acknowledge, respect, and recognize others. Key team-building behaviors are bridging, pacing, playing it back, and deflecting hot button attacks.
- Asking questions invokes listening and broadens thinking.
- Transparency and active listening are keys in developing positive team communications.
- Helping people reach more positive and productive states includes changing elements (content, process, or behavior) and moods, switching polarity, and spinning forward.
- To break a negative cycle, change thinking to change behaviors.

You cannot control another person's behaviors, but you can use the techniques in this chapter to better manage and cope with conflicts. Focus on what you can control. Rising to a higher behavioral level and helping others reach a higher level are the essence of good teamwork and leadership.

Those Who Break Through Will Never Go Back

Not all people who exhibit lower-level behaviors are difficult people. Some are simply trapped: they have a low set point, exhibit lower-level behaviors, and have been unable to find a way to improve. They have been in their lower level for so long that it is protective and safe for them despite the impact they may have on themselves and others. Unlike difficult people, trapped people do not impede the progress of others; they impede their own progress. They have fallen into a lower-level state, which limits their ability to perform on teams. Their behaviors have persisted because they have been internally or externally reinforced. In other words, either their upper-level behaviors have been negatively reinforced or their lower-level behaviors have had positive consequences for them. For example, people take risks in projects because they feel fulfilled by the challenge and excited by the prospects of achievement (internal positive consequences). They are likely to continue that behavior unless they are negatively reinforced by their management or past failures.

For many people, lower-level behaviors are coping behaviors in response to insecurities, stress, fear, or conflict. It is natural to take flight to one's defensive side once in a while, but when it occurs more and more frequently, it becomes a norm.

285

At that point, people are trapped and blind to their downward shift. It is a gradual erosion of behaviors and leads to poor performance.

As people move downward, their behaviors become more self-centered and closed-minded. Here are some examples of statements from people who reside in their lower state:

"If people don't understand it, then that's their problem."

"That will never work!"

"You make no sense at all."

"That person is so frustrating to work with!"

"I can't work with him."

"That's how I've always done things, and it works fine for me."

"I don't need people to tell me what to do."

"I like to be direct and to the point. Sometimes that intimidates people. They need to learn to deal with that."

"I couldn't go along with what the team was doing; I just worked on my own."

Difficult and trapped people have blind spots that prevent them from seeing their way out of their lower levels. Difficult people feel they are doing and saying what is right. They may be absolutely right in their content, but it is their behavior that is coming across poorly. They should not change their convictions and values but improve how they interact and communicate with others. Difficult people come across badly because they do not recognize other behavioral options, they lack flexibility in their interpersonal behaviors, and no one has made the effort to help them.

When difficult and trapped people learn to use their upper-level behaviors, dramatic changes can happen. They become more expressive, interactive, open-minded, patient, confident, and optimistic. They are less afraid, defensive, and self-centered. As a result, they feel more appreciated, see more opportunities, and establish better relationships. It becomes a breakthrough for them: a dramatic improvement in their behaviors and a step change in their set point. What is most significant is that those who have a breakthrough will never go back.

Here are five stories of personal breakthroughs.

BREAKTHROUGH OF A TRAPPED GUARDIAN

Helen is a thirty-two-year-old industrial engineer who has worked several years for a large company in the San Francisco Bay Area. A second-generation Filipino American, she grew up in the Bay Area and went to school in southern California. She had a quiet family who lived by all of the traditional Asian values: education first, respect your parents, and children are seen but not heard. Her parents were very strict, and they worked hard to support their family. They knew how difficult life could be and were both self-driven. Helen proudly remembers that "they pulled their own weight" and made a life on their own, and they expected others to do the same. School was serious business, and "having fun was not a priority," she remarked. The most feared behavior was expressing your opinions. She recalled, "Talking back to your parents was never considered." It was a sign of disrespect. She commented, "You kept quiet, and when their friends came over, I would hide in my room so that I wouldn't do something that would embarrass my parents. I purposely did not show myself; expressing yourself was an embarrassment, a weakness."

Love and praise were not topics they talked about. They stayed humble in everything they did and said. She continued, "Speaking up and showing yourself were rude behaviors, never disrespect yourself, and embarrass others, and you needed to be quiet about your feelings." Her parents were very proud of Helen but never told her that.

This upbringing made Helen feel awkward, introverted, serious, and structured. She was able to play high school softball and join school clubs only because she was able to convince her parents that extracurricular activities were necessary to get into college. As a Guardian, Helen enjoyed school and took well to the structure and discipline of engineering. Her parents were pleased with her good grades, compliant behaviors, and her motivation to do well in school. Helen says, "I grew up afraid to cause any conflict or draw any attention to myself."

Helen's breakthrough occurred one day on a conference call with her project team. The team was having a rough time with Linda, a team member who never seemed satisfied with anything that the team was doing. She was outspoken and emotional and intimidated the team with her behaviors. This made their team meetings slow and painful. On this conference call, the team was reviewing their work products when Linda again expressed her dissatisfaction with the team. She thought the work was subpar and well short of what she had expected. At that point, Helen mustered up her courage and said, "Linda, why don't you appreciate the work we do?" That simple question brought sudden silence to the proceeding and caught Linda completely off-guard: she was speechless.

Quiet and reserved Helen had expressed what the team had felt for weeks. She said afterward, "My heart was pounding, but I said what was on my mind. I couldn't believe I blurted it out. It felt good. It felt really good." Helen had just given Linda a gift: honest feedback. This question broke the negative cycle that Linda had been in and broke the ice as well. The team then had a long heart-to-heart discussion. Throughout the discussion, Helen cried, Linda cried, and, Helen said, "I believe the whole team cried." She said, "In the past, I would have just kept quiet and tolerated it to let it go. This time, I felt differently." She told me that she had applied what she had learned about difficult people, lower-level behaviors, and negative cycles. She commented, "From what I learned, I felt that speaking up was an acceptable thing to do. For the first time, I felt I had permission to speak out." She learned that she should not accept lower-level behaviors from others and that when they occurred, as in this case, she should speak up and not let difficult people drag the team down.

Helen said, "I have been a victim all my life. I can think of many times in my life when I felt I could have made a difference if I had said something."

Helen's story is not so much about speaking up as much as becoming less self-centered. Being trapped in her lower level, Helen kept to herself and was afraid of embarrassing herself and her parents. She was catering to and supporting lower-level behaviors. Certainly her behaviors were shaped by her parents, culture, and experiences growing up. She grew up fearful of what others would think if she spoke critically.

Her real breakthrough was in the way she saw herself and others. She raised her set point, so that she now operated from a higher level and spent much of her time "up" and not "down." She no longer saw herself as a victim. She said, "I now enjoy people for who they are. I still play softball. Regardless of whether we win or lose, what matters most is how we treat each other in the game. When I make an out and feel badly, the team gives me a lift by saying it's okay, good try, and we'll get 'em next inning. What matters most is how I make others feel and how others make me feel." By raising her set point, Helen has a broader view of herself and others. She cares more about other people and how she treats others. She now operates outside herself more. Helen gives more and takes less. She has more energy, greater self-esteem, and stronger confidence. You can tell by her voice and enthusiasm when she says, "I now enjoy people for who they are."

Helen now sees a bigger playing field. She mentioned that she compliments people and acknowledges others when they do something well. She gives feedback to others and has become much more transparent. She admits that she sometimes reverts to her former self but says, "I catch myself and don't go there anymore." By adopting these human factor principles, Helen is happier: "I feel relief. I'm not worried anymore. I don't have words to describe it. It has changed my life. In fact, I now tell my parents and sister that I love them."

BREAKTHROUGH OF AN ISOLATED RATIONAL

Peter is a thirty-eight-year-old computer scientist employed by a medium-sized computer technology company. He was born and raised in Pakistan, where his father was an accomplished legal writer and publisher. His family had migrated to Pakistan from India in 1947 after India gained independence from Great Britain. They worked hard, studied hard, and lived in a small rented apartment with his sister and brother. They lived above some commercial shops.

Growing up in Pakistan, Peter attended substandard schools and has strong memories of the poor instruction and conditions. But he never complained to his parents. He recalled, "I was very introverted, uncomfortable in talking to my parents about my problems." He kept to his home and studies and had few friends. He said, "I felt different, unique, not socially engaged growing up. I had no circle of friends and stayed focused on school."

Peter especially had problems communicating with his mother and found it easier to remain detached from her to avoid conflicts. They never saw things eye-to-eye. Peter recalled that "she was not open, very autocratic, and I just kept my conflicts with her inside me." He confessed that he was never a top student and struggled with his school work through college. He also kept himself isolated from his siblings and father, who was occupied with his profession.

One of Peter's disappointments in life was not being recognized by his family for his academic accomplishments. He commented, "I had hoped my father would attend my graduation, but he chose not to. When I returned home, no one really cared. My family did not understand what I was doing."

As a pure Rational, Peter pursued education. His motivation to learn and achieve was so strong that he had continued to take classes despite his limited free time. Education was a refuge for Peter. In my interview with him, education and schools dominated his memories of his childhood and early adulthood. Relationships with family, friends, and colleagues were almost nonexistent in conversation. The three people who had influenced his life the most were his teacher, college adviser, and a major professor.

As a quiet Rational, Peter was not accustomed to showing emotions and expressing himself much. He preferred to "keep everything inside of me," he said. He added, "My isolation and environment kept me down." When I asked him what drove him to be so introverted, he said that he never felt a need to express himself. He could read people well and knew what they wanted without much conversation. He expected others to do the same: "I expected people to know what I wanted; I didn't feel I needed to say anything." Also, expressing his feelings would make things worse. He commented, "Every time I spoke up, I was angry, felt mad that people did not understand me. How could you not know what I want? They did not do what I wanted, and they should. So when I spoke up, I always made things worse."

Being an introvert, Peter was uncomfortable working on teams, especially with people who had expressive personalities. He felt like an outsider looking in. His quiet, independent, nonengaging nature distanced himself from teams, and his teams would isolate him. They assumed he was uninterested in the work and moved forward without him. But being isolated by the team disturbed him: "I was afraid that I was abnormal. I have all these thoughts in my head, but they just don't come out of my mouth. Why was I so different?" Yet he accepted his fate with the team. He added, "I suppressed everything. I would hold it in, not letting anything out. I had a fear that if I spoke, it would make matters worse."

Peter's breakthrough story involved a class project that he had to complete to receive his certification in project management at a local university. Peter was on a team of five people. In the first meeting, Peter found himself in familiar territory: he was quiet and passive, while the team was planning their work. By the third meeting, the team was convinced that Peter was a weak team member and would not be an active contributor. In fact, he did not even show up for their third team meeting. "He didn't seem to care about us and checked out," said one of his teammates. However, Peter was angry that the team was not accepting him, and he was not even informed of the team's third meeting. He felt totally rejected. Actually, there was a simple mix up in the meeting announcement, and two other team members were left off too, but they had heard about the meeting another way. Needless to say, Peter was in conflict with the team.

Instead of letting it go and retreating, Peter decided to speak up and confront the team at their next meeting. True to his style, he came across angry and upset.

He was mad that he was excluded by the team and that "they did not understand me." The team got angry too. A team member later wrote, "What right did this non-team player have to be mad at the team who was doing all the work, and this do-nothing is mad at us!" After everyone vented, they came to an agreement on future communications to try to include him more in the decision making. The team was emotionally wasted and still angry, but they agreed to try harder to improve communications. In reality, this encounter was a step forward for Peter, but he was still angry. Right after this, Peter was introduced to the concepts of human factors, upper and lower levels, and set points, and he participated in a one-day learning session with other Rationals. This exchange opened Peter's mind: "I finally understood myself and why I did the things that I did. I saw myself in a very low state."

Peter's real breakthrough came the following week when his project team had to give a class presentation. The team had about thirty minutes, and each team member was asked to share their team experience. Peter went last. He stood up before the class, took a glance and a breath, and instead of reviewing a piece of the project, he surprised everyone by saying, "I want everyone to know that I was the one who held up the team. It was my fault. I did not communicate well with the team, and that led to conflicts and problems." It was the first time that he had ever openly shared his feelings in front of a group and admitted that he was wrong about anything. It was a total change for him: he had never shared his feelings and had never admitted to a mistake. This was his breakthrough.

Why did it happen now? Peter said he felt "it was now or never. I suddenly realized that not speaking up was worse than speaking up. I realized that I was a Rational who was deep in the lower level. I had to help myself out." More important, he realized that "I was always trying to pull people down to my level, and that never worked. I took a 180-degree turn. Before, I felt that if I spoke up, I made things worse. But now, I believe that when I speak up, I make things better! I am not afraid anymore. I am not afraid to show myself. I need to show myself so that I can help others see the middle ground. I never looked for middle ground with others. I now pay attention to other people and listen to what they want and then share where I am in order for us to compromise."

Peter summarized his breakthrough by saying, "I will never go back. I will never go back to the lower level. It was so dark and isolated. When I open up and face others, I feel much lighter, energetic, and confident about my relationships. I am more open with people at work, with my director, and with my wife."

When I last spoke to Peter, he was about to start another graduate program at a local university.

BREAKTHROUGH OF A RUNAWAY IDEALIST

Cathy is a twenty-nine-year-old planning and marketing consultant for a large bank in San Francisco. She grew up in Texas and California, where she was raised as a fundamentalist Christian and received home schooling by her father. She has two brothers and a sister, and Cathy recalled that "we had no TV, movies, or games. I had a strict upbringing, and my siblings were my best friends. I learned a lot by using my imagination and reading." She read everything that she could get her hands on and had a love for the outdoors and painting. She did not have a lot of friends growing up but made friends easily when given the opportunity.

When she was twelve, her family moved to California, and Cathy began encountering serious family problems. Her parents were divorcing, and she was being physically abused. She tried to escape by going to the movies and hiding out in her room, but by seventeen, she had to leave home for her personal safety. Just like that, she was on her own and had to work and go to school. Although she suffered many hardships and was not well socialized by her family, Cathy was determined. She recalled, "Being away at school, I wanted to heal myself, repair my social flaws, and prove to myself that I could make it." This escape was actually a blessing for Cathy. "I became exposed to so many things, and it made me want to know more and more," she said. Learning and personal growth were deep motivators for Cathy.

In addition to her Idealist behaviors, Cathy possessed values and behaviors common to generation X. She wanted to be judged on the merits of her performance, and she preferred to work at home over commuting and reporting to work at eight o'clock every morning. She remarked, "Time is very valuable to me, and I want to prove that I can be effective working at home." She liked an unstructured work environment. Also she did not look at anything long term and admitted that she "liked to turn over after a year or two and move on to new stuff and ideas. I want mental and physical freedom in my work life."

Cathy had difficulty dealing with conflict and confrontation, from her early days growing up to her relationships as an adult. She was an escape artist. She acknowledged that she avoided conflict, ran off when things got rough, and headed for the movies or her room when things got heated "to escape and clear my head at the same time," she said. As an Idealist, removing herself gave her time to think through problems and assess them in a less emotional state. She said, "I just froze and locked up when confrontations occurred; I dealt with it by getting away from it. I think I purposely avoided having to be in a position to make a tough decision, especially those that may have a potential negative impact on people. Black-and-white decisions, such as honesty and integrity or life and death, were no problem, but I never put myself in a position to have to make a hard decision in life—no gray decisions." She added, "I didn't like conflict situations and having to confront them when I don't see a benefit."

Unfortunately, when Cathy did her escape act, she was really running to her lower level for relief. In this lower level, she found solace, but she also left others in a wake of frustration. Her hot buttons were people who ignore others, talk over them, or shout them down. She loathed the aggressive types who prey on others and did not care about whom they hurt. She commented, "They react quickly in disagreement and shut people down; I don't like to see people get hurt. I look around the room, and people are slammed, yet this person doesn't seem to care at all." This personality type had frustrated and upset her for as long as she remembered. She had an especially hard lesson in one incident where she had thrown away some trash that was lying on the floor. It turns out that these papers were not trash but written ideas that belonged to another team member. When he realized that she had inadvertently thrown out his marketing ideas, she recalled, "He exploded and began screaming at me over the phone. It was so bad, I had to escape, so I just hung up on him." She acknowledged that "I don't like people to say things that are critical of others, especially to me."

Unbeknown to Cathy, she was dealing with a Rational. Tossing out a Rational's list of ideas is almost criminal to them. It was like throwing out the artwork of a painter. This kind of act will drive a Rational to his or her lower level. Rationals' values are fundamentally grounded in their thinking. On top of that, hanging up on a Rational was adding insult to injury. Rationals need an explanation of what happened and a chance to analyze and mourn the tragedy (albeit they can overdo it at times). Denying Rationals that opportunity fuels their volatility.

The breakthrough for Cathy occurred when she took an interest in learning human factors and discovered that she had conflicts with Rationals. Their behaviors of shouting down others and moving forward without buy-in by others were normal lower-level behaviors of Rationals. Understanding these tendencies, Cathy dramatically changed her perception and behaviors toward Rationals. She understood that they were more content focused than people focused and their aggressiveness was really aimed at the content, not at people. When they hurt people, it was just collateral damage. The way to deal with Rationals was to use logic and reasoning, not emotion.

Using this understanding, Cathy had a breakthrough during a team meeting. She remembered, "Ted was a creative Rational who talked a lot but caused chaos by constantly switching gears and wanting to make changes all the time. He ignored what others think and paid no attention to the people aspect. This behavior was frustrating and upsetting to me. With my knowledge of Rationals, I confronted him, focused on the facts, and used logical thinking to present the team's position. I spoke strongly and with confidence. To my surprise, he listened, agreed with my points, and said he was okay now. He told me he was glad we talked about it and he would now go along with the direction of the team. I was shaking but elated that I was able to speak up and say what was probably on everyone's mind. I stuck with the facts, and it worked! I feel more comfortable with Rationals now, understanding why they don't react as I do. I also realized how ideas are important to people. I find working with Rationals to be challenging but rewarding. I am no longer afraid of confronting them. It takes different people and perspectives to succeed as a team."

When asked about her avoidance behaviors, she said, "I rarely go down to my lower level anymore. I just don't. I let people know where I'm coming from and try to facilitate and coordinate. I get people to talk, and I avoid negative gossip. I am also able to step away and look for the right behavioral tools to use. I now admire other personality types. Before, I didn't understand them and avoided them. I speak up in all areas of my life now."

Cathy is still "very sensitive when people say I didn't do my job, didn't get it done, or did a lousy job. It's unfair and unjust. It hurts my integrity, professionalism, and work ethic." Also, she sometimes over-commits herself but is learning to say no. One coping method that she has adopted is to observe how other people make decisions. She said, "I've watched what other people do when they are on the spot, how they stay in their upper level. Now I prepare myself by storing a library of possibilities. I borrow techniques from a lot of people."

Cathy's biggest shift was that she doesn't "avoid anymore. Now I want to incorporate people into my life. I try to see positive things in people and bring that into my own life."

THE IDEAL GUARDIAN

Karen is a thirty-six-year-old software developer and artist who received her bachelor's degree in photography. She grew up in a blue-collar family of ten; her father worked in a local automotive shop, and her mother held several jobs doing mostly bookkeeping. She remembered her family as having high moral standards and was very strict about respecting other people. It was a working-class life with high ideals for racial equality and giving everyone an even playing field. She recalls that although her family was "as white as you can get, we believed in civil rights, Martin Luther King, and rooting for the underdog." Her family instilled Puritan work ethics. She said, "You did what you were told to do, and if you were given a job, you were expected to do it to the best of your ability." This strong work ethic was a fundamental value for Karen growing up. But it was not all hard work and no play. She was encouraged by her mother to do what she enjoyed, which was photography, and her mother let her take photography classes after school. It was evident that Karen's mother had a significant influence on shaping Karen's perspective of the world.

Karen's biggest trauma came early in her life when she was nine years old, and her parents divorced. It was a messy affair, and the divorce was devastating to her family. Karen became neglected and forgotten in the process. Despite this loss and emotional pain, she learned to be independent: "I learned to take care of the important things for myself. No one was taking care of me, being shuffled from home to home, so I spoke up and got the things that I needed, like clothes, health care, and food." She learned to be assertive with others. She added, "I would put my foot down and control the situation to give myself sanity." Control became the overriding feature of her life. She remarked, "I became aggressive and driven, which carried over into college."

After graduating from college in 1992, Karen was briefly a star in the art world, where she had art exhibits in a few cities. These exhibits, however, were not enough to pay the rent, and she realized that she needed to work in an occupation that allowed her to use her artistic skills yet paid enough to support herself. Besides having a strong independent work ethic, Karen's biggest need in life was security. Maybe it was due to the divorce or the unstable childhood; nevertheless, Karen's top priority was personal security: to have a home and to have emotional and financial security. She tried freelancing for awhile but got out because she said, "I never knew what my next job was going to be." So she went to work in developing children's software and was successful in applying her artistic talents to commercial products. She loved the drive, the rush to get products out, and the blind commitment to meet ridiculous deadlines. It was not the project management work that excited Karen. She said, "Project management was like herding cats—not a lot of satisfaction day-to-day, but I got lots of satisfaction by hitting targets." Early on, Karen was successful in marrying her love of art and her craving for financial security.

Karen had control of her life and enjoyed it very much. She commented, "Having control gave me comfort, knowing what was going on. Not knowing what was coming around the corner scares me. My parents had nothing and lived paycheck to paycheck. I need financial security. I have to have money in the bank, a job, a home, a place to be." In her heart, art was her love; in her head, security was her need. She believed that her ideal job was one that blended her creative energy with daily work tasks. She knew some people who could work part-time doing mindless work in order to save their creative energy to pursue their art. She could not seem to do that; it would be like separating her own life. Duty and heart go hand in hand. Doing a job well and enjoying her job always must go together. She was taught that growing up.

Karen was not a great people person at work. Her controlling attitude and demanding work style turned off many cohorts and friends. "I was pretty driven and always got what I wanted," she said. She did not care to work with people who did not share in her drive and commitment. She was highly ambitious and highly passionate about doing the best job possible and worked long hours to get the job done. This was fine unless she applied those same expectations to others. She said, "I expected everyone to have the same commitment level as me. I assumed everyone was into their careers like me. It never occurred to me that people would have things in their life other than work! Why would anyone get up early in the morning to go to a job that they didn't love?" I noted that Karen used the word *love,* not *like.* She assumed everyone must love what they are doing; otherwise why would they be there? Her underlying belief was that people must enjoy what they do, and do what they want, and if not, they would go somewhere else.

Karen's strength was her weakness. She was so passionate and self-driven about her job that she had to be involved in everything and expected everyone else to follow suit. If she was responsible for the project, she had to go all out to make sure the job got done. She always gave her best and accepted accountability for the results. If the job had a bad outcome, she blamed herself: "I gave it my all since my butt was on the line."

Karen's breakthrough came when she realized through human factors that not everyone was like her. She said, "I was running myself into the ground, trying to do everything myself. It was crazy. One late night working alone at the office, it struck me that my human factors were pushing people away from me. Here I was, working all alone. I realized that I was not motivating others but isolating myself by applying my personal values to everyone who worked with me. I finally decided to let go. I now find that life goes on whether I'm doing the work or not. It was ironic, because I discovered that I really didn't have control. I didn't have to control things for things to get done. Now I trust others and make suggestions from the back seat. I didn't have to be the driver; I'm content to be in the back seat. I made useful suggestions and tried to guide the process instead of running the process. I learned that I didn't need to be so organized, controlling, and driven. I can let things go now. I can operate outside my comfort zone and survive fine. I am more flexible in dealing with other people and allow people room and space to operate. I can enjoy the journey instead of rushing to the destination."

Karen was able to look outside herself to let others succeed and do things differently from the way she did. She was taking on a heavy burden by expecting so much of herself and others. I asked her if she lowered her own standards and became less productive. She smiled. "Not at all, I find that I can get the same result by letting people do their jobs and by coaching from the sidelines. I didn't have to be on the front lines controlling everything to get things done." Also, she felt a lot better about herself and was able to do more things she enjoys. She said, "I feel less worried, less stressed out, and much lighter." She has learned to let go and shifted herself to a higher plane. She learned to adapt to others rather than require everyone to adapt to her. "I find the end result is no big difference, and I feel much better," she remarked.

Karen's long-term goal is "to keep a roof over my head." Spoken like a true Guardian.

BREAKTHROUGH OF A SUCCESSFUL ARTISAN

Lee is a forty-two-year-old self-employed, semiretired investor who grew up in Houston and has lived in twelve different cities during his lifetime. He is divorced, married twice, and has two daughters. He lives in a five-bedroom home on a golf and tennis club. Lee drives a BMW but gets around the neighborhood on a golf cart that looks like a small Cadillac.

Lee grew up in a large family and attended public schools in a large city. He recalled that "I didn't have a lot growing up, but I always found money. I would scrounge for change in the telephone booths, vending machines, and gutters. I would collect bottles for deposit money and find student bus passes on the street." He proudly proclaimed that "I always had money and did what I wanted."

He was a city kid. His favorite activity was traveling across town on the bus and seeing movies with friends. Lee enjoyed the action in the city and was not afraid to explore. However, his father was very strict and his mother was "passive" but "strong-minded." Lee and his father did not get along well. He recalled, "He was a disciplinarian, and I was not in that mode, so he would get upset, yell, and punch me often. I just stayed away from him and did my own thing. I was very independent."

Lee was successful in school and did well "in classes that I enjoyed and felt challenged," he said. He loved sports: basketball, tennis, baseball, bowling, football, and even Ping-Pong. He said, "I loved to compete and just do different things as well as I could. Playing sports came easy to me. I wasn't the most athletic, but I used my head and outthought my opponents."

When he finished high school, Lee attended the local state university and majored in political science and art. He had a scholarship in college but did not reapply for it each year, so he had to work to pay for his fees and tuition. He worked at a local manufacturing plant that "had a subsidized cafeteria with the best beef sandwiches and paid the highest salaries in town," he said. He did not care for fraternities and social clubs but had lots of friends. He organized parties and outings, and even helped form a rock band that played on Friday nights and weekends around different colleges and bars.

When he graduated from college, he was most interested in business and applied to a large M.B.A. program. He remembered, "I didn't really have to apply; I went to the admissions office, talked to the dean and the administrators, and they liked me. I had the grades and test scores, and they wanted me. I filled out some stuff, but the staff did a lot of the work for me, and I got in." Lee attended business school part time for about two years and took classes that he knew he would need. Apparently he got what he wanted and left business school before finishing.

Lee met some real estate investors, and they wanted him to help them on contracts and land development strategies. This turned out to be highly successful for him, and he started making real estate deals on his own. He invested in real estate, small businesses, and even in movies. It was not clear what succeeded or failed, but Lee enjoyed making deals. His eyes lit up as he described his conquests as "sweet," "crazy," and "incredible." He was especially proud of the deals he made that were "totally unheard of." Lee was outgoing, talkative, and expressive and engaging in his speech, inflections, and body language. You cannot help but get excited just listening to him. He talked about food, his favorite restaurants, and great deals he found on the Internet. Lee was a successful entrepreneur.

Lee was always looking for new things to do. He taught classes for awhile and gave investment seminars for a couple of years. One year he was intrigued by the concept of human factors and joined a work team to learn more. He said, "I wanted to see if this could improve my negotiating skills and also make new contacts." The project team that Lee joined was a lively mix of Guardians, Idealists, and Rationals. Lee was the only Artisan. Right away, he added a great deal of spirit to the team and designed some Excel templates and tracking sheets for the project. The team liked Lee and found his style to be open and fun. But some team members grew resentful of his constant tardiness, inattention to detail, and distracting behaviors. He was stimulating, but others found him too unfocused and pushy. Lee claimed "the work was so slow. They didn't seem to trust me, but I knew what I was doing."

By the third project meeting, Lee and the team were in chaos and had no consensus on a work plan. After the meeting, Lee recalled, "I was not happy, and two team members stayed behind to talk with me. I'll never forget what they told me: that I was smart and creative but also insensitive, disruptive, and rude to others. I thought they were crazy. I told them they were overreacting and that their behaviors were a lot worse than mine. I was the doer, and I made things happen. They should be grateful. I couldn't believe it."

Later that evening, Lee met with a friend he had known for over twenty years and shared what had happened. He explained, "Robert is a smart guy; I trusted him, so I wanted to hear what he thought about my clash with the team. Well, I was surprised what he told me. He said that people who do not know me feel threatened by my aggressive style and that I unknowingly acted and made remarks at the expense of others. I was too critical and people felt hurt and turned off." Lee remembered, "His remarks hit me like a ton of bricks. I never thought I was insensitive to people. I have lots of friends. I tend to say what's on my mind, and I don't pay much attention to how others may take it. I never thought much about it. I thought people appreciated my openness and honesty. I don't go around hurting people." Robert said, "Look, you asked me, and I told you. Just think about it." Said Lee, "I reflected hard on it, and that conversation really changed me. It was such a wake-up call. I know that I am outspoken and frank, but I didn't realize I stepped on people and drove people to their lower levels. Here I thought I was act-ing upwardly, when in fact I was in my lower level, trying to get attention, and in the process I was taking others down. I realized that people were not like me at all. I found I got too deep into myself, becoming self-absorbed with things. I realized that I needed to be more sensitive to how others react to me. I need to look out-side myself and get beyond my space."

With Lee's breakthrough, the team went on to finish the project successfully, and Lee was even given an award by the team. I do not know where Lee ended up, but I heard he went to Alaska to start another business.

WHAT THESE STORIES HAVE IN COMMON

Behaviors are driven by values that are strongly shaped by family background, ex-periences, culture, and events in life. Human factors are about understanding how these values and behaviors affect personal effectiveness and interactions with oth-ers. Through trial and error, people settle into a personality style that is comfortable and natural to them. These behavioral preferences are highly related to personality type and experiences.

Understanding human factors enables people to learn their behavioral strengths (upper level) and weaknesses (lower level) and improve their teamwork and re-lationships. The people in these stories had hidden truths that kept them trapped in their lower levels. They all assumed others understood them. Their intentions were always good, but their impact was often negative. Just like the tale of the hos-tile brothers (Chapter Four), they meant well, but their behaviors pierced people the wrong way.

Everyone in the examples had real fears that drove their behaviors. Their fears created a perpetual, self-defeating internal dialogue. Helen had a fear of speaking up and expressing her opinions. Peter had a fear of being wrong. Cathy had a fear of conflict and confrontation. Karen had a fear of insecurity. Lee had a fear of being insignificant, constrained, and uninvolved in life. Fear is not abnormal, but letting those fears take you down, diminish self-esteem, or lower the quality of life is not healthy.

Their breakthroughs helped to raise their set point and transcend their fears. They were able to face the factor that drove them downward: fear. They were able to operate outside themselves. When people stay within themselves, they stay dark and isolated. They take on selfish, defensive, and sometimes detrimental behaviors that drive them further into themselves and downward. Being more outside yourself enables you to be less judgmental and more accepting of others. Being more external opens your mind to accepting different views and opinions. Suddenly you see more good than bad, because you are filtering less and seeing more. People who have had breakthroughs talk about how they are now bringing in the positive things from people as opposed to judging and finding faults.

It is self-consuming and stressful to operate in your lower level. As a result of their breakthroughs, the people whose stories have been told felt "lighter," "less worried," "free," and "more confident." These were consistent feelings among them. Can you imagine the pressure of never being wrong about anything? Can you imagine the stress of always being permissive and conceding in conflict? Can you imagine the effect on your self-esteem by running away all the time? Can you imagine the stress of having to control everything?

What helps facilitate breakthroughs is the personal realization that change is needed and that current behaviors are detrimental to themselves and others. The pain of the status quo was greater than the perceived pain of change. They were ready for a change. They were willing to make that emotional investment and take the risks that go with change. People who become trapped are often harder and more critical of themselves than anyone else. But more important, human factors gave them an alternative pathway for change. People do not fully comprehend that they have a real choice and control on their behaviors. Human factors are about knowing yourself and what alternatives you have to make another choice on how you live your life.

There is a bit of sadness to the stories. Lower-level behaviors creep in because no one lifts them up. Lift is when someone praises you for your efforts and achievements, when you feel valued, and others care about how you feel. We seek appreciation and validation in our lives, yet when the natural sources for that emotional support dry up (through, for example, divorce, separation, neglect, poor parenting, no network of friends), we shrink our scope of human interaction and become independent and self-supporting. It is a natural coping mechanism and a way to gain personal stability and sanity. We control what we can control. But when it is sustained in life, it becomes a defensive and limiting state.

In the next chapter, we explore what the emotional and intellectual needs are for the different personality types and discuss the challenges that we all face in reaching our desired balance in life.

Hearts and Minds
of Human Factors

We all seek the same things in life. We want to be challenged intellectually and valued for our contributions. In previous
chapters, we learned that each personality type has unique intellectual and emotional needs. All of us are striving to reach a positive set
point in our personal space. Raising our game is about self-motivation and demonstrating upper-level behaviors in the face of constant
environmental change. This is achieved through continued fulfillment
of our intellectual and emotional needs (Figure 16.1). If we believe
that our intellectual and emotional needs can be met or exceeded,
then we are motivated to act and even inspired to go above and beyond that. Inspired people are self-motivated, upper-level players.

Chapters Nine and Twelve described personal space and human factors and explained the role they play in shaping how we see, interpret, and respond to the world.
External information is internalized in personal space and intellectually and emotionally processed through internal dialogue (Figure 16.2). I defined personal space
as a place where internal interactive thinking occurs and human factors are formed.
Internal dialogue occurs as we mentally process new information, interpret its meaning against our human factors, and express those perceptions in our behaviors. We
process information in two ways: intellectually and emotionally. Some people think
intellectually and factually, while others think emotionally and spiritually. We engage

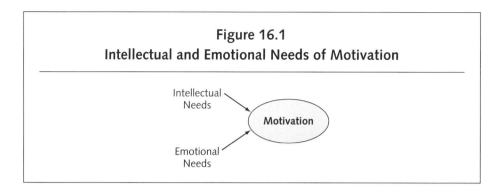

Figure 16.1
Intellectual and Emotional Needs of Motivation

Intellectual Needs

Motivation

Emotional Needs

in an internal dialogue as we judge and interpret that information against our human factors. That internal dialogue is the way we have learned to cope with things that life throws at us. "Getting results" appeals to our intellectual side, while "getting results and feeling good about it " meets emotional expectations and personal values. We need both intelligence and passion to get the job done. We have the ability to do both, but we usually have a strong preference for one or the other. Intellectual and emotional thinking generates human energy and motivation, and we need both types of thinkers on project teams in order to succeed.

The best team leaders and team performers consistently exhibit intellectual and emotional balance. They are also keenly sensitive to the intellectual and emotional balance of others. That sense comes from personal experiences working with different personality types, an appreciation and sensitivity to generational and cultural differences, and a good understanding of what motivates people. Good team players adjust their behaviors to accommodate others and sense when they need to lead and when to follow. They are happy to share in the credit and take great pride in mentoring others and seeing others grow and develop. They push you to succeed and catch you when you fall. They create an emotional acceptance by valuing and encouraging diversity in thinking and appreciating cultural differences in interactive styles. They invite differences and make people feel comfortable and safe in being themselves and expressing their opinions. Good team players think beyond themselves to draw out the best from others.

High-performing teams consistently show two strong intellectual traits—clear vision and an ability to solve problems—and two specific emotional traits—a positive, forward-looking mind-set and inclusive behaviors. These intellectual and emotional traits are powerful motivators.

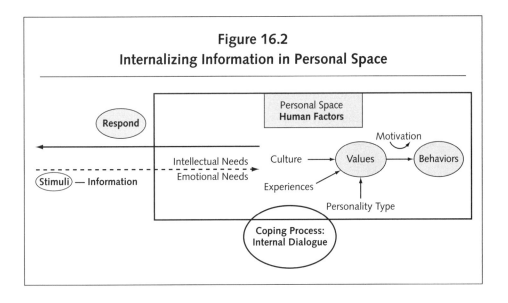

Figure 16.2
Internalizing Information in Personal Space

Intellectually, a team is defined by its purpose and charter. The objective is to complete a project on time, on spec, and within budget. To do this successfully, the project must be well planned and executed with excellence. It takes intellectual vision and problem-solving abilities. People have a need to know where they are headed and why. If the payoff is clear, people will be motivated to participate. If the benefits are fuzzy, they will work with less commitment. It is critical to envision and map the strategies and processes to achieve the milestones and goals. In addition, not all plans are perfect, and it takes effective problem-solving skills to execute a project successfully. Teams must be able to think ahead and anticipate problems. This requires team innovation and diversity of ideas, which provide intellectual horsepower for the team: Rationals are excellent strategic planners and analysts, Artisans are creative problem solvers, Guardians are task driven and accurate, and Idealists are purposeful and visionaries.

People's emotional needs are less apparent, and intellectual needs are more open and objective. In traditional business culture, intellectual needs are hard, and emotional needs are soft. Furthermore, intellectual needs are considered a sign of strength, while emotions are perceived as being a weakness. When it comes to emotional needs, people tend to use words with negative connotations, such as *stressed, concerned, challenged,* and *feeling overwhelmed.* Intellectual needs are expressed as competencies, skills, and know-how: *intellectual capital, core competencies,* and *knowledge management.* Intellect is treated as a valued asset, while emotions are treated as liabilities.

High performers are positive and inclusive. They genuinely care about how other team members are doing and feeling. When they interact through verbal and nonverbal communications, team players support each other and build trusting relationships. They have both an intellectual and emotional commitment. The team feels free and open to discuss new ideas, problems, people issues, and processes without feeling guarded and competitive. Lower-level performers are focused on individual success before team success ("Team success is nice, but I get more satisfaction from personal success"). Upper-level performers truly believe in team success first ("I will succeed when the team succeeds").

Each team member has emotional and intellectual needs and looks to the team as a source of support. A supportive team generates motivation by fulfilling the needs of its team members. Unfulfilled needs accumulate in our personal space and weigh us down. As we learned from the breakthrough stories in Chapter Fifteen, people's emotional support may be absent at home, and therefore they rely heavily on their careers or their workplace for appreciation, friendship, and respect.

There is an old African saying, "Those who throw rocks forget; those who get hit remember forever." Emotionally, people want to feel appreciated and valued. How you make someone feel has a much greater impact than what you do or say. I was involved in a team-building exercise where each team member shared a personal past experience when they were belittled or put down by others. As I was listening to everyone's stories, I was struck by not only the piercing emotionality of the experience but how vivid their stories were and how strongly they had held these negative feelings. Although many of these stories occurred years ago, they described the experience as if it were yesterday. Bad feelings are hard to shake.

Good and bad team experiences are emotionally stored in the team's memory. Negative feelings can weigh a team down like baggage. Baggage is a personal storage of bad feelings that you have mentally retained about people or situations. Baggage can come in different sizes, shapes, and weight. The worst baggage is old and heavy and you cannot let go; you carry it with you all the time, and it weighs you down and prevents you from stretching and doing something different. Your ability to adapt to change becomes limited. Baggage mentally ties you up. The weight anchors you down and makes it hard for you to rise to your higher level. It is the same for a team. A team creates its own baggage. Chapter Seven discussed storming and the techniques for escaping the storm. As a result of disagreements and conflicts, team members may hold on to negative emotions and baggage. All teams will somehow get through the storm, but good and bad feelings from the experience may be long-lasting. On the good side, conquering adversity together can strengthen a team and draw people closer together. The shared experience may yield a greater understanding of each other and forge mutual respect and trust. Such an outcome qualifies as a good conflict.

I remember an experience that I had with a new supervisor who was in charge of quality assurance (QA) for our team. We had a new employee who was learning our system and had just completed her second assignment, which required her to collect data from previous studies and consolidate them into a single summary. The data had to be accurately assembled and analyzed. She worked extremely hard on the project and put her full energy in making it perfect. She constructed data tables and colored figures and showed tremendous ability in presenting information in a creative way. She was proud of her work. My new QA supervisor reviewed her work and then later met with her to discuss it. I was not at the meeting, but I could see the interaction through the window of her office. It started out fine, but I noticed soon that the new employee was visibly upset and they were debating the report. Their meeting ended suddenly, and the QA officer left her office.

After letting some time pass, I approached the new employee and asked her how her meeting went with the QA supervisor. At first, she said that everything was fine, and then I noticed that all of the figures and diagrams in her report were crossed out. When I inquired why they were crossed out, she remarked that the QA supervisor told her to take them all out because "they added nothing to the quality and accuracy of the data and that putting in extra things was just asking for trouble." She appeared discouraged, but I indicated to her that the QA supervisor was very experienced and had the responsibility for accuracy and was helping her keep from making mistakes. I then commented to her that although her drawings were not appropriate for the report, they were graphically wonderful and that I would like to use them for a future presentation. Her mood suddenly brightened, and I could see that she was lifted by my comments.

I caught up with my QA supervisor and asked him how he felt about the outcome of the discussion that he had with the new employee. He pointed out some problems with the data but felt sad that she did not appear to like him. I mentioned to him that I had had a conversation with her and she felt disappointed too. I first told him that I felt he did his job well in reviewing and correcting the problems with her report and that his work of ensuring accurate documentation was critical. I told him that he was a leader and we needed his analytical skills and knowledge. However, leadership also requires satisfying the emotional and expressive side of people. In this case, her expressive spirit was contained in her graphics. We need to recognize that some people are emotional thinkers and think with their hearts first and then with their minds. It is sometimes hard to get people to listen and appreciate your guidance if your style is to recognize your intellectual side first and leave out the emotional element entirely. The employee deserved emotional support because she was new to the job and was still learning and also because she obviously had artistic talent and we needed to encourage that talent, not discourage it. In this case, getting results and feeling good about it was critical. We want people to have a good experience, not a bad experience, with QA. It was a short message, but I think meaningful to the supervisor: people need to be emotionally and intellectually recognized.

Teams have good and bad experiences in any project. Successful teams learn, adapt, and use what they have learned to support each other intellectually and emotionally, while low-performing teams will recycle and use the information in a more destructive way. For example, passive-aggressive behaviors from Guardians and Idealists can consume enormous energy and stall the team's progress.

When we develop some negative feelings for each other over some disagreements, it can be difficult to let some things go if they are tied to our core values. For example, if respect is a core value for a person and she feels disrespected or denigrated by others, she will carry that hurt for some time.

People react to behaviors, not to values. We cannot change values, but we can manage behaviors. High-performing teams manage behaviors by establishing behavioral norms, reinforcing desired behaviors, and providing emotional outlets for people. The plus/delta, pulse checks, and other team feedback processes serve as ways for people to share their conflicts and discomforts. The project leader should make time to touch base with each team member individually during the project to uncover any problems. It is important to maintain a balanced participation in team discussions and to solicit input from quiet members. These are inclusive team behaviors.

MANAGING THE MIND AND EMOTIONS IN CONFLICT

In a team conflict, it is important to support the intellectual and emotional needs of people. The techniques described in this section will help you manage conflicts and cope with difficult people.

Switching Brains

Each of us has a creative and emotional side (the right brain) and an intellectual and analytical side (the left brain). Some of us are predominantly left brain, while others are more right brain in the way we think and express themselves. Rationals and Guardians are more left brain operators and tend to use logic and processes to express themselves. Idealists and Artisans are more people focused and are more expressive and transparent about their feelings. Knowing these tendencies can help you manage conflicts by motivating people to "switch brains," that is, change their right and left brain thinking.

Switching Brains in a Left Brain Attack   A left brain attack occurs when a person is speaking pointedly and aggressively and is trying to intimidate you with information. To break this attack, switch the person off with a short right brain question, such as:

"Gee, I'm sorry. Did I say something that upset you?"

"Gee, are you mad at me about something?"

"Why are you yelling at me?"

I remember a heated discussion over how much to bid on a project. My lead engineer was spewing out some strong technical arguments in an intimidating way with the finance person, and tension was building. Reading the situation well, the finance person stepped back and calmly said, "Why are you shouting at me?" This stopped the engineer absolutely cold. The finance person was expressing her feelings. Saying "at me" was a personal statement, not a technical response. The question actually brought much-needed relief to the proceeding. After a few seconds, the engineer good-naturedly smiled and smartly said, "I'm sorry. I think my brain had too much coffee." That broke the tension, and we successfully agreed on a bid. The finance person knew that getting into a technical argument with the engineer was a losing proposition, so she switched his brain into another mode. Unless you are willing to fight and risk a relationship, never escalate an emotional or intellectually heated disagreement. It is better to switch brains.

Switching Brains in a Right Brain Attack   A right brain attack is an emotional assault against another person. The person may yell, rant, and rave at you. To defend yourself, ask a left brain question to snap the person out of it:

"May I ask you a question?"

"What do you feel is the source of your problem?"

"What would you like to see happen?

Dick, an Idealist staff member, one day rushed into my office upset. He told me he just came out of a "horrible meeting." The team members arrived late and never followed any of the meeting processes. He started to blame people by name, when I suddenly stopped him with a question: "Excuse me, Dick, may I ask you a question?"

He stopped his flow of whining and said, "Yeah, sure."

I asked, "What was the purpose of your meeting?"

He reflected a few seconds and answered, "Let's see, to get ideas for next year's technology plan."

I followed by asking, "Did you get some good ideas?"

He responded, "Well, yes, I collected a lot. Some were pretty good."

"Sounds like you met the purpose of your meeting. I would feel good about that."

"I do feel fine about that, but it was chaotic to get there."

"What do you think you could have done differently to improve it?"

"I'm not sure what you mean."

"For example, did you do a plus delta or ask how the participants felt about the meeting and how it could have been improved?"

"No, I got frustrated with the process and didn't think anyone would be interested in it."

I encouraged him to try it next time even though the participants may not be into process: "You'll be surprised what you may get in the feedback. It would have been a good way to improve it for next time." He agreed that he should have taken time to air it out instead of running into my office to vent.

It is best not to reinforce whining behaviors or transfer the person's problems to you. Instead, keep the ownership and focus on the other person, and offer positive suggestions. Keep the tone and conversation in the left brain mode, and avoid supporting the right brain behaviors. By coming into my office, Dick wanted to vent and wanted me to join him by sympathizing with his plight. The best way to coach Dick was to turn down his invitation and help him move to a higher level of thinking. Shifting his thinking was likely to shift his behaviors as well.

In summary, whether it is a left brain or right brain attack, it always seems that when we use only one side of our brains, our ears stop listening. Switch brains to regain balance and reset the mind to a positive problem-solving mode.

The Price for Being Right

As we strive to meet our emotional and intellectual needs, we share a common desire to be right in the eyes of others. Being right drives many behaviors, both good and bad. Being right is a power that drives us to seek validation intellectually or emotionally, or both. Have you ever been in an argument where a simple, "You're right," could have ended it? Many arguments start out as an intellectual conversation, then evolve into an emotional conflict. Being "right" switched from being intellectually right to being emotionally right for pride and ego. It seems as if once one side of the brain gets overloaded, the other takes over. You may start by debating the facts, then facts become opinions, the opinions become emotional, and before you know it, people are fighting. The conflict gets so deep and long that someone finally says, "What were we arguing about? I've forgotten." Have you ever had a heated emotional argument over nothing and could not understand how a trivial issue became a major conflict? Isn't that what road rage is all about? Being right has both an intellectual and an emotional side. Have you ever noticed with some people that even when they are wrong, they still have a need to feel right? This comes from the intellectual and emotional sides of being right (Tables 16.1 and 16.2).

Intellectual and Emotional Needs of the Temperament Types

- Rationals need to be *intellectually right* to be logical and technically correct.
- Idealists need to *feel righteous,* free of any conflict and dishonesty, the beacon of team harmony, and the need to do the right thing.
- Guardians need things to be done the *right way,* to be true to the process, to be accurate, and to play by the rules.
- Artisans need to do things *right now,* to obtain immediate gratification, to be right in the middle of the action, and not wait for others.

All people need intellectual validation when working on teams:

- Rationals seek validation of their ideas and strategies.
- Idealists want external validation of their unselfishness and sensitivity to people.
- Guardians need validation of their work and effort.
- Artisans want validation of their risk taking and spontaneity.

We need to be good listeners and observers to identify these different needs. They are important factors for individual motivation and team cooperation. On

Table 16.1
Intellectual and Emotional Motivations of Different Personality Types

Idealist	Guardian	Rational	Artisan
Intellect			
Having a purpose	Realistic	Competent	Fast-paced thinker
Believing in a cause	Process orientation	Logical thinker	Creative
Helping others	Responsibility	See the big picture	Risk taking
Philosophical	Rules of conduct	Goal oriented	Leadership
Truth	Clear course of action	Strategic orientation	Nonconformist
Principles	Defined roles	Continuous learning	Must have social impact
Objective	Plans	Seeks challenge	Pathfinder
Mission oriented	Institution		Multitasking
	Authority		
	Practical		
	Get the job done		
Emotion			
Romance	Security	Must be right, fear of failure	Stimulation: "Thrill of the hunt"
Support	Money	Achievement	Impulsive
Loyalty	Control	Independence	Excitable
Social interaction	Acceptance	Privacy	Engaging
Collaboration	Belonging	Passion for perfection	Sensitive
Growth and improvement	Order	Not emotional, does not show feelings	Appreciation of their boldness
Appreciation of their authenticity	Organization		Expressive
Team harmony	Clear direction		Freedom
Honesty and integrity	Appreciation of their work		
	Fairness		
	Compliant		

Table 16.2
How to Support the Different Personality Types

Idealists	Guardians
• Respect their feelings.	• Respect their need for structure, schedules, and systems.
• Be compassionate and supportive.	• Recognize their need to follow process and rules.
• Compliment them on their ideas, insights, and feelings.	• Thank them for their hard work and organization.
• Express what you feel, not what you think.	• Follow the rules (such as being on time, meeting their promises, and keeping things organized).
• Help them to keep small things small.	• Be accountable and dependable.
• Treat them fairly.	• Use examples and details to explain ideas.
• Always be inclusive.	• Finish what you start, and try not to change course in midstream.
• Remind them it is not personal.	• Explain why change is needed.
• Build a positive relationship.	• Give them the road map and time to adjust to change.
• Recognize their tendencies to procrastinate or not follow through.	• Never criticize them in public.
• Help them with resolving conflict.	• Do not step on their toes or territories.
• Be flexible, even on little things.	• Do not belittle them.
• Give them time to think.	• Work with them.
• Listen to their concerns.	
• Help validate their feelings.	
• Be gentle, kind, and empathetic.	
• Be honest and open; look them in the eye.	
• Appreciate them for their sensitivity toward others.	
• Be open and honest with them.	

Table 16.2
How to Support the Different Personality Types, continued

Rationals	Artisans
• Respect their thinking.	• Plan to be spontaneous.
• Ask for their insights and reasoning behind their ideas.	• Be flexible.
• Seek their advice.	• Be willing to change rapidly or shift gears on a whim.
• Recognize their intelligence, creativity, and good thinking.	• Be direct, open, and transparent.
• Compliment them on their work, achievements, and competence.	• Be their best audience, and applaud.
• Help them become more transparent.	• Respect their actions.
• Stand up to them; do not be intimidated.	• Respect their need for action.
• Be willing to engage in a lively debate.	• Do not force them to conform.
• Understand their need for perfection.	• Recognize that freedom is important to them.
• Forgive their insensitivity and defensiveness when they are challenged.	• Forgive them for being late, not following through, and being unfocused at times.
• Give them independence, privacy, and time to think and work.	• Give them lots of attention.
• Excuse them if they withdraw from social scenes.	• Give them a stage, and allow them to perform.
• Be direct and logical.	• Avoid imposing meaningless limits or deadlines.
• Validate their thinking.	• Support their need for risk taking.
• Think with them.	• Recognize their need to physically get involved.
	• Have some fun.
	• Play with them.

the job, people want to be challenged intellectually. But as this need is satisfied, they begin to look for greater emotional satisfaction from the job. As you consider new assignments, the heart comes first and then your head in making career decisions. If it is a matter of money and security, then it is an intellectual decision. It is important to note that Idealists and Artisans tend to think emotionally, while Rationals and Guardians emote intellectually.

On the emotional side

• Rationals want to feel appreciated for their good thinking and planning. They have a strong need to say smart things and to provide bright insights. That is where they feel they make the greatest impact. The biggest emotional hit for a Rational is failure. They mourn losses and mistakes for long periods and cannot let them go. Rationals are uncomfortable in emotional situations (crying, yelling, complaining) and dislike people who do not follow through on their commitments.

• Idealists need mutual team respect and trust. They want to be loved and appreciated. They are wonderful relationship builders and yearn to be liked and regarded as a good person. Idealists are givers and have a strong emotional need to help and extend themselves to others. They suffer most when there is conflict, turmoil, and chaos. They hate it when people hurt other people.

• Guardians need to feel wanted, valued, and accepted by the team. They have an emotional need to make a contribution and be recognized for their work. They need to be needed. Guardians are hard, conscientious workers who want to be valued for their strong work ethic. They suffer most when they are ignored, unfairly criticized, left out of decisions, minimized, belittled, or put down. They are disappointed when their expectations are not met.

• Artisans look for instant gratification, speed, action, and engagement. They want to be appreciated for their boldness and risk taking. Boredom and isolation are their biggest enemies. Artisans have a tendency to be self-centered and will play only their own games, not other people's games. They thrive on activity and human interaction. They have a special sensitivity to people who are hurting physically or emotionally. Artisans suffer most when they have to work within a slow bureaucratic process and are forced to do a lot of routine work.

Emotionally, all types need praise and recognition for what they contribute to the team. Rationals have an emotional need to be successful and right. They suffer most when the team gets bogged down in details. Getting Rationals to change takes reasoning. Idealists have a strong need to feel connected with others, feel valued by others, work in harmony, and experience personal growth. Idealists and Rationals share the need for continuous learning and intellectual growth. Both types are likely to take courses at colleges and universities or find enlightenment in religious faith and spiritual pursuits. Rationals explore new things to hone and broaden their thinking skills, while Idealists seek a higher level of spiritual wellness and tranquility. Idealists are romance seekers, while Rationals seek knowledge and application of their know-how. Intellectual need drives the emotional state for Rationals, and for Idealists, the emotional need drives the intellectual state. Rationals and Artisans have a strong need to say and do smart things all the time. Tremendous internal pressures can build when people carry high expectations of themselves.

When people are in a good intellectual and emotional balance, meaning that they are getting their needs met, it is easy to maintain an upper-level state. Remember that stress and frustrations are feelings that stem from not meeting personal expectations. When we have good balance, we start to look outside ourselves, become more transparent, and care more about others. When we are under pressure to complete a task on time, we are consumed and occupied by the activity. It is hard to think about others. When we have good balance, we also have a good sense of the intellectual and emotional needs of others as well as our own. That is why good leaders have strong influence and the ability to motivate others so well. People sense this balance in others and can be de-motivated when that balance is absent. When your personal needs are met, you show it in your behaviors.

HOW INTELLECTUAL AND EMOTIONAL NEEDS ARE COMMUNICATED

So how do these intellectual and emotional needs play out in real life? In our interactions with others, we constantly send out emotional and intellectual messages. Their impact on others can be subtle but significant. Much of what we say is miscommunicated. This occurs most often when we are seeking to satisfy our own emotional and intellectual needs over the needs of the other party. We do not think about what others may want from us. Sometimes we are blind to what messages we are sending to others and how those messages are being received. When we are in conversations, we should be sensitive to the emotional and intellectual impact that we have on others. We want to fulfill our own needs but not at the expense of others. When you are engaged in conversations, are you trying to listen for the emotional and intellectual needs of others? If your answer is yes, then you possess a strong sensitivity and feelings for others. That is a gift. If your answer is no or you do not know, you have a wonderful opportunity to improve your listening and communications skills.

The best way to illustrate this concept is through a short exercise. This section presents three cases in which two parties are engaged in conversation. After reading the story, you will be given several choices on how you would respond as one party or the other. Select the response that feels most natural to you or comes closest to what you would say. The responses are listed again after the three cases but expanded to include what message each response may have communicated and what impact that message may have had on the other party.

Case 1: FDA Testing

Rich and Laura work for a large pharmaceutical company. Rich is the R&D manager, and Laura is the laboratory supervisor. One day Rich came into Laura's office to discuss an issue about their new drug in development. Rich had just learned from the Food and Drug Administration (FDA) that some of the laboratory tests were insufficient to prove its efficacy. The FDA wanted more testing done on the new drug. Rich was anxious to please the FDA and wanted to see if Laura could do the additional testing and complete the final report by the end of the month. He said to Laura, "I need your help. Can you get the final report out by the end of the month?" Laura responded by saying, "I think we can get the blood tests done in two weeks, and finish the analyses eight days later. Yes, I think we can complete the test by the end of the month." Of course, that is not what Rich was asking; he needed the final report. If you were Rich, which response comes closest to what you would say?

A. "No, Laura. You weren't listening to me. Let me say it again: Can you get the report done by the end of the month?"

B. "Did you hear what I said? My question was: Can you get the final report done by then?"

C. "Laura, my question was: Can you get the final report done by then?"

D. "That's good, Laura, but I'm sorry, I didn't make myself clear. I need both the test and report done by the end of the month. Can you help me?"

Case 2: Going on Vacation

Last summer, Matt was embarking on a three-week vacation in Europe. To protect his house during his absence, he had advised the sheriff's department and the state police yesterday about his absence. Before leaving, he called his neighbor, Kathy, to tell her of his vacation plans. He mentioned to her how long he would be away, who would be visiting the house, and whom she could contact in case of emergency. After some light conversation about his big trip, she said, "Oh, Matt, did you contact the sheriff's office about your absence? You know that would be a smart thing to do. We do that when we leave on trips." If you were Matt, which response comes closest to what you would say?

A. "Of course, I did even better. I contacted both the sheriff's department and the state police. That way I have more coverage during the three weeks."

B. "Yes, that's something I always remember to do when I go away."

C. "Yes, I did."

D. "Thanks for asking, Kathy. Yes, I just remembered yesterday. I'm glad to hear that you do that too."

Case 3: Where Are the Meeting Minutes?

A team meeting was held to review the team's project schedule and workload. The team had seven staff members from different departments. The project had been running for about eight weeks, and the team had been making good progress. It had a meeting with its management two weeks ago, but the team had not met since then, and things had become disorganized. The objective of the meeting today was to identify any issues that required follow-up actions. As the team was discussing the meeting, Mike remarked that he had not seen the minutes from the last meeting yet. (Internally, he was disappointed that the minutes had not been distributed. As a result, he felt ill-prepared for the meeting.) The team turned to Glen and asked, "Glen, weren't you supposed to type them up?" Glen remarked, "No, I haven't had time." Mike added, "I thought our ground rule was to post minutes promptly?" Glen replied, "I have my hand-written notes. If you really wanted them, you could have just contacted me for them. It's not easy to find time to type notes. I have too many things on my plate, and besides, most of it was covered in the action items anyway." Tension rises. If you were Mike, which response comes closest to what you would say?

A. "This is a problem. I do not feel prepared for our meeting since I didn't see the minutes, and I also think we need to revisit our ground rules as a team before we start."

B. "Well, I think the minutes are important, and I think following our team ground rules is important."

C. "I guess we'll just have to go ahead without them."

D. "Glen, I appreciate your taking the minutes, and you've had a busy week. How about if we spend some time now going over the highlights of the meeting and then talk about the follow-up issues? That would help me a lot."

The Case Messages and Their Impact

Here are the messages that the various responses send and their impact:

Discussion on Case 1: FDA Testing

A. Rich: "No, Laura. You weren't listening to me. Let me say it again: Can you get the report done by the end of the month?" *Message implied:* You were not paying attention, and now I have to repeat the question. *How Laura felt:* He's unhappy with me, and I feel blamed.

B. Rich: "Did you hear what I said? My question was: Can you get the final report done by then?" *Message implied:* Try to listen this time! *How Laura felt:* I missed his point. I better listen up.

C. Rich: "Laura, my question was: Can you get the final report done by then?" *Message implied:* My question did not get answered. *How Laura felt:* Did I miss the question? Does Rich think I'm not paying attention to him?

D. Rich: "That's good, Laura, but I'm sorry, I didn't make myself clear. I need both the test and report done by the end of the month. Can you help me?" *Message implied:* What you said was fine, but we had a miscommunication here, and I take responsibility for having to ask this question again. *How Laura felt:* Rich wanted to make sure I didn't feel badly for the miscommunication. He respects my feelings.

Discussion on Case 2: Going on Vacation

A. Matt: "Of course, I did even better. I contacted both the sheriff's department and the state police. That way I have more coverage during the three weeks."

Message implied: I know more than you. I have great intelligence. *How Kathy felt:* I guess you are better than I am.

B. Matt: "Yes, that's something I always remember to do when I go away." *Message implied:* I have my act together; please recognize my intelligence. *How Kathy felt:* He doesn't need my advice.

C. Matt: "Yes, I did." *Message implied:* It has been done. *How Kathy felt:* I'm not sure if he appreciated my advice.

D. Matt: "Thanks for asking, Kathy. Yes, I just remembered yesterday. I'm glad to hear that you do that too." *Message implied:* Thanks for caring, and I recognize your intelligence too. *How Kathy felt:* He appreciates my asking. I feel accepted.

Discussion on Case 3: Where Are the Meeting Minutes?

A. Mike: "This is a problem. I do not feel prepared for our meeting since I didn't see the minutes, and I also think we need to revisit our ground rules as a team before we start." *Message implied:* I am not happy. I feel victimized, and I can't go forward until I get [emotional and intellectual] satisfaction. *How Glen felt:* We have a conflict. I feel punished.

B. Mike: "Well, I think the minutes are important, and I think following our team ground rules is important." *Message implied:* I'm not happy. I feel I have a legitimate issue here [intellectual and emotional needs]. *How Glen felt:* I feel blamed.

C. Mike: "I guess we'll just have to go ahead without them." *Message implied:* I'm not happy, but I won't impede the team. *How Glen felt:* I'm glad Mike is not going to make a big issue out of this, but he appears unsatisfied. Is he mad at me?

D. Mike: "Glen, I appreciate your taking the minutes, and you had a busy week. How about if we just spend some time now going over the highlights of the meeting and then talk about the follow-up issues? That would help me a lot." *Message implied:* I understand Glen's situation. I am willing to compromise and move forward as a team. *How Glen felt:* Mike wants to maintain a cooperative relationship. He is being transparent and gracious and is not blaming me.

For all three cases, here are some questions to consider in terms of your responses:

- Do you naturally think about your needs first or the needs of the other party?
- Do you find it challenging to have to think about your needs and the needs of the other party at the same time?
- Do you recognize behaviors first?
- Do you feel you are compromising yourself when you consider the needs of the other party in your response?
- Did you like the responses that were more transparent or less transparent?
- Who do you think feels better in each response: you or the other person?

The value of these cases is to get a sense of how you instinctively respond under these various scenarios, to raise your awareness of the range of options that exist, and to see how different responses can change the impact on people. Upper-level players and people who have good sensitivities to others tend to give D responses, while lower-level players and self-centered individuals tend to give A and B answers. Answer C is a neutral, nontransparent response that keeps the other person guessing. For response D, you are extending yourself to others and caring about the intellectual and emotional well-being of the other party. Keep in mind that these narratives capture only what is said, and it represents only a portion of the actual communication that is occurring. Nonverbal communications have a significant impact on how things are said and received. Facial expressions, speech volume and tone, eye contact, and general body language have profound effects on communications.

SUMMARY

Motivation is the human energy behind our behaviors. It requires satisfying both the intellectual and emotional needs of people. We process information intellectually and emotionally and interpret its meaning against our human factors. Those perceptions are then expressed in our behaviors. "Getting results and feeling good about it" means meeting the intellectual and emotional needs of the project team.

High-performing team players always show two strong intellectual traits—visioning and problem solving—and two specific emotional traits—a positive mind-set and inclusive behaviors. Intellectually, people want to be challenged and connected with the team's objectives and goals. Emotionally, they want to feel appreciated, respected, and valued by others. These emotions are signs of strength and should not be treated as a liability. Ultimately how you make someone feel has a much greater impact than what you do or say. Negative feelings can weigh a team down like baggage.

This chapter discussed several effective techniques for supporting the intellectual and emotional needs of others. Among them are speaking to the internal dialogue of others (that is, some people think emotionally, while others think intellectually), helping people use both the right and left side of their brains for improving collaboration, and recognizing the intellectual and emotional needs of others in your interpersonal communications. Each personality type has a unique set of intellectual and emotional needs. However, all types want to be right in their own way, and emotionally, all types need praise and recognition.

Personal Leadership
Putting It All Together

Leadership is the final topic of this book. This does not imply that leadership is last in importance or void of human factors. Quite the contrary, leadership is essential to good project management, and future project leaders will require greater knowledge and skills in managing human factors. The previous chapters have captured the best concepts of human factors in a series of ten models that can be used to develop superior leadership skills.

The Ten Models of Human Factors

1. Three Spaces of Project Management (Chapter Two)

2. Three Key Elements of Team Performance: Content, Process, and Behaviors (Chapters Three to Six)

3. Five Stages of Team Development and Meeting Facilitation (Chapters Seven and Eight)

4. Personal Space: Culture, Experiences, Personality Type, Values, and Behaviors (Chapter Nine)

5. Four Temperament Types: Rational, Idealist, Guardian, and Artisan (Chapter Nine)

6. Passive-Aggressive Threshold (Chapter Eleven)

7. Expanding Your Personal Space (Chapter Twelve)

8. Managing Good and Bad Behaviors (Chapter Thirteen)

9. Raising Your Game and Set Point (Chapter Fourteen)

10. Intellectual and Emotional Needs of Motivation (Chapter Sixteen)

The three spaces of project management represent interactions between people and systems (organizational space), between team members (team space), and within an individual (personal space). Personal space contains human factors that define individuality and diversity. These factors are the source of our motivation and drive our daily behaviors. Human factors define who we are—our inner self—and serve as a filter by which we perceive and respond to the world. They are also our source of emotions, which produce tremendous human energy and motivation. By tapping into human factors, we are able to better understand each other, understand the motivations behind our behaviors, and ultimately learn how to bring out the best in ourselves and others. Having the ability to bring out the best in yourself and others is personal leadership.

In this chapter, we review each model and explain how they can be used to develop your personal leadership.

THREE SPACES OF PROJECT MANAGEMENT

Organizational space provides the necessary scope and boundaries on which we develop our leadership roles and responsibilities (Figure 17.1). Organizational space has a leadership role in defining values, goals, content, and expectations for its leaders. Team space is where the work gets done through the intelligence and passion of teams. However, personal leadership stems from personal space, not organizational or team space. Strong leaders shape the elements of organizational space, such as setting new policies, standards, and strategic direction, while weak leaders are shaped by the elements of organizational space and struggle to build positive influence. Effective leaders expand team space by creating team synergy from good team processes and behaviors. Personal leadership has influence in all three spaces and makes things happen. It has power, authority, and impact on organizational behaviors. Leaders guide behaviors by setting the vision, direction, expectations, and processes. They translate organizational objectives into team and personal strategies.

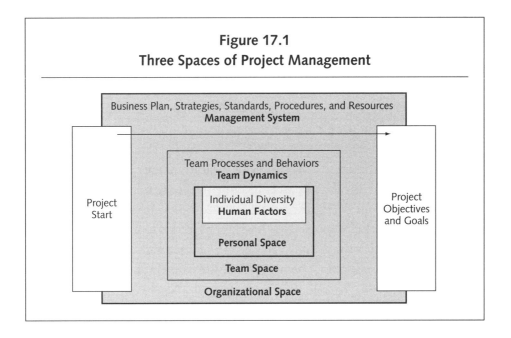

Figure 17.1
Three Spaces of Project Management

Business Plan, Strategies, Standards, Procedures, and Resources
Management System

Project
Start

Team Processes and Behaviors
Team Dynamics

Individual Diversity
Human Factors

Personal Space

Team Space

Organizational Space

Project
Objectives
and Goals

Leaders have access to more information and knowledge than others in the organization. Understanding the strategies of the organization builds personal influence; translating that information and knowledge into priorities and actions for the team creates personal leadership. Respectively, these attributes appeal to all personality types: Rationals, Idealists, Guardians, and Artisans. Good strategies have a pulling effect on people, not a pushing effect.

No matter how good a team may be, poor leadership can single-handedly bring a project down. Effective leaders are motivators and bring out the best in people and teams. To bring out the best in people, you must be able to bring out the best in yourself. It is the same for leadership. To lead, you must be able to first lead yourself. That is, you must be able to model your organizational values and leadership behaviors before you can expect project teams to do the same. You must understand yourself and know what motivates and demotivates you before you can motivate others.

Through superior leadership behaviors, great leaders get results and they consistently meet or exceed project expectations and people's expectations. That kind of performance can be generated only from your personal space.

THREE KEY ELEMENTS OF TEAM PERFORMANCE: CONTENT, PROCESS, AND BEHAVIORS

A strong leader knows the power of content, process, and behaviors in driving team success (Figure 17.2). Leaders clarify and translate organizational content (goals and objectives) into executable work plans. They have a knack for bringing together the right set of people, assets, technology, and business plans to meet organizational goals.

For process, good team leaders ensure that their teams are employing high-performing processes in conducting team meetings, defining roles and responsibilities, communicating, decision making, measuring performance, and giving feedback. They are skilled in selecting the right processes to drive desired behaviors. For behaviors, leaders actively demonstrate and support the six key team behaviors: mutual trust, interdependence, accountability, respect for diversity, transparency, and learning and recognition in project teams.

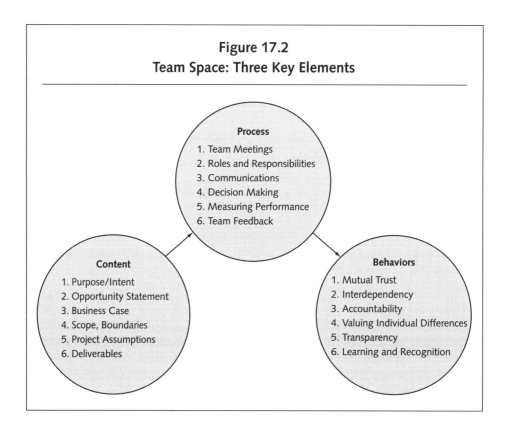

Figure 17.2
Team Space: Three Key Elements

Process
1. Team Meetings
2. Roles and Responsibilities
3. Communications
4. Decision Making
5. Measuring Performance
6. Team Feedback

Content
1. Purpose/Intent
2. Opportunity Statement
3. Business Case
4. Scope, Boundaries
5. Project Assumptions
6. Deliverables

Behaviors
1. Mutual Trust
2. Interdependency
3. Accountability
4. Valuing Individual Differences
5. Transparency
6. Learning and Recognition

Effective leaders recognize and differentiate among content, process, and behavior in resolving team problems and conflicts. In conflict, they ensure parties are addressing the same element. They attain maximum negotiating power by establishing an advantage in at least one of the three elements, and they know how to move to that strength as needed. When they face negative behaviors, good leaders know when to switch elements and reset discussions. Unlike most other people, who are content focused, strong team leaders are well balanced among content, process, and behaviors. In fact, they understand the power of recognizing behavior first and personalizing their feedback.

Personal leaders are able to speak to the diversity and internal dialogue of others. They speak process to those who need a way forward, give vision to people who want inspiration, provide courage to people who are afraid, give heart to those who fail, and award recognition to those who succeed.

FIVE STAGES OF TEAM DEVELOPMENT AND MEETING FACILITATION

It is normal for teams to go through stages of good and bad teamwork and productivity. Good team leaders are skilled facilitators who can help guide their team from project start-up (forming), through the stages of conflict (storming), execution (norming), and recalibration (reforming), to project success (performing) (Figure 17.3). Getting a team through the stages of team development requires well-developed facilitation skills. A team leader needs to be knowledgeable of the tools and techniques, experienced in applying them in team meetings, and knowing which tools to use for the situation. Facilitation is an art of skillfully using process to guide teams. Project leaders must know how to use process to help their team reach timely agreements through effective discussions and collaborative behaviors.

Strong leaders have the ability to see all sides of an issue. They are open to other ideas and options, listen for understanding, and judge the quality of the ideas, not the people who proposed them. They see other people's perspectives because they take the time and effort to listen, and then they ask questions to understand their views, concerns, and needs. They constructively probe to understand the drivers behind the comments and listen for content as well as the emotion and nonverbal messages behind the words. They seem to have an internal radar system that constantly scans the mood and feelings of people, so they are able to read people emotionally and intellectually.

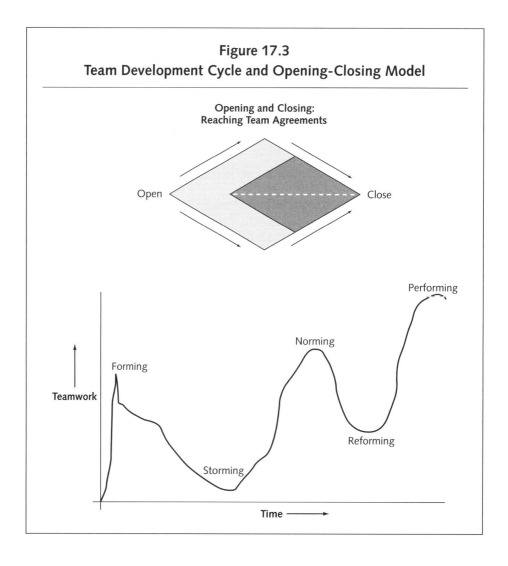

Figure 17.3
Team Development Cycle and Opening-Closing Model

Opening and Closing:
Reaching Team Agreements

Open

Close

Performing

Norming

Forming

Teamwork

Reforming

Storming

Time

They establish open and honest communications in all directions: with management, peers, and those they supervise. These leaders value the uniqueness of individuals and the different perspectives they bring to the team. They seek to discover the unexpressed needs of their team members by encouraging participation, and they treat everyone's contributions as important and valuable to the team. Effective leaders are open to different opinions but are also timely and decisive in knowing when to close a process. Most important, they know when to make a decision.

Leaders foster collaboration and consensus among team members. They look for commonalities among different points of view and propose viable alternatives and compromises to break disagreements. At times, the project leader must make the tough call and risk disappointing some team members. This risk is reduced by being transparent and explaining the reasons behind their decisions.

A strong leader helps drive teams to agreement by

- Helping the team narrow and achieve consensus by playing back what was discussed, summarizing agreements and disagreements, and clearly expressing his or her decision

- Proposing compromises and options to bring people together

- Not accepting the silent yes and seeking confirmation

- Facilitating problem solving and thinking forward, not backward

PERSONAL SPACE: CULTURE, EXPERIENCES, PERSONALITY TYPE, VALUES, AND BEHAVIORS

Superior leaders understand the power of organizational values and how values drive successful behaviors (Figure 17.4). It is a belief system that supports diversity, individual differences, and people over process. This system fits processes to people, not people to processes. Our behaviors are strongly driven by our values, but they are also shaped by our consequent history. Leaders are in the most influential position to deliver positive and negative consequences to improve team

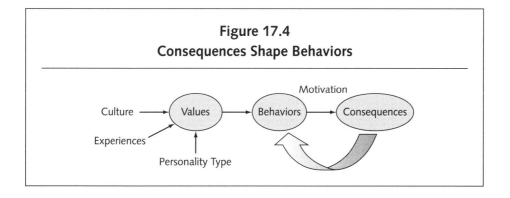

Figure 17.4
Consequences Shape Behaviors

performance. Whether it is a pat on the back or a formal reward, leaders are critical in reinforcing and shaping desired behaviors. High-performing organizations seek and achieve discretionary performance through effective use of positive reinforcement. Behaviors that are positively reinforced will be repeated. Although consequences can be both positive and negative, positive behaviors have been shown to have a much greater effect on sustaining desired behaviors (Daniels, 1994). Here are some ways to give consequences:

- Catch people doing the right things, and acknowledge them on the spot.
- Recognize desired behaviors, and tailor the form of recognition to the individual.
- Give negative consequences when necessary to increase compliance or reduce unwanted behaviors.
- Be sincere with your praise, and personalize how the person's behaviors helped you or the organization.
- Give meaningful reinforcement: quality reigns over quantity.

FOUR TEMPERAMENT TYPES: RATIONAL, IDEALIST, GUARDIAN, AND ARTISAN

Each personality type has a unique set of leadership skills (Table 17.1). All personality types make good team leaders, and each brings different leadership styles to an organization. What makes a good team leader is not leadership style, but how well the leader blends his or her style to fit the needs of the team, project, and organization. A great leader in one organization may not necessarily be a great leader in another. Smart leaders recognize what capabilities and resources they need to achieve success.

Rationals as Leaders

Rationals are strategic, independent, and competitive leaders: they play hard and work hard. They are great thinkers, analyzers, and planners. Failure is their greatest fear, so they have tremendous drive to succeed. They are able to bring the pieces of a project together and design a winning plan. They are able to see ahead, find creative options, and know how to position an organization for success. Rationals make decisions based on good analyses, research, and logic. They like to conquer,

Table 17.1
Leadership Styles by Temperament Type

Idealist: "Let's all work together"	Guardian: "Let's get the job done"	Rational: "Let's achieve our goals"	Artisan: "Let's go for it"
• Visionary leader style	• Steady, reliable, consistent leadership style	• Strategic thinker	• Gets out in front
• Values-based approach	• Well organized	• Logical decision maker	• Strong communicator
• Participative leadership	• Authoritative thinking	• Initiator of ideas	• Engaging leadership
• People-sensitive thinking	• Follows protocol and policies	• Methodical	• Persuasive
• Values relationships and partnerships	• Does all the right things	• Systematic	• Charismatic
• Highest honesty and integrity	• Fair minded	• Performance-based leadership	• Entrepreneurial
• Thorough thinker	• Accountable	• Welcomes change	• Risk taker
			• Resilient

solve problems, and move to the next challenge. They value efficiency, initiative, and results. Rationals lead by their relentless drive for achievement.

Idealists as Leaders

Idealists are dedicated, caring leaders who are motivated by both purpose and people. To an Idealist, an organization represents a system where people work together and contribute value, and in return they are rewarded and appreciated by the enterprise. Both the enterprise and the people grow together. When Idealists strongly believe in the mission of the organization, they lead with great commitment and passion. They want people to feel good about coming to work and about what they do. They want to see people and organizations grow, develop, and succeed. They build organizations through consensus, alignment, and cooperation. They are good listeners and are well connected to the issues and problems of the organization.

Idealists make decisions after thorough examination and consideration of options and consequences. Idealists lead by compassion and vision.

Guardians as Leaders

Guardians are well-organized, hard-working, and purposeful leaders. They know how to get the job done and are driven to do it well. They lead by example and always walk the talk. They are excellent implementers and are committed to meeting all of their goals and objectives. They do it with reliable systems, structure, order, policies, rules, and process. Guardians believe in proper protocol, where there is a right way to do everything and proper execution will lead to success. Their leadership style is based on clear goals and plans, cooperation, and quality execution.

As leaders, Guardians believe in hard work, competence, compliance, loyalty, and accountability. Guardians lead by example and hard work.

Artisans as Leaders

Artisans are active, high-energy, and charismatic leaders. Leadership represents an opportunity to make a difference, have a real impact, and move without constraint. Artisans enjoy being in the middle of the action, and leadership gives them the freedom to act. They have the temperament to be potentially good leaders: they are bold, confident, willing to take risks, unafraid of failure, and quick to adapt. They are strong communicators, persuasive, and brave. They have the courage to take leaps into places where most other people dare not go. Their entrepreneurial spirit and enthusiasm build excitement and energy in an organization, especially in high-risk endeavors. Artisans lead by courage and creativity.

PASSIVE-AGGRESSIVE THRESHOLD

The best project leaders are assertive and well centered in their passive-aggressive model (Figure 17.5). They have developed the flexibility in their personal space to assert passively and aggressively when needed. They have a big sweet spot, which enables them to respond rather than to react to conflicts. They are competent in managing conflict and using the classic four response tracks (aggressive, passive, avoid, and cooperative) and the three spaces (organizational space, team space, and personal space) to resolve conflicts.

A big part of personal leadership is managing fear. We learned from the passive-aggressive threshold model that people naturally fear conflict, rejection, failure, embarrassment, and accountability. We are expected to lead people who are

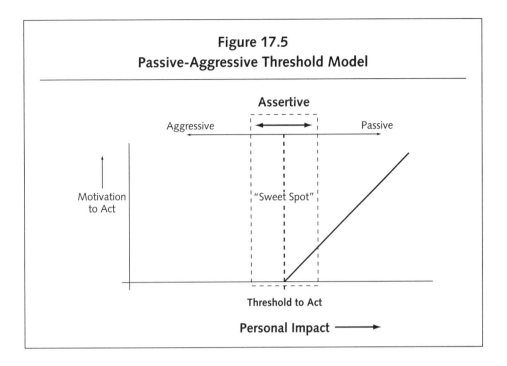

Figure 17.5
Passive-Aggressive Threshold Model

Assertive

Aggressive ←——————→ Passive

Motivation
to Act

"Sweet Spot"

Threshold to Act

Personal Impact ——————→

highly passive or aggressive. Leaders must be good at driving away fears and encourage risk taking in organizations. We need to create a safe working environment to allow people to not fear making mistakes or challenging the status quo. It is amazing how much effort goes into managing fear. We are afraid to speak up, confront difficult people, make hard decisions, and take risks. We prefer to avoid risks, transfer risks (giving problems to someone else), and hedge our risks, such as inflating budgets, extending time lines, adding extra review steps, and overanalyzing data. The Abilene paradox is one example of how fear affects team decision making. We can fill pages with examples of the impact of fear on performance. It affects all aspects of project management. Good leadership drives fear out of the system and enables people to perform at their best.

EXPANDING YOUR PERSONAL SPACE

Good leaders expand space, and bad leaders take and shrink space. Expanding personal space builds personal influence, while helping others expand their space, and encouraging them to take action outside their space demonstrates personal leadership (Figure 17.6). By expanding space, we are increasing our sphere of influence, scope of responsibilities, and personal capacity. High-performing leaders expand space by raising the bar, stretching teams and organizations to do more, pursuing higher goals, and embracing change. Superior team leaders speak to people's diversity and help people internalize change. Moreover, they help people adopt a positive internal dialogue and stretch their confidence. They set a positive emotional tone.

Successful leaders are forward thinkers and visionaries. They possess a contagious can-do attitude. They move forward but never leave people behind. They do not accumulate excessive emotional baggage; however, they do not ignore the past. They learn from the past to apply to the future. They apply learnings and invite continuous improvement and new ideas. Effective leaders give people hope and optimism about what can be possible about the future—not what can go wrong but what can go right. Setting that mind-set illuminates the future. Good leaders expand and illuminate space by defining future expectations and strategic direction, providing a sense of purpose and urgency that motivates all personality types.

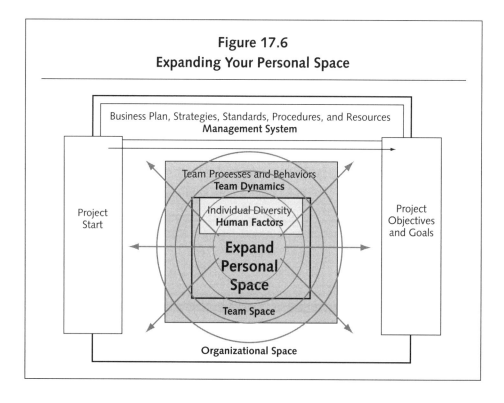

Figure 17.6
Expanding Your Personal Space

That is the secret to visionary leadership. Purpose is driven by a compelling strategy that is idealistic (which appeals to Idealists), logical (Rationals), practical (Guardians), and meaningful (Artisans). Vision creates hope, which is one of the most powerful motivators of all.

Remember that winners expand space, and losers take space. Winners play large; losers play small. Leaders create bigger spaces by bringing people together to build a vision of what is possible.

MANAGING GOOD AND BAD BEHAVIORS

Each personality type has both positive upper-level behaviors and negative lower-level behaviors (Figure 17.7). These two psychological states exist within our personal space. High-performing leaders are upper-level dominant and build upper-level organizations by establishing high values, standards, and expectations. Upper-level organizations promote teamwork, mutual trust, diversity, active communications, feedback processes, peer recognition, and continuous learning. Upper-level leaders are open, honest, inclusive, transparent, positive, caring, and accountable for their actions.

When you operate from your upper level, personal leadership is visible. Upper-level leaders are not hidden from people. They make themselves visible by walking

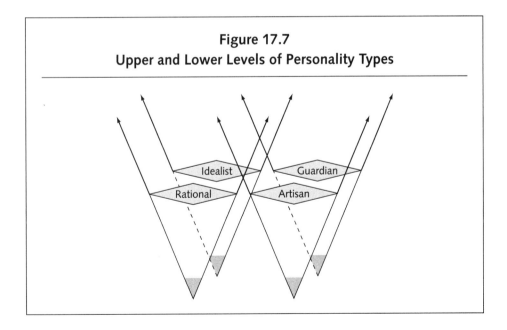

Figure 17.7
Upper and Lower Levels of Personality Types

around and talking to people, visiting employee work locations, modeling desired behaviors, leading change, and showing their passion (emotional) and intellectual motivation. When leaders show themselves, people are able to see what they stand for.

RAISING THE GAME AND SET POINT

Personal leaders do not accept lower-level behaviors (Figure 17.8). Lower-level behaviors drag an organization down and create low motivation, while an upperlevel culture creates synergy and high human energy. The role of personal leadership is to raise the culture, motivate high performance, and help people make breakthroughs.

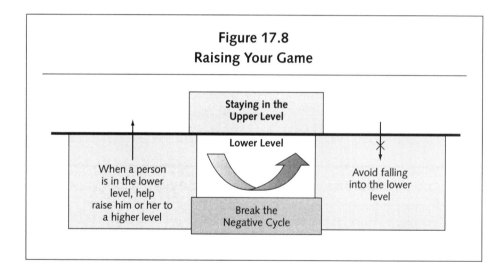

**Figure 17.8
Raising Your Game**

Staying in the Upper Level

Lower Level

When a person is in the lower level, help raise him or her to a higher level

Break the Negative Cycle

Avoid falling into the lower level

Great leaders have a high set point—they set a high bar and inspire their teams to rise above it. Leaders are in the best position to raise the level of performance in others by supporting upper-level behaviors. They can help others rise to a higher level in these ways:

- Have an interest in what people are thinking and saying.
- Regularly express confidence in others and in their ability to do the job. Raising performance involves a certain degree of risk taking and confidence.
- Coach and mentor others. Help guide others, and give timely and effective feedback. Freely share your know-how with others.
- Empower team members to make decisions and act independently in their areas of responsibility. Empowerment builds trust.
- Challenge employees with specific opportunities to grow and succeed.
- Invite debate and different points of view. Ensure all team members understand their role and responsibilities, share information, and create a participative work environment. Encourage all team members to show their individuality and diversity.

With a high set point, leaders do not just react to conflicts; they defuse them. Good leaders defuse conflicts between people in these ways:

- Avoiding win-lose competition between people. They bring focus to differences on issues rather than differences between people.
- Understanding that people have different problem-solving skills, and they react differently with conflict. Some people do not like to deal with conflict directly, while others like to meet conflict head-on. Good leaders recognize these types of differences and resolve conflicts in a manner that is consistent with their style and problem-solving abilities.
- Training and educating the workforce on conflict resolution techniques and processes. They provide resources, such as facilitators, counselors, and employee assistance programs, to support employees in conflict. Conflicts are not necessarily between people; for example, the disagreement may be with company policies, procedures, or values.
- Supporting the intellectual and emotional needs of people in their work assignments and day-to-day interactions.

Personal leadership is about having the ability to bring out the best in people. You cannot bring out the best in people when you are in the lower level. Leaders with high set points will raise the performance standard of others.

INTELLECTUAL AND EMOTIONAL NEEDS OF MOTIVATION

Leaders have strong intellectual and emotional balance (Figure 17.9). They are able to positively influence others. They think outside of themselves, are not afraid to show themselves, and help others grow and develop. Intellectual and emotional strengths enable leaders to communicate effectively, manage change, and motivate people. It is a combination of what they say and how they say it, and a feeling they instill. Others feel their personal confidence, commitment, passion, and faith in their people and organization. Their message is clear. They show no fear, no filters, no spin, and no hesitation. They inspire others by speaking to their hearts and minds.

SUMMARY

Personal leadership has influence in all three spaces and makes things happen. It has power, authority, and great influence on behaviors. Leaders guide behaviors by setting the vision, direction, expectations, and key processes. Effective leaders are motivators and bring out the best in people and teams: that is personal leadership.

All personality types can make good team leaders, and each brings different leadership styles to an organization. Yet all good leaders seem to share some common human factors and leadership behaviors:

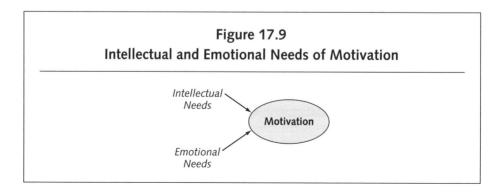

Figure 17.9
Intellectual and Emotional Needs of Motivation

Intellectual Needs → **Motivation**

Emotional Needs →

- Effective leaders recognize and differentiate among content, process, and behavior in resolving team conflicts.
- Leaders expand space by bringing people together to build a vision of what is possible.
- Upper-level leaders welcome change and are skilled in facilitation and change management.
- Personal leaders are able to speak to the diversity and internal dialogue of others. They give people courage to do things differently.
- Successful leaders are forward thinkers who illuminate a vision for the organization.
- Upper-level leaders possess a high set point and help others elevate their team behaviors and performance.
- Personal leaders have a strong intellectual and emotional balance and are able to think outside themselves. This enables them to foster team agreements, promote collaboration, and defuse potential conflicts.
- Personal leadership is visible.

As we go forward, technology, globalization, and socioeconomic development will continue to change the dynamics of human interactions. As we broaden our knowledge of the world, we will need to expand our personal capacity to work with people who have different backgrounds, cultures, and personalities. We face an enormous challenge as we try to extend project management practices and teamwork across continents, regions, and countries. Organizations need to improve their capabilities to manage a global workforce and multinational partnerships. Human factors will be more visible in project management in the future.

Project management can make leaps and bounds beyond where it is now by understanding and managing human factors better. We need to loosen our hold on content and process and devote more time and resources to improving team behaviors and motivating human performance. These are the greatest opportunities in project management. As global businesses evolve, demands on human performance, in terms of creativity, productivity, and teamwork, will continue to rise over time. To raise the bar on human performance, we must increase our competencies as project managers in understanding, respecting, and motivating people. To do that, we need to go where we have never gone before and understand personal space, human factors, and the values and behaviors of people. Most organizations try to drive behavioral change through organizational space and team space with minimal impact. We lack resources and trained personnel to reach people in personal space. If we can reach people in their space and tap that tremendous source of human energy, we can bring out the very best in others and achieve great success in project management.

To integrate human factors in our organizations, we can begin by better operationalizing diversity and practicing human factors in projects. We can spend more time understanding the temperament types, cultures, experiences, and values of people; treat people the way they would like to be treated; recognize people more often; pinpoint and reinforce desired behaviors; and create a more inclusive work environment. Second, we can invest more in improving the skills and knowledge of trainers, mentors, coaches, facilitators, and managers in the tools, techniques, and models of human factors. Third, and most important, we can begin with ourselves. To bring out the best in other people, we must be able to bring out the best in ourselves. To lead and motivate others, we must be able to lead and motivate ourselves first. To do that, we must be happy in our own skins. We have the power to choose our own level of behavior. Being in the upper or lower level is a personal choice. Why not show the best part of yourself? Rise to your upper level by shedding the fear and baggage that are weighing you down, seeing greater opportunities, and maximizing personal success and leadership. We can develop our personal capacity by expanding our values to accept things outside our comfort zone, increasing our set point for higher performance, thinking outside ourselves, and raising our game. All of these expand our personal space and happiness.

I hope this book has given you valuable insights into yourself and others. I hope the concepts, discussions, and stories have broadened your awareness and understanding of the differences and similarities that exist among people. These differences and similarities are the basis for improving interpersonal behaviors, motivation, and leadership. I hope you will take these learnings, live them, and enrich your relationships and life.

REFERENCES

Adams, J. S. "Toward an Understanding of Inequity." *Journal of Abnormal and Social Psychology,* 1963, *67,* 422–436.

Blake, R., and Mouton, J. *The Managerial Grid: The Key to Leadership Excellence.* Houston: Gulf Publishing Co., 1964.

Bolten, R., and Bolten, D. G. *People Styles at Work: Making Bad Relationships Good and Good Relationships Better.* New York: AMACOM, 1996.

Briggs, K. C., and Myers, I. B. *Myers-Briggs Type Indicator.* Princeton, N.J.: Educational Testing Service, 1957.

Covey, S. R. *Seven Habits of Highly Effective People.* New York: Simon & Schuster, 1989.

Daniels, A. B. *Bringing Out the Best in People.* New York: McGraw-Hill, 1994.

Flannes, S. W., and Levin, G. *Essential People Skills for Project Managers.* Vienna, Va.: Management Concepts, 2005.

Gardenswartz, L., and Rowe, A. *Diverse Teams at Work: Capitalizing on the Power of Diversity.* Chicago: Irwin, 1994.

Graham, R. J., and Englund, R. L. *Creating an Environment for Successful Projects: The Quest to Manage Project Management.* San Francisco: Jossey-Bass, 1997.

Harrington-Mackin, D. *Keeping the Team Going.* New York: AMACOM, 1996.

Harvey, J. B. *The Abilene Paradox: The Management of Agreement.* New York: AMACOM, 1974.

Herzberg, F., Mausner, B., and Snyderman, B. B. *The Motivation to Work.* (2nd ed.) Hoboken, N.J.: Wiley, 1959.

Hiatt, J. *ADKAR: A Model for Change in Business, Government and Our Community.* Loveland, Colo.: Prosci Research, 2006.

Holpp, L. *Managing Teams.* New York: McGraw-Hill, 1999.

Jung, C. G. *Psychological Types.* New York: Pantheon Books, 1923.

Katzenbach, J. R., and Smith, D. K. *The Wisdom of Teams.* New York: HarperCollins, 1993.

Keirsey, D. *Please Understand Me II.* Del Mar, Calif.: Prometheus Nemesis Book Co., 1984.

Kerzner, H. *Conflict in Project Mangement: A Systems Approach to Planning, Scheduling, and Controlling.* Hoboken, N.J.: John Wiley & Sons, 2001.

Kübler-Ross, E. *On Grief and Grieving: Finding the Meaning of Grief Through the Five Stages of Loss.* New York: Simon & Schuster, 2005.

Lancaster, L. C., and Stillman, D. *When Generations Collide.* New York: HarperCollins, 2002.

Lencioni, P. *The Five Dysfunctions of a Team: A Leadership Fable.* San Francisco: Jossey-Bass, 2002.

Maslow, A. *Motivation and Personality.* New York: HarperCollins, 1954.

McClelland, D. C., Atkinson, J. W., Clark, R. A., and Lowell, E. L. *The Achievement Motive.* Princeton, N.J.: Van Nostrand, 1953.

McGregor, D. M. *The Human Side of Enterprise.* New York: McGraw-Hill, 1960.

Parker, G. M. *Cross Functional Teams: Working with Allies, Enemies, and Other Strangers.* San Francisco: Jossey-Bass, 2003.

Pinto, J.K.K., and Trailer, J. W. *Leadership Skills for Project Management.* Newtown Square, Pa.: Project Management Institute, 1998.

Scholtes, P. R., Joiner, B. L., and Striebel B. J. *The Team Handbook.* (2nd ed.) Madison, Wis.: Oriel, 2001.

Thomas, K. W., and Kilmann, R. H. *Thomas-Kilmann Conflict Model Instrument.* Tuxedo, N.Y.: Xicom, 1974.

Tuckman, B. W. "Developmental Sequence in Small Groups." *Psychological Bulletin,* 1965, *63*(6), 384–399.

Verma, V. K. *Managing the Project Team.* Newtown Square, Pa.: Project Management Institute, 1997.

Vroom, V. H. *Work and Motivation.* (Rev. ed.) San Francisco: Jossey-Bass, 1995.

Zenger, J. H., Musselwhite, E., Hurson, K., and Perrin, C. *Leading Teams: Mastering the New Role.* New York: McGraw-Hill, 1993.

INDEX

A

Abilene paradox, 211–213, 222, 231

Accommodate, 236–237

Accountability, 70, 72–72, 75–77, 88; as a guardian behavior, 178, 331; as a pitfall in storming, 115; fear of, 213, 322

Achievement theory, 23

Action register, 57

Adams, J. S., 23

Aggressive track, as conflict options, 236–237

Aggressives, behaviors of, 105, 114, 171, 206, 217; expanding space of, 226, 234–235, 253; in rationals, 183. *See also* Passive-aggressive threshold model

Air cover, 32–33

Antagonism, team, 201, 204–205

Artisan personality type, 168–169; breakthrough story of, 297–300; controlling behaviors of, 256; fear of, 213, 216; getting to a higher set point by, 269; impatience of, 257; in conflict 221–222; in times of change, 198; intellectual and emotional needs of, 311–315; leadership style of, 331–332; recognition and respect of, 259; team behaviors of, 179–183; upper and lower behaviors of, 248–249, 252

Ask assertive, 273–274, 278

Assertiveness, 227, 232–236, 246

Assumptions, project, 32–34

Avoidance 235–236; as a conflict option, 238

B

Baby boomers, 161–162

Baggage, emotional, 306

Behaviors, as a key element of team performance, 27–28, 67–68; as related to values, 150–151; exclusionary, 200, 237; conflict of, 200–201, 206; controlling, 256–257; dominant, 256; fear, 209–219; impatience, 257–258; in team scorecard, 59; in team space 18–19, 25; inclusive, 87–88, 158, 186, 231; leadership 325–327, 338–339; most common lower level, 255–258; of personality types, 166–169; poor listening, 258; to expand personal space, 227; top six team, 71; upper and lower levels, 249, 251; versus content, 96–100; versus process, 104–108; whining, 255–256

Biases, individual, 30; in scorecard, 61; methods to break, 134, 143; team, 33

Boundaries, project, 31

Brainstorming, 133

Breakdowns, team, 201–202, 206

Breakthroughs, personal stories of, 285–300; key learnings from, 300–301

Brains, switching left-right, 309–310

Bridging, 271–273

Bring out the best in people, 15, 25; in personal leadership, 324–325, 338; by understanding personal values, 151

Business case, 29; for change, 197

C

Cause and effect tool, 135

Change, 34; as a concern to Guardians, 178; as part of learning, 81; behaviors in personality types, 181–182, 198; conflict of, 195–198, 205; in enabling personal breakthroughs, 301; in reforming phase, 120; management of, 123, 196; resistance to, 120

Charter, 31–32; communicating it, 34

Cherry picking, 140

Chevron Way, 13

Classic Conflict Model, 235–239

Closing processes, 131. *See* Narrowing techniques

Collaboration, 236, 239; ladder of, 269–271

Commitment, 29–30, 73, 214; definition of, 35

Communications, 46–48, 87; channels, 48–49; e-mail, 50–52; in creating a safe zone, 48–49; in cultural languages, 152–153; in team norming phase, 116; leadership, 328; nonverbal, 155–156, 231; overload, 48

Community orientation, 153–154

Compete, as a conflict option, 236–237

Compromise, 236, 238

Conflict, by personality type, 219–222; change, 195–198; conflict cycle, 196; definition of, 191; dynamics, 224; emotional, 283; fear of, 212, 216; good and bad, 192–193, 205; in team storming phase, 115; of behaviors, 200–201, 206; management of, 197–198, 243–245; model, 193; of values, 198–200, 206; response options, 235–245; scenarios, 245; sources of, 195; team curve, 201

Confrontation, as a conflict option, 236, 238

Consensus, team, 53–54

Consequences, 75–76, 219; as a pitfall in team development, 117; how to give, 330; shaping behaviors, 329

Content, 28–35; definition of, 28; in team scorecard, 59; versus behaviors, 96–100; versus process, 100–104

Control, loss of, during change, 197; due to behaviors of others, 216, 224–225, 232

Controlling behaviors, 256–257, 264; by personality type, 221

Cooperative, as a conflict option, 236–238

Coping, 218–219, 222–224, 269

Cost benefit matrix, 144–145

Culture, aspects of, 152–159; definition of, 152

D

Decision-making, 53–57; decision support package, 46; cultural differences, 157

Deliverables, project, definition of, 32

Difficult people, 250–258; definition of, 250

Diversity, valuing, 15, 25, 77–78, 88; cultural, 158–159; in decision-making, 215; in expanding personal space, 227–228; in leadership, 334; in personal values, 150–151, 188

Dominant behaviors, 114, 256, 264. *See also* Aggressives

Down cycles, team 112, 123, 197

Drivers, key, in a team charter, 31

Dual factor theory, 22

E

Electronic communications, 50–52

Elephant in the room, 213

E-mail, 50–51

Equity theory, 23

Expanding your space, 225; benefits of, 226–227; how to, 227–243

F

Facilitation, 126–147; definition 125; key concepts of, 126–127

Facilitator, 42, 44–45

Fear factors, 211–215; by personality types, 216

Fear, in aggressive-passive threshold model, 209; of conflict, 83, 212, 216–217; of embarrassment, 213; of failure, 171, 212–216; of losing control, 197; of rejection, 212, 216; of taking risks, 214; weakness, 213

Feedback, meeting, 42; how to give feedback, 82–86; team, 49, 54, 62–67; to raise your behaviors, 267

Fishbone diagram, 135–136

Fist of five, 55–56; 142

Force field, 133–134

Forcing, as a conflict option, 236–237

Forming, in team development cycle, 111–113

Free-wheeling, 133

G

Gap analysis, 137–138

GE values, 13

Generational diversity, 159–165

Generation X, 162–164

Golf, 248

Go slow to go fast, 127–128

Ground rules, 42; for e-mailing, 52; for power dotting, 141

Groupthink, 134, 211, 222

Guardian personality type, 168–169; breakthrough story of, 287–289, 295–297; controlling behaviors of, 257; impatience of, 257; in getting to a higher set point by, 269; in conflict, 220–222; in self-disappointment, 248; fear of, 212, 216; in times of change, 198; intellectual and emotional needs of, 311–313, 315; leadership style of, 331–332; recognition and respect of, 260; team behaviors of, 177–179; upper- and lower-level behaviors of, 248–249, 252

H

Herzberg, F., 22

Hidden agendas, 30, 33, 40, 113

Hierarchy of human needs, 21

High performing teams, core processes of, 41; list of key behaviors of, 71; general behaviors of, 28–30, 43, 119, 126, 199; inclusive behaviors of, 87–88; in team space, 261–265

Hoarding information, 82

Hot buttons, managing, 281–282, 284

Human Factors, definition, introduction, 1

Humor, 200, 279; ethnic, 202

I

Idealist personality style, 168–169;
  breakthrough story, 292–294;
  controlling behaviors of, 257; fear of,
  212, 216; getting to a higher set point,
  268; impatience, 257; in times of
  change, 198; in conflict, 220–222;
  intellectual and emotional needs,
  311–313, 315; leadership style, 331;
  team behaviors of, 174–176; upper
  and lower behaviors of, 248–249, 252;
  whine behaviors of, 255
Idioms, 153
Impatience, 120, 257–258, 264
Inclusive behaviors. *See* Behaviors
Influence diagram, 135 137
Informal power, 226, 246
Inner strength, 219, 227
Inspiration, by vision and hope, 27, 30, 35;
  from the 3 R's, 261; inspiring others,
  71, 265; meeting individual desires,
  149, 184, 264; in leadership, 276, 338
Interactive spaces, 18, 218
Interdependency, 73–75
Internal dialogue, 20, 150, 218, 303–305,
  in passive-aggressive model, 209; in
  personal space, 216–217

J

Jung, C., 165
Juran, J., 11

K

Keirsey, D., 166, 188
Knowledge manager, 45–46

L

Ladder of collaboration, 269–271
Language, 152–153
Lasso, 142

Learning, 80–86, 88; different styles of, 80;
  obstacle to, 82
Leadership, personal, behaviors, 96–97,
  102, 338–339; by personality type,
  330–332
definition of, 324; during change,
  197–198
Listening, in team communications,
  119–120, 269–270, 274, 278–279; poor,
  258, 264

M

Maslow, A., 21
Mayo, E., 21
MBTI, 166
McClelland, D., 23
McGregor, D., 23
Measuring team performance, 57–62
Mediocrity, road to, 215–216
Meeting, agenda, 41; monitor, 64–65;
  technology, 52
Mentoring, 266
Metrics, team, 32, 57, 115. *See* Measuring
  performance
Millennial generation, 164–165
Milestones, definition and examples of, 58
Minority report, 146
Moderator, 52
Motivation, from personal space, 20, 149,
  188, 265, 324; from leaders, 338; from
  personal stake, 73; from seeking intel-
  lectual and emotional needs, 303; power
  and human energy of, 14–16, 303–306,
  321; self, 261; theories of, 20–24
Myers-Briggs Type Indicators, 166

N

Narrowing techniques, 132, 140–147
National Aeronautics and Space
  Administration, 254

Need to be right, 311
Negative cycles, ways to break, 276–281
Negotiations, methods in, 93–95, 103–104
Nokia Way and Values, 13
Nonverbal communications, 85, 155 156, 321
Normalization of deviance, 254
Norming, in team development cycle, 112, 116–117

O

Off-line voting, 141–142
Opening processes, 131–140
Openness, 33, 48, 156–157, 199, 273
Opportunity statement, 31
Organizational space, affecting behaviors, 217–219, 225; change conflicts from, 195; definition, 18; general, 19–25; in conflict management, 240–241; in leadership, 325, 334; processes in, 37; resolving conflicts in, 240–241; values in, 184
Overcompromising, 215

P

Pace, 275–276
Parking lot, 130–131
Passive-aggressive threshold model, 208–210, 222, 234, 333
Passives, 105–106, 217, 234, 253
Passive track, as a conflict option, 236–237
Patience, 251, 257, 269. *See* Impatience
Performing, in team development cycle, 112, 121–123
Personal account balance, 228
Personal capital, 228–229
Personality types, as part of personal space, 165–167; description of types, 167–169; in conflict, 219–222; intellectual and emotional needs, 311–312; leadership styles, 331; motivating, 275; upper- and lower-level behaviors, 249. *See also* Artisans, Guardians, Idealists, and Rationals
Personal space, definition and introduction of, 18–23; description of, 149–151; expanding, 225–227; fear factors in, 211–216; in conflict, 207, 217–219, 224; leadership, 325; speaking from, 232–233; staying in your upper level of, 259–261
Pinch points, 54–55
Playback, 280–281
Plus Delta, 63–64
Polar, go 280
Positive account balance, 228–229. *See also* Personal capital
Power dotting, 140–141
Pressure, 251
Processes, 11–15, 37–68; change, 34; in team scorecard, 59; in three spaces model, 18–19; key attributes, 39–40; list of the key six, 41; strategies, 40; team meeting, 41–43; three critical roles of, 38; versus behaviors, 104–108; versus content, 100–104
Process checks, 62, 117; in facilitation, 127, 129; in reforming phase, 117–119; techniques with difficult people, 256–257
Project management expectations, 14
Purpose, 30
Put it in neutral, 274

Q

Quality Management, 11

R

3 R's, 259–262, 264
Raise your game, 276–279

Rational personality type, 167, 169;
breakthrough story, 289–291;
controlling behaviors of, 257;
dominating behavior of, 256; fear of,
212, 216; getting to a higher set point,
268; impatience, 257; in conflict
219–222; in times of change, 198;
intellectual and emotional needs,
311–312, 314–315; leadership style,
330–331; recognition and respect, 259;
team behaviors of, 170–174; upper
and lower behaviors of, 248–249, 252

Recognition, 80, 86–87; as a common
emotional need, 315, 322; in building
account balance, 229; in performing,
122; in valuing cultural diversity, 158;
leadership style, 330–331; raising to
upper level, 259–260; *See also* Positive
feedback

Reforming, in team development cycle,
112, 117–120

Reinforcement, 64, 80, 84, 86, 108; as a
leadership behavior, 329–330

Relationship with peers, 154–155

Relevance, 260–261

Respect for authority, cultural, 154

Respect and trust, 260

Risk, 214–215, 333

Road to Abilene. *See* Abilene paradox

Road to Mediocrity. *See* Mediocrity

Role model behavior, 276

Roles and responsibilities, 44–46, 88

Round-robin, 133

Roundtable, team 48

Rule, 80:20, 130

S

Safe zone, 48–49

Sandwich technique, 51, 85

Schwarzenegger, A., 198

Scorecard, 58–62

Selection criteria, 40, 143–144

Set point, definition of, 250; how to raise
it by personality types, 268–269; in
difficult people, 252; in great leaders,
337; to raise, 265, 283–284

Signals, 227, 231–232

Silent yes, 55, 329; as a cultural behavior,
154, 159

Silver mining, 266

Six Sigma, 11

Slip method, 133

Smile Index, 65–66

Smoothing, as a conflict option, 236, 238

Spider diagram, 66–67, 74

Spin forward, 282–283

Sponsor, project, 31

Stages of team development, 85–94

Stake in the game, 73

Stake-in-the-ground, 56–57

Stalemates, methods to break, 145–147

Storming, in team development cycle,
112–116

Strategy table, 138–140

Straw model, 54

Stress, 122, 216–219

Success metrics, 32

Sweet spot, in passive-aggressive threshold
model, 233–234; in leadership, 332

Switch key elements, 279

Switching brains, 309

Synergy, 28, 34, 71; definition and from
interdependency, 73, 203; team,
201–204

T

Team, agenda, 41; agreements, 42; antagonism, 201, 204–205; behaviors,
69–89; charter, 31–32; cross-
functional, 12; development cycle, 112;

dynamics, definition, 18–19, 25; expectations, 261; feedback, 62–67; involvement, 261; key elements, 27–28, 34, 91; leader of, 44; learning, 80–82; meetings, 41–43, 125 126; metrics, 57–62; natural, 12; networks, 12; self-managed, 12; space, 17–20; synergy, 201–204; terms of reference, 31, 35; workload distribution, 46

Techniques, in facilitation, 126–130; in building personal capital, 229; in opening and closing discussions, 132; in managing difficult people, 255; to avoid dropping into lower level, 281–283; to break a negative cycle, 276–281; to break stalemates, 145–147; to expand personal space, 227, 246; to help team stay in upper level, 258–263; to identify personality types, 170; to raise your game, 270–276, 284

Temperament types, 166–169. *See also* Personality types

Theory X and Y, 23–24

Three spaces of project management, 18–26

Threshold to act, 208–210

Time, value of, 157, 257

Timekeeper, 45

Traditionalists, 160–161

Transparency, 78–80, 88, 279; in cultures, 158–159; 262–263; 275

Trapped, 285–286

Trojan horse, 274

Trust, 30, 70–72, 79, 88; definition of, 71, 93, 260

Tuckman, B., 111

U

Upper level, definition of, 247; help others to reach, 269–270; shaping behaviors in, 268–269

V

Values, as it drive behaviors, 115–117; company, 184–185; conflict of, 198–200; definition of, 150; personal and organizational, 184–187

Valuing diversity, 227–228. *See also* Diversity

Valuing individual differences, 77–78

Visible, be, during change, 198; in expanding space, 230; in leadership, 330

Visuals, use of, 158

Vroom, V., 23

W

Web-based meeting techniques, 52

Whining behaviors, 255, 264

Withdraw, as a conflict option, 236–237

WorldCom, 267